DEFIANT MOMENTS

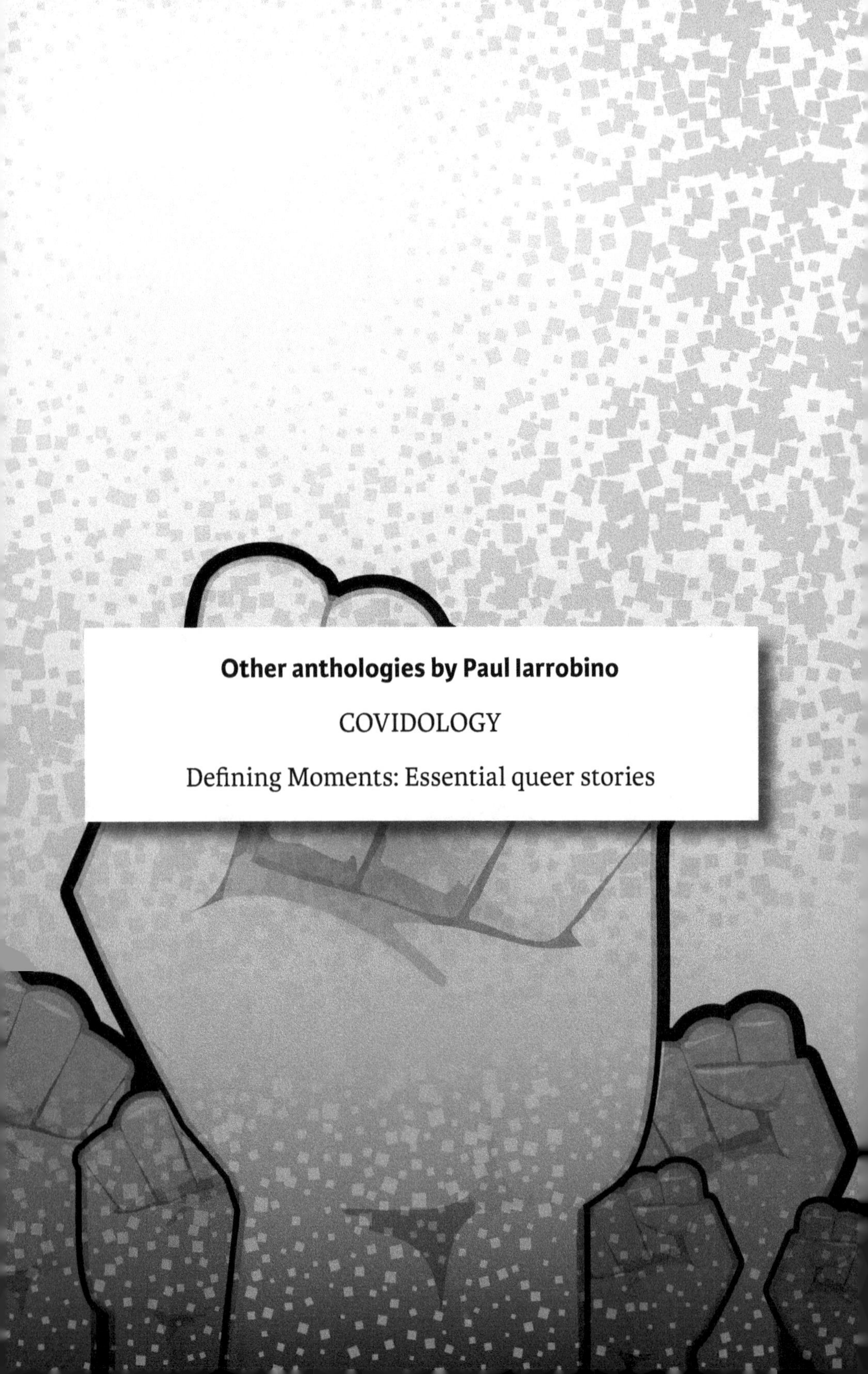

Other anthologies by Paul Iarrobino

COVIDOLOGY

Defining Moments: Essential queer stories

DEFIANT MOMENTS

Unyielding queer voices. Unstoppable change.

EDITED BY PAUL IARROBINO

OUR BOLD VOICES
PORTLAND, OREGON

www.ourboldvoices.com

Defiant Moments is set in TypeTogether's Karmina and Karmina Sans, My Creative Land's Above the Sky Extras, and Latinotype's Informative.

Cover photo credits: Envato (monkeybusiness, LightFieldStudios, ghostlypixels, iheartcreative, Olivija_photos, wirestock, aetb, and YuriArcursPeopleimages). Letters courtesy John Lucia and AleX Dean. Poster courtesy Eric Zimmerman.

Cover design by Arnel Mandilag

ISBN EBOOK 979-8-9901940-5-2
ISBN PAPERBACK 979-8-9901940-3-8
ISBN HARDCOVER 979-8-9901940-4-5

Queer erasure is real, and we see it happening now on government websites. We will not be silenced. We are strong and resilient people. We will keep sharing our creativity and stories. This book is a tribute to our authors and our promise to fight against those who try to hide us. We will continue to speak out, celebrate our identities, and ensure our voices are heard loud and clear.

CONTENTS

Foreword

Russell Alexander-Orozco's story, "It's Not Fiction, It's My Life," sets an appropriate time frame for this collection of intimate chronicles. At the Metropolitan Community Church in San Francisco in the 1970s, Russell met an older man who worked for the US government in the 1960s. The older man experienced the terror of the Lavender Scare, which began with Joseph McCarthy in the 1950s when government employees could be fired and outed if their sexuality became known. It was a time of demagoguery, conservative political hysteria, and repression—a time similar to our politics in 2025. (See *The Lavender Scare, the Cold War Persecution of Gays and Lesbians in the Federal Government*, by David K. Johnson, 2004, U. of Chicago Press.)

While many of the stories begin in the 1970s, after the beginning of the Gay Liberation Movement following the Stonewall riots of 1969, others center on the 1980s and 90s during the AIDS epidemic. The Vietnam War, in which the

US military became more intensely involved between 1964 and 1973, is another important reference point. John Lucia's story "Bus to Oakland" describes his experience with the military draft before the Stonewall riots. Still other stories are influenced by the COVID-19 pandemic from 2020 to 2022—although COVID is still with us.

You will find here a number of recurring themes. The important influence of parents shows up as a toxic and devastating element, but alternatively as a positive, supportive relationship. Likewise, religion appears as both a toxic or in other cases a positive influence. Police violence is portrayed as a significant factor in some stories, even before the George Floyd murder in 2020. And, of course, transgender issues and gender roles are a prominent feature in many. Yet others point in unique directions not touched on by any other chapters.

But besides historical touchstones and varied thematic content, these heartfelt accounts pack an emotional punch. Reading them I felt tense with trepidation for the authors' situations, or in other cases I was so touched that tears welled up in my eyes. I defy you to read these narratives without feeling some emotions.

This is a compilation of wildly different localities, time settings, people, and personal concerns. But what these stories have in common is immense courage, emerging as these diverse individuals turn their backs on the status quo and defy convention. This is what makes them so inspiring.

—Jeff Stookey, author of the novel trilogy *Medicine for the Blues.*

Introduction

Like many Americans, I was shocked when the 2024 election results were announced. At the time I was on a small group tour in Nepal and Bhutan with a few dozen gay men from various countries. It felt strange to be in a foreign land away from the constant discussions and debates about politics back home. I could not help but feel disconnected from the excitement and tension that filled the air in the United States. While I enjoyed the beautiful scenery and rich culture of Nepal and Bhutan, my mind often wandered back to the implications of the election results.

When the official election results were announced, a heavy silence fell over us. We felt the weight of the moment. I remember an Australian traveler turning to me with wide eyes and asking, "How could that happen?" My mind raced as I tried to find an answer, but I was still in shock. It was difficult to understand the situation, and the uncertainty added to our confusion.

Before traveling abroad I thought it would be a perfect opportunity to reflect on my experiences and write my short story for this anthology. I imagined hiking in quiet, peaceful areas and admiring views of mountains, waving prayer flags, and watching Buddhist monks walking around temples in their colorful robes. I was certain these new surroundings would inspire my creativity, and the words would flow. That was not my experience.

Fortunately, the wheels were already in motion for this anthology with our defiance theme. That was a result of a story that one of our writers had, and I set out to build an entire anthology around it. In hindsight, it was brilliant. The book was half-written by the time we were away, with most authors actively working on their stories.

While this election was not the impetus for this book, the aftershock served as a motivational force to inspire our authors and for me to craft my own story. When we had our first in-person rehearsal, it was just a few months into our new, chaotic federal administration. Even though we had heard each other's stories on our Zoom calls, somehow that day was different. It was as if we had heard the stories for the first time. Some of us cried while listening to others or reading our own stories. It was a crystallizing moment for us, knowing these stories need to be out there, both in their written form and our upcoming book tour.

—Paul Iarrobino

It's Not Fiction, It's My Life

By Russell Alexander-Orozco

It's the early 1970s in San Francisco. I'm in my second year away from home and living in an all-boys dorm at my Catholic university located four blocks from the Haight-Ashbury district, once home to the Grateful Dead and the iconic Janis Joplin.

On breezy days, the aroma from the Flower Power Era lingers enticingly in the air, often thicker than the bay area fog. As students, we've been advised to stay away from the birthplace of the 1960s counterculture movement. The word is that bad influences lurk there. We know those warnings are overblown because most of what we see is ongoing, passive resistance and nonviolent demonstrations against the Vietnam War.

I set out to explore the magic wonders of San Francisco—the architecture, the diversity of people and languages, the clanking of the street cars, and of course, the breathtaking views. I'm definitely in *Oz*. During one of my many escapades, I discover the weekly underground newspaper that would change my life, *The Berkeley Barb*[1]. The journal covered subjects that I've never been exposed to and are never talked about at my conventional academic institution. I'm enthralled and moved by what I read about the Civil Rights and Free Speech movements, anti-war, and social changes advocated by youth culture.

That exposure ignites a longing to learn more about the Social Justice movement, its needs, and its impact. I recall the first 11 years of my life in Mexico where my father had several businesses. Both of my parents worked, so I was raised by indigenous women, and through them, I witnessed major socio-economic status discrimination just because of the color of their skin. My parents separated by the time I turned 11, and I returned to the states with my mom, but I've never forgotten the rage I felt at seeing those injustices.

And that's when I began to educate myself about the ongoing state of affairs regarding people of color. As it turns

1 A weekly underground newspaper published in Berkeley, California, from 1965-1980 to serve the civil rights, anti-war, and countercultural movements. It mixed radical politics with psychedelic art, guerilla comics, local happenings, opinions, reviews, calls to protest, as well as gay and straight classified ads.

out, in the city of Oakland just across the bay, the Black Power movement is in full bloom with immense community programs being developed. Then I read about the Chicano movement and a call for Black-Brown unity. Long-ignored topics affecting our quality of life are finally being addressed, such as school inequality, police brutality, the lack of political representation, health care, and jobs.

Galvanized by the material, I form a campus Brown Power Society along with Carmen, a fiery Chicana from San Diego, our mutual hometown. It comes as a shock to many, particularly since I was already a member of a very preppy business fraternity. Our peers definitely don't see it coming when we decide to change our look and get afro perms. We want to make sure that no one doubts our commitment and solidarity to social advocacy. Our intentions are honest, but in retrospect, I realize we didn't have the experience to carry it very far, and it fell on deaf ears.

But another part of me is awakened as I make my jaunts into the heart of the city to get my *Berkeley Barb* and stay informed. I can no longer ignore that a third of the newspaper consists of an extensive array of ads for X-rated films, mail-order novelties, and both gay and straight classifieds. And so my explorations take another path.

I'm awestruck when I discover the films of Andy Warhol featuring his most popular star, Joe D'Allesandro. *Rolling Stone* magazine previously named *Trash* as the best film of the year, and the *New York Times* wrote, "D'Allesandro's physique is so magnificently shaped that men as well as women become disconnected at the sight of him." My new escapades are all done without the knowledge of anyone back at school. In fact, I now have a different swagger of confidence that is attracting more attention from the popular girls—the ones who are known to only date the captain of the football team and are referred to as "the student bodies."

It isn't long before I'm exploring the city by night. I'm still underage, and the gay bar nightspots that pepper the city are not easy to enter—except for the Alley Cat. It is, indeed, nestled at the end of a short alley just off a major street. As much as I enjoy the attention—particularly the free drinks—the age of the crowd is a lot older than I expected, and Joe D'Allesandro is nowhere to be seen. But all is not lost as there's an area at the front of the bar with an array of throwaway newspapers that are new to me. As if by divine intervention, I spot an ad that calls to me. "Spiritual Renewal Day— we have 1000 seats to fill—sponsored by Reverend Troy Perry, founder of the Metropolitan Community Church (MCC), where everyone is welcomed."

On Sunday evening I make my way to historic California Hall along with 800 other folks. MCC is a church that is primarily an inclusive ministry that welcomes gays, lesbians, bisexuals, and transgender people. The Reverend Perry stirs a spiritual awakening in me that I've never experienced. I'm in a faith-based environment where I'm not being judged or ridiculed for the feelings that have been stirred up within me. I'm home.

My double life is now more opposite to what is expected of me than ever. The only person I share my secret with is my best friend, preppy Greg. He opts not to attend church with me because of his Catholic upbringing, but he is more than willing to join me for an underground movie. I immediately become a regular at Sunday services, not quite realizing that my call to organize and serve social justice causes will soon be heading in a new and unexpected direction.

Word gets around the university that I am now more radical—so accepting of others that I even associate with gay people and support their causes. The big identity shift happens when I see Doug walking my way on the campus courtyard. We've never met, but he stands out for a number of reasons. He's always impeccably dressed, he's one of a handful of Black students, and he makes no bones about being out as a gay man. He slows down as he nears me, gives me the once over, and says, "Hello Miss Thing." I stop in my tracks and bend over in laughter. Doug will become a great ally and incredible friend.

Soon, I'm more involved in spiritual and social activities at my new place of worship. Through this process, I witness the vastness and diversity of the gay community, along with experiencing the joy and creativity of my new village. It's also the time that Gay Liberation is unfolding, and although I'm a neophyte, I'm more than ready to join the first pride marches.

Despite my attempts to remain involved with my fraternity and other social clubs on campus, my lack of attendance draws unwanted attention. It's just a matter of time before folks figure it all out. Even my appearance has changed. My afro has grown out and is replaced by my naturally wavy hair with added long sideburns. I'm going for an Engelbert Humperdinck/Tom Jones flair, but I end up looking more like Tony Orlando.

There's an upcoming fraternity house party, and for some reason, I feel it's time to face the music and spend some time in my university environment. The festivities are in full force as I swagger in. And sure enough, a handful of guys that I used to just kick it with are now pretending to not know me. Maybe they've forgotten the radical part of me because their actions propel me to head directly towards them. As I approach, the tallest one says, "He's a fag." I feel my adrenaline kick in, along with my civil rights activism. I grab him by his shirt collar and shove him against the wall saying, "What did you call me?" He doesn't respond, so I declare, "If you have something to say, say it to my face." The entire room stands in silence. No one has ever seen this side of me—not even yours truly.

That night is a major turning point for me. I'm embraced by a sense of strength for standing up for myself. At the same time, I feel a sense of pride for defending and championing my newfound family. It immediately reactivates the organizer in me. I take a deep look into what is needed and how I can best be of service. I don't have to look very far.

Our church youth population is slowly growing, and with it the necessity for an array of services, particularly mentoring and social activities. With the approval of Reverend Howard Wells, San Francisco-MCC's first pastor, I hold a meeting after Sunday morning worship for all our youth—enticing them with punch and cookies, something I learned from leading a handful of the social clubs during my high school years. I announce that we are officially becoming a recognized group within the church, and therefore we can raise money for activities of our liking. The room initially goes silent, then breaks into thunderous applause and yays of approval and excitement.

I'm elated, and then tell them, "We'll need a mission and vision statement, goals, and a name." Once again the room goes silent, but this time applause and yays don't fill the space. Instead, there's a look of bewilderment. From experience, I know this could be an overwhelming task, so I assure them that several of us will put those formalities together. Truth be told, I'm the "several of us."

Within a couple of weeks, at the age of 19, I'm elected president of what is to become known as The Chicken Coup. It all happens so quickly that I don't remember ever questioning it. It all just feels right, and I'm joyous. What I don't realize is that I'm now the acknowledged spokesperson for gay youth. It's a group growing by leaps and bounds in San Francisco—catapulted by the birth of the Gay Liberation movement. I realize that if I'm to be a leader, I need to educate myself not only about our current social and political climate but also our rich history.

MCC and the Chicken Coup become a lifeline for many of us. We bond as a community, united in raising consciousness in a safe, fun, and loving space. Being seen out in public is crucial for us. With that come car washes, weekly chats, and outdoor social events in addition to our ever-growing dances. It's a delight to see us growing in self-confidence and self-worth. Then a great honor is bestowed upon us when we are asked to lead Sunday service. Our theme is love. Love for one another, for community, and for oneself. I wish I had kept my sermon, because in addition to a smiling and attentive congregation, there isn't a dry eye in the house.

A number of adults and elders notice my efforts and encourage me to join them for after-service coffee hour. These men and women, some who had been teens and young adults just 20 or 30 years prior, share with me a trove of insightful stories about their own struggles maneuvering through life as a gay person.

Dale, a gay man in his mid-forties, is luckier than most. He shares his experiences about working for the federal government during the 1960s Lavender Scare[2], where thousands of gay employees could be fired because of their sexuality. He kept his sexuality secret for fear of losing his

---

2 The Red and Lavender scares. The former was the congressional witch-hunt against Communists in the 1950s.The latter lasted far longer and impacted many more lives—up into the 1960s. Dubbed the Lavender Scare, thousands of gay employees were fired or forced to resign from the federal workforce because of their sexuality. The wave of repression was bound with anti-Communism and fueled by the power of congressional investigation labeling gays, along with communists, as subversives.

job. And yet, after all these years, he continues to keep a low profile by usually attending work-associated social occasions accompanied by a female friend. I'm shocked to hear why he still does this. Although it's not currently enforced, the provision to fire someone for their sexual orientation is still on the books. I develop a close kinship with this incredibly kind man who, unbeknownst to either of us, would soon guide me into a similar career path.

I consider this time to be a major renaissance period in my life. No university can compete with what I'm learning and experiencing. Coming to terms with this realization, I leave my institution mid-way through my studies. I tell my parents that I'm going to remain in San Francisco and explore other options. Truth be told, I don't have a clue where I'm going to live or how I'll earn a living – since, up to then, I've been surviving on a full university business school scholarship. The only area that I can afford, even though I'll be sharing the rent with my boyfriend Marty, is in the Tenderloin. It's a neighborhood known for low rents, dive bars, and street walkers—both women and crossdressers.

Finding a job is another learning curve that I quickly master. One morning, walking past Marinello's School of Beauty, I see a sign that reads, "Earn While You Learn." By that afternoon, I have an assigned spot for my own mannequin head, a locker, and a cosmetology kit with an apron, cape, brushes, combs, clips, and scissors. And to boot, a full scholarship. Who knew I would be good at this? Within six weeks I'm working with paying customers. I find out they are assigning me the older clients that no one else wants—

the ones known for never being satisfied and being bad tippers. I go to town backcombing and teasing those updos, beehives, and half updos (popularized by sex icon Bridgette Bardot). Those ladies make their next appointment right after I do my magic, something the school has never seen. And these women tipped quite well.

But alas, although I'm having fun, the money isn't enough to survive on, and all that hair spray is making me nauseous. So within three months of this colorful adventure, I officially become a beauty school dropout.

I continue my involvement with MCC and the Chicken Coup. It's at this time that the use of inclusive, gender-neutral language is introduced in worship services and church hymns. And in a genius marketing campaign to increase overall attendance, the "Bring A Trick to Church Campaign" is launched. This is a true embracement of the cultural uniqueness our community is developing during these days of newfound freedom and pride.

Living in the Tenderloin exposes me to even more incredibly creative social ways of identity and communication. As I make my way back into the city streets—looking for work and enrolling in university evening extension courses—I interact more with my newfound neighborhood. In the early hours, quite a number of cross-dressing hookers are heading home or working the morning pedestrian flow. As I walk by, they yell, "Hi honey, looking good." Then one day, as I'm passing a large store window at Macy's in Union Square, I notice a slim young man meticulously dressing the display.

He looks familiar, but I can't place him until he waves, and I notice his long, manicured fingernails. I've never seen Jay in the daylight or out of drag when he's working the streets. Here again is another gifted soul who will soon introduce me to an entirely new world that I would have never imagined existed.

During my job search, my mom suggests that I apply for a civil service job since they're known to be quite secure and with benefits. During high school, she encouraged me to take typing classes as my elective; a skill that would serve me in the future. When other boys were taking shop and auto mechanics, Russell was accomplishing 90-words-a-minute on that typewriter. Mom was right. It turns out to be a lifeline. I pass the civil service exam and quickly start another unexpected chapter in my life as a clerk typist with the personnel department of the U.S. Customs Service, an entry-level position in the federal government, which soon allows me an array of unforeseen opportunities.

I like my job, and I'm fortunate to have an incredible supervisor. Marguerite is a middle-aged Japanese American, living in Oakland and raising a family along with her husband, who is Black. They met while students at UC Berkeley in the late 1950s, a time when interracial marriages were frowned upon and illegal in many parts of the country. Knowing her story teaches me that activism doesn't need to be confined to outward public displays. She becomes one of my heroes.

Every once in a while, I run into Jay while having lunch at Union Square. I learn that he arrived from Honduras to study design and was able to immerse himself in an accepting and loving community—one he had longed for his entire life. It's such a delight to see someone be so comfortable in their newfound gender nonconformity. His sense of freedom and personal expression is truly inspiring.

And then, as luck would have it, the universe decides it's time for me to have another unexpected diversion. Although Patrick doesn't attend MCC, I meet him through mutual church friends and am quite taken by his charm and striking good looks. On our third date, he introduces me to his family at their ranch in Petaluma, just an hour's drive from the city. It's my first time riding a horse and certainly not the last since I become enamored by them. Then comes an unforeseen surprise. He invites me to come see him perform at the Hungry i—a straight strip club in San Francisco's famous Broadway district. Patrick performs a tightly-choreographed, steamy, striptease act with his dance partner, Clare. I'm completely mesmerized, to say the least, but this isn't my ultimate surprise. Later that evening he makes a proposition. "I spoke to management, and we all agree that you have a great voice and presence. We'd like you to come work with us." I can't believe what I'm hearing. "Doing what?" Patrick chuckles at my reaction. "We need to elevate the show and would love for you to be our master of ceremonies and introduce the acts."

It also turns out that Patrick makes his own costumes and has already started on mine. The night of my debut I wear tight-fitting, flared pants and a vest minus a shirt. I'm like a fish to water as I introduce the various acts including the headliner "Lolita," a classy, platinum blond beauty whose claim to fame is stripping down until all she has on is a string of pearls around her neck. She then gracefully kneels down, leans back, and sensuously unloosens the clasp. The audience is spellbound as the string of pearls makes its way down her front and somehow manages to stay dangled at the end of her nipples. The crowd goes wild.

Although I'm having a great time, my night gig as an MC at a straight strip club only lasts a few weeks, as does my relationship with Patrick. Luckily, my day job doesn't suffer from my most recent escapade. In fact, I'm doing so well that human resources sends me an announcement advertising an upcoming position with a department whose purpose is more aligned with mine.

I become a specialist with the Office for Civil Rights[3], working on Title IX issues at predominantly underserved school districts in Southern California. Obtaining this assignment is a dream come true. It allows me the opportunity to further my knowledge in the ever-growing area of civil liberties, which will serve me a lot sooner than I expect.

Our country is going through a major turbulent time, reflecting the polarity in our society. Richard Nixon is in the

---

3 The Office for Civil Rights (OCR), is a sub-agency of the U.S. Department of Education and, at that time, was expanding due to the approval of Title IX, which prohibits sex-based discrimination in any school or education program that receives funding from the federal government.

Oval Office for the second time, and the Vietnam War continues in full force. That summer (1973), the UpStairs Lounge in New Orleans, frequented by parishioners of our MCC sister churches, is torched and claims the lives of 32 people. And sadly, a few weeks later—in what seems to be a copycat, hate-motivated arson—our own church building burns down. That Sunday I feel an intense re-kindling of my passion for advocacy as we march from our burned-out church to a nearby Presbyterian Church that had invited us to hold service. With teary eyes and a defiant spirit, we sang, "We Shall Overcome."

I treasure that I am blessed to have forged a bond with a number of elders to guide me during this emotionally fractured time, particularly Dale. He tells me that, not only is he overjoyed that I'm a fellow federal employee, but that my timing is impeccable. A federal judge finally rules that a person's sexual orientation cannot be the sole reason for termination of federal employment.

Armed with a steady income, I eventually move into a Victorian flat in Haight-Ashbury. Unbeknownst to me, it is just down the street from a safe house where the Symbionese Liberation Army had been keeping kidnapped newspaper heiress Patty Hearst. Other than that, it's a pretty mellow area.

My new responsibilities call for me to up my dress attire; a coat and tie become the norm. I once again run into Jay. This time he makes an unexpected proposal. He takes a step back as he checks me out from head to toe and says, "No doubt about it. From now on I'm going to call you Miss Man." His words are followed by a slight head turn and a snap as he waves his hand—a physical expression that I have certainly not seen at church. Then he lays out his carefully thought-out plans. He invites me to be his escort to an upcoming event hosted by the International Court of San Francisco[4]. I'm speechless, mostly because I don't have a clue as to what he's referring to. But Jay speaks with a deep excitement and joyous energy that I've never seen from him. The event is sponsored by the second largest gay LGBT organization in the world, surpassed only by MCC. They build community relations for equality by raising funds through the production of several large-scale drag events.

I have nothing to compare it to since the biggest dance party I have ever attended was my high school prom. And with that as my previous schooling, I show up with a wrist corsage when I appear at Jay's front door. He looks radiant in his bell-bottom pantsuit with a form-fitting vest accentuating his tiny waist. His hair is so big that we have to do some creative maneuvering to fit into the cab. Once we arrive at the hall, reality hits. A group of evangelicals is gathered outside with hateful signs, yelling that we are doomed to hell. It was a disturbing scenario that sadly was gaining

4 Founded in 1965 by legendary gay political activist and prominent drag performer Jose Sarria, the Imperial Council of San Francisco is the founding mother court of the International Court System and the oldest LGBTQ+ nonprofit with over 65 chapters in the U.S., Canada, and Mexico. They work with prominent drag queens, gay community leaders, and activists to share the vision of a greater united, politically active, and charitable gay community.

momentum across the country, and I would eventually come face-to-face with on a more regular basis.

Once inside we have pictures taken as if we are attending a world premiere. Flashes everywhere. Jay knows exactly how to pose; never exaggerated, always glamorous and elegant. One thing he hadn't warned me about is that each couple would be announced as they enter the big hall. "The Imperial Court welcomes Mr. Russell and Miss Jay." Thank God they didn't say Miss Man. I have the time of my life—so much so that I send my mom a picture of us, figuring she'd think Jay was a real girl. Oddly enough, she never asked about that evening or the girl with the Cleopatra eyeliner.

During my handful of years with the Office for Civil Rights, I continue to expand my academic education by pursuing a graduate program in holistic health. Once again, I'm at the perfect place and the perfect time since Northern California is at the forefront of the Holistic movement. The Holistic perspective of combining physical, mental, emotional, social, and spiritual components in the healing process captivates me. Classes are in the evenings and on weekends in San Francisco and eventually on the UC Berkeley campus.

Instead of a thesis, we're required to complete a capstone project integrating the knowledge and skills that we've learned and apply them to clinical settings. The head of our program makes sure to prepare us for our final presentation, which is to be in front of professors from UC Berkeley and outside Holistic practitioners. "Be fully prepared and expect to be asked questions beyond what's in your project." I'm incredibly excited and don't have a clue that my life will once again take a 180-degree turn.

It's a large empty room, probably used for dance and movement classes. A chair has been placed in the middle of the space facing a series of expansive, fold-out tables like the ones in school cafeterias. To this day, I don't remember how many people were behind those tables or any questions except "the one." The woman in the dance leotard speaks. "Russell, tell us, what is your fantasy?" I think I hear her incorrectly. I mean, being a gay man I certainly have many, but this is hardly the place to discuss them, so I say, "Uh, my fantasy?" "Yes," she replies. "If you could do anything in your life, what would that be?" As I dig deep for the answer, my body temperature rises, and I begin to get teary-eyed. "I can't answer, it won't do any good." "Why not, Russell?" she asks. "Because it's too late, so why torture myself?" I'm sobbing. "What is it, Russell?" I take a deep breath and carefully respond, "I've always wanted to be a dancer, but because of circumstances due to my parents being separated, I never did, and now it's too late, I'm too old." She never takes her eyes off me the entire time. "How do you know this is what you truly want to do?" The answer is in my heart, "Every time I'm sitting in the audience and dance is part of the performance, I'm miserable because I've always wanted to be up there on stage, like I had been as a kid."

The professor in the leotard gets up and walks over to me. "Russell, take a look at my feet." She's wearing Birkenstock sandals. I glance down and see that she only has four toes on each foot. "I was born this way, and all my life I knew

I wanted to be a dancer. I'm not only the head of the dance department at Berkeley, but under my leadership, our dance program is now rated among the top 10 in the country. If you really want something, don't let any circumstance stop you from pursuing your dream." The next day I pay a visit to one of the most respected ballet teachers in San Francisco, Yanina Cywinska.

The following week I begin taking classes. Within four months, I'm there every day after work and on Saturdays. After six months, I quit my job and am now studying full time. Yanina believed in me from day one and never asked my age. She has several numbers tattooed on the inside of her wrist—Yanina had survived the Holocaust and became a prima ballerina later in life. I'm blessed with one of the most knowledgeable and inspirational teachers in the dance world. Within three years, I'm touring as a member of a professional ballet company. Yanina is not only my hero, she is also an angel in my life.

During all of this time, I never forget the hateful scenario I witnessed outside the venue at the event I attended with Jay. That's why I find it even more joyous to learn that we enter a period when support for our gay community is increasing, including straight advocates of civil progressivism. San Francisco elects our "People's Mayor," George Moscone, who appoints Blacks, Asians, and gay people to city commissions, reflecting the diversity of the city for the first time. Assemblyman Willie Brown, along with Moscone, initiates and fights for Assembly Bill 489[5]—state-recognized legislation decriminalizing homosexuality, referred to as the Consenting Adults Law.

Despite all the jubilation, I can't ignore the arrows of ignorance and oppression that are still aimed at us. Even our first-term Governor Jerry Brown signs Assembly Bill 607[6] banning gays from civil marriages, an act that perplexes us all.

But even more menacing is witnessing the loathsome actions taking place in Dade County, Florida, with the goal of repealing a recent ordinance prohibiting discrimination on the basis of sexual orientation. Singer Anita Bryant heads the campaign, naming it "Save Our Children[7]" and stating, "If gays are granted rights, next we'll have to give rights to prostitutes and to people who sleep with St. Bernards and to nail biters."

Once that ordinance is overturned, I help form a group of local, astute, young gay professionals (lawyers, architects, business owners, etc.) to strategize about how we

---

5 California legislation decriminalizing private and consensual gay sex. Signed into law on May 12, 1975.

6 The first California statute expressly limiting marriage to "a man and a woman." It wasn't until 2008 that the state's court struck down the same-sex marriage ban.

7 An anti-gay campaign headed by singer Anita Bryant. It was formed after Dade County, Florida passed an ordinance prohibiting discrimination on the basis of sexual orientation. Her campaign ended successfully with a majority vote to repeal the ordinance later that year. Dade County restored the ordinance in 1998.

can best address this wave of hostility before it reaches our own shores. The consensus is that, in order to better understand and address the mind-set of this movement, we must work within the Republican party by attending their functions.

The threat to our civil liberties kindles an enormous statewide mobilization unlike anything we've seen before. The entertainment industry is now one of our biggest allies, with Bette Midler's manager, Aaron Russo, producing "A Star-Spangled Night for Rights" at the Hollywood Bowl—a concert to benefit the Save Our Human Rights Foundation on September 18, 1977. Some of the performers on the lineup include Lily Tomlin, Helen Reddy, Tanya Tucker, War, Richard Pryor, and Bette Midler. This outpouring of support is also rattling the homophobic wave taking place. Senator John Briggs (R-Fullerton), a name we will soon recognize, threatens to blacklist every Hollywood performer or politician who supports the show or even attends.

As I approach the entrance, we are all met by sign-carrying religious fanatics yelling that we're scum, degenerates, doomed to hell—what we now call "hate speech." I don't see anyone confronting them. Nothing can deter 17,000 people moving forward in anticipation of experiencing this momentous, unifying extravaganza in support of our rights. Some of us are lucky enough to be able to eye the VIP section, where I spot the likes of Paul Newman, Olivia Newton-John, Valerie Harper, and Robert Blake.

Although the event starts later than scheduled, the crowd is so amped up that no one cares. Once Lily Tomlin appears, a propulsion of excitement is unleashed, lasting for the next three hours. Then an unimaginable scene takes place that brings our joyous, celebratory occasion to a stifling pause. Richard Pryor steps on to the stage sputtering his anger, which had been triggered by the fact that a young, Black dance group didn't receive the same thunderous applause bestowed on two White ballet dancers. "How can faggots be racists?" His tirade continues as he weighs Black rights against gay rights, Black rights against women's rights, and makes pejorative comments about gay sex acts. In a state of shock and anger, the majority of us respond with deafening boos. Before finally walking off, he concludes with, *"Where were you faggots when niggahs burned down Watts?"* Then he bends over and raises his backside, *"All you, can just kiss my happy, rich Black ass!"*

There we are, a sea of stunned faces. How could this be happening? This was to be a night of unity, and it's collapsing. But the show isn't over, and I'm sorry to say, I don't remember the next couple of acts until the spell is broken. Bette Midler struts on stage to an exhilarating, deafening response. Once we all quiet down, the Divine Miss M delivers the one-liner that will squash Pryor's bitterness. *"Is there anyone here tonight who wants to kiss this rich, White ass?"* We are all instantly on our feet, and the show goes on.

Two months later, a jewel emerges in the presence of Harvey Milk—one of our most prominent gay activists—who became the first openly-gay man to be elected to public office in California as a member of the San Francisco Board of Supervisors. Harvey quickly sprang into action by ensuring the passing of a city bill banning discrimination based on sexual orientation in public accommodations, housing, and employment. It passed 11-1.

I enthusiastically continue to take part in our gay professional advocacy group, attending Republican political gatherings and forums. We are gaining a voice in those sessions, so much so that a few gay allies within the party identify themselves as gay to us, but never at the functions, only after. I'm always dumbfounded by gay Republicans, thinking of them as self-loathing, until I meet Bruce Decker at one of the meetings.

Bruce is a political consultant in his late twenties who moved to the city after serving as the advance man for President Gerald Ford and Vice President Nelson Rockefeller. We quickly become friends. He reveals to me his ongoing frustration at publicly remaining in the closet while doing his best to enlighten his party on gay issues. Bruce lives politics 24-7. By simply observing his interactions with politicians and other decision makers, I learn a lot about how to engage with them—skills that will serve me for the rest of my life.

The timing for our group couldn't be better as the hateful tide quickly shows itself in the form of the Briggs Initiative, also known as Prop 6—a ballot referendum to ban gays and lesbians from working in California's schools. I make sure to be more actively involved as we set out to engage in dialogue and ensure that the Republican party won't be able to hinder our movement to defeat Prop 6. It's an effective tactic that, although slow moving, will eventually have a measurable impact.

The next few months could have become a discombobulated period of panic, hopelessness, and surrender, but it was not to be. Instead, our gay community never loses focus and moves into overdrive by homing in on acts of unity and empowerment. This is when artist Gilbert Baker, with prompting from Harvey Milk, creates the Rainbow Flag as a symbol of gay pride. I feel so much love as I walk with the MCC contingency on June 25, 1978, the day our flag first flies at our San Francisco Gay Freedom Day Parade.

As voting day approaches, political forecasting shows a very close outcome. This is when President Jimmy Carter and California's Governor Jerry Brown announce their support for our cause. Soon after, former president Gerald Ford and upcoming presidential nominee Ronald Reagan finally follow suit.

Although never publicly acknowledged, I know in my heart that our small but vocal group, along with Bruce Decker's influential voice, played a major role in obtaining the Republican party's turn-around. On November 7, 1978, Prop 6 was defeated 58% to 42%. Mission accomplished.

And from that moment on, the pulse of our community is euphoric. Then on November 27, 1978—just 20 days past that historic occasion—Harvey and Mayor George Moscone are assassinated by Dan White, a disgruntled former city supervisor who cast the sole vote against Harvey's bill.

While in a complete state of shock, I let out several powerful angry screams from the open window in my third-floor Haight Ashbury flat. That evening, I headed to the Castro, knowing that our community would band together. On my way, I notice that the usual traffic noises and bustle of crowded city streets are now silent.

I'm one of thousands gathered for a candlelight march, making our way to City Hall where the killings had taken place. When we arrive, Joan Baez leads us in singing "Amazing Grace." That is the first time in my life that I cried for what seemed like hours.

Six months later, while touring the Pacific Northwest with Western Ballet's *Giselle,* I'm in my hotel room watching the news when I learn that Dan White has been sentenced to a mere seven years in prison for the two killings. The jury buys the Twinkie Defense—claiming that his depression and mental illness caused him to binge on junk food including Twinkies. I immediately call several friends in San Francisco, but no one answers. Then the national news carries the riots that followed. Even though I'm miles away, I'm experiencing the same rage that I see in the faces of my angry brothers and sisters.

When I return to the city, I receive a lunch invitation from Bruce Decker. He encourages me to turn my internal rage into action and continue to work for change within the conservative sector. At the time, he's working with Pete Wilson, mayor of San Diego, who is already exploring his candidacy for state and national public office. Because of Bruce, I also believe that Wilson will be one of our allies. And since I'm in the process of producing a major photography exhibit, Bruce suggests I raise my level of influence by dedicating opening night to Wilson's pursuits. The George Hurrell/ Philippe Halsman photography exhibit is a major hit. It's the first time the works of these two renowned, iconic Hollywood portrait photographers appear together.

Fast forward 20 years later. My artistic pursuits lead me to the entertainment industry in Los Angeles as a working actor, writer, and producer. This particular evening, I accept a dinner invitation from Richard, an older gentleman from old Connecticut money who is wooing me with his lavish lifestyle. A chilled bottle of Moët & Chandon awaits my arrival at his three-story, old Mediterranean, palatial home. After a tour of his extensive art and antique collection, we head over to his garage where he asks, "Which car should we take?" I decide not to be fussy and choose the Bentley.

We are heading to a Republican party fundraiser in Beverly Hills. I think to myself, "This could be interesting." Upon entering we are guided to a meticulously-manicured, outdoor courtyard filled with elegant dinner tables. It doesn't take me long to notice that I'm the only person of color among the 60-plus guests. Some things never change. I don't interact with Richard for the rest of the evening. He sits at the front with the host and the guest speakers while my place card positions me towards the back of the patio.

I don't recall the table conversation or the topics emanating from the rotating speakers. What I do remember is experiencing the onset of claustrophobia from the mightier-than-thou attitude permeating the atmosphere. I'm trying to find the humor in all of this, anything to stop my head from exploding. That's when I spot the guest speaker stepping up to the mic. It's Pete Wilson.

A lot has happened since I last saw him, in particular the AIDS epidemic that still raged during his two terms as senator during the Reagan and G.H.W. Bush years and continued well into his two terms as Governor of California. I don't take in a single word that he utters. All that's playing in my head are memories of Bruce Decker.

By the early 1980s, Bruce had founded Concerned Americans for Individual Rights, a national group with the goal of expanding Republican awareness of gay issues and to counter the rising influence of the religious right. And once he learned that he was HIV+, he devoted himself to advocacy for people with AIDS, a disease that took him from us just five years prior to this evening at the age of 45.

Before long, I spot Richard signaling me to follow him out the door. Luckily, at that very moment I notice that the "bid farewell" line for Pete Wilson has dwindled. Trusting my instincts, I patiently wait my turn to speak to him. "Pete, it's been a long time. I'm Russell Alexander-Orozco. I produced a distinctive and successful fundraiser for you in San Francisco back in 1980—The Hurrell/Halsman Exhibit." After a short, awkward pause he remarks, "Oh yes!" That's when

I went at full throttle. "That was Bruce Decker's idea. He believed in you. How sad that, after devoting his life to the party, most of you turned your backs on him when he chose to come out of the closet." The seasoned politician doesn't say a word as his eyes desperately search for the host, as if to say, "Save me." But I'm not finished. "I miss Bruce. He was truly a great man, not many are." And I walk away.

I realize now that, in that moment, I was finally able to release the inner rage that I've learned to keep hidden. And I am not alone. I feel Bruce's presence, along with the embracing energy of love and support from all the heroes and angels that I've been blessed to know and to work with throughout my life. They are the ones that continuously fuel my spirit as the struggle continues.

Author's Note

One of the overarching descriptions of the 1970s and gay culture is that it was all about pleasure, freedom, and play as gay people cohered publicly in greater numbers than ever before. But what many of us forget is that during all that euphoria, incredible injustices were still being perpetrated on our gay brothers and sisters. The wounds around us were still fresh. It had been less than two years since the New York City Stonewall Riots of 1969. Credited with being the catalyst igniting the movement, the confrontations were influenced by the civil rights movement, the counterculture of the 1960s, the anti-war demonstrations, and the feminist movement. And let us not forget the impact from the socio-political climate spilling over from the late 1960s when Martin Luther King Jr. and Robert F. Kennedy were assassinated. Fires were burning everywhere.

Russell Alexander-Orozco (he/him) is a multidisciplinary artist of Latinx and Native American heritage: teaching artist, actor, writer, filmmaker, storyteller, community organizer, and advocate for social justice. As a teaching artist, he utilizes Theatre Arts Integration to create art that impels action and uplifts community beyond barriers of race, gender, class and geography. Russell is the recipient of the Guardian Award for extraordinary leadership & years of service to the Community of Los Angeles. He can be heard sharing his stories at the Autry Museum of the American West, the_NDA_show, *and* Strong Words—Voices of the City.

Run Kiddo Run

By AleX Dean

Growing up as a young girl in a rural Idaho farming community, Mormonism was all I knew. With the exception of two families, everyone in our small town of 557 people was Mormon. After our chores were done, my sisters and I were free to run about and play on the farm. Rare visits from my boy cousins brought the excitement of Matchbox cars, catching frogs, and other outdoor adventures.

Sometimes we would visit my great Uncle Rasty. I always counted on him to reach out and shake my hand, swinging my full arm gently back and forth while saying,

"How ya doin' ol' kiddo kiddo kid?" When he released my hand, I delightedly discovered a whole nickel in my palm!

When I was 5, I started kindergarten. Succumbing to pressure from my paternal grandmother, my parents began going to church regularly at this same time. They attended the temple and took vows of strict obedience to church doctrine. I was required to attend church all the time, not just twice on Sundays but also on Wednesday afternoons when we were released early from public school. I hated wearing the required dresses! They were uncomfortable and awkward. I couldn't move around freely or run and play. My legs got so tired from trying to keep my knees together that I resorted to sitting on my hands to hold my legs in place.

Church was so boring! There was no joy or celebration. Only reverence. God was not a source of comfort to me. He saw every move I made and knew everything I was thinking. I envisioned a large tablet where he took detailed notes about me for Judgment Day. I was afraid, so I obeyed! I had no friends, and I felt so different than all the other kids. No one was like me, and nobody liked me.

The one thing I did like about church was singing the hymns. My Dad had a deep singing voice, and I loved to hear him. When the whole congregation sang in unison, it gave me a sense of comfort, warmth, and belonging.

My feelings about my dad confused me. He was so powerful! On one hand, I felt he could protect our family from any harm. On the other hand, I was constantly afraid of getting into trouble with him. I was extremely sensitive, and a raised voice or a stern look from him was enough to make my stomach churn.

Boys and girls were separated in church at a young age, and activities were based on prescribed gender roles. The boys had Cub Scouting. I admired their bright blue uniforms with their many pockets. They earned merit badges by mastering outdoor skills like knot tying and fire building. They got to go hiking, biking, and camping. Then there was the Pinewood Derby where they made little wooden cars and raced them for a prize. I longed to do all those things. I wasn't the least bit interested in any of the girls' activities, like cooking, embroidery, knitting, and crocheting. I wasn't very good at them either. I also saw the power that men had. They were the ultimate authority over their families. Wives and children were subservient to them and duty-bound to obey them.

These changes brought with them the loss of freedom I felt as a younger child. Now it was my job to figure out what the rules were, to try and comply, and to stay out of trouble.

One warm spring Sunday, as we approached the church entrance, I saw the boys running up the grassy hillside. I watched them as they lay down sideways and rolled their bodies down the hill, laughing and screaming. Over and over. It looked like so much fun! But I couldn't run over and join them because I was wearing a stupid dress! It just wasn't fair! I let out a big sigh and thought, "Sometimes ... I wish I were a boy."

When I turned 8 years old, it was time to be baptized. My parents never asked me if it was what I wanted. It's just what was done. They didn't explain anything about it. My family didn't talk about anything! I was relieved that my baptism by immersion would wash away all my sins. However, I'm not sure what sins I had committed at such a young age as I always tried my best to be good and stay out of trouble.

On my baptism day, twelve families gathered at the stake[1] center for the ritual. It was going to be a long evening. My mother and I were sent to one of the empty classrooms, and my mom was handed an all-white jumpsuit for me. It was knee length with short sleeves and buttons all the way up the front. I tried it on, but it was too tight. I was way too fat! Embarrassed and ashamed, I realized that this was one more way I didn't fit the mold. My Mom simply sent the jumpsuit away and requested a larger one. That one was also too tight. My tubby belly was busting out of it, but it was the largest jumpsuit they had, so I stuffed myself into it.

My family joined the other families in the baptismal room, along with the stake president and other authorities. I anxiously watched as others ahead of me were baptized so I would know exactly what to do. When it was my turn, my dad and I entered the hip-high water. After my dad recited the baptismal prayer, I felt nervous and out of control as he leaned me back and dunked me into the water. When he

---

1 Stake: A congregation is called a ward, and a group of congregations is organized into a stake. Each local ward is led by a bishop, and a stake is led by a stake president.

pulled me back up, the stake president told us my foot had stuck up out of the water, and I had not been completely immersed. "Oh no!", I thought. "It didn't work! My sins didn't get washed away!" He told my dad it was not necessary to recite the prayer again. All he needed to do was dunk me again, making sure I was completely immersed. So he did just that. No prayer—just a dunking.

It was a mistake! What kind of baptism was that? Just a dunking without the prayer? We didn't follow the rules exactly! My sins had not been washed away. I was not going to get a fresh start! My foot sticking up was clear evidence that I was an unworthy person.

The next morning at church, I was confirmed as a full and responsible member of the Mormon faith. I sat on a chair at the front of the chapel, facing the congregation. My father, along with the bishop[2] and several other men from the ward, formed a closed, tight circle around me. Each man placed their right hand on the shoulder of the man on their right and their left hand on my head. There were so many of them surrounding me. My neck was strained with the weight of their hands. It felt like they were actively pushing my head down. The air in the tight circle was extremely stuffy, and I had trouble breathing. I felt trapped. I tried to resist, but it made no difference. I couldn't lift my head against the weight of all these men's hands. With the recitation of the prayer, I was confirmed as an official member

2 Bishop: The leader of the local congregation, similar to a priest in other Christian churches.

of the Mormon church. I was now required to obey all the commandments, and I was responsible for all my future sins. Due to my failed baptism, I felt I was still also responsible for all my past sins. I did not believe my sins were washed away as I thought about my foot sticking up out of the water. Ugh! My head ached, and my body felt heavy with guilt and dread.

As time went on, my feelings of unworthiness grew. This way of life I was required to live was gradually draining my life force. I did my best to suppress my anger and frustration because I thought it was wrong to have those feelings. I became more and more contained and subdued.

As teenagers, we attended youth group on Tuesday evenings, and I had to go. The gender-based differences were apparent and now even more significant. Our classes prepared us for our purpose in life. Women were to marry, raise children, and serve and support our husbands. We were always the ones to provide refreshments and decorate for the occasional mixed-gender dances. The boys just showed up.

When boys turn 12, they are ordained at the first level of the priesthood[3]. They get to participate in the church service by passing the sacrament, a ritual similar to Communion in other Christian churches.

Their program included Scouting, and they spent most Tuesday evenings playing sports and learning outdoor

3 Priesthood: The priesthood is the power and authority to act for God. Mormons believe they're the only organization on earth with this authority. All worthy males are ordained with incrementing levels of the priesthood starting at age 12.

skills. I was sitting in class one evening, hearing "Thump, thump, thump. Thump, thump, thump...Kerswish." There was a basketball hoop out there, and instead of being taught a lesson on how to become good husbands and fathers, the boys were running wild on the basketball court. It was so unfair! I longed to be a boy!

During my teenage years, I tried to behave as I was supposed to. I can't tell you how many times I heard my mother say in exasperation, "Diane, can't you please try and act like a lady?" And I tried, I really tried, but I just couldn't do it. Trying to "act like a lady" was just like trying to stuff my fat, 8-year-old self into the too-small baptismal jumpsuit. I was a complete failure as a "lady." I recoiled just hearing that word.

I believed there was something quite wrong with me. My sense of joy and freedom had been replaced by a sense of unworthiness and failure as a girl. I was not the young lady I was supposed to be. And yet, at the same time, I began to get a sense of, "There is something wrong with this picture." I couldn't yet articulate what it was, but something just wasn't right. And it had to do with how women were treated.

When I was 14, Congress passed the Equal Rights Amendment[4], and the states were in the process of ratifi-

4 The Equal Rights Amendment, or ERA, would constitutionally guarantee equal rights for women. Approved by Congress in 1972, it has lacked enough political support to be signed into law. Title IX, which also passed in 1972, provides equality for women and girls in education. It had a huge positive impact on me as a teenager, opening the avenue for competitive women's sports. It continues to disappoint me that the ERA has not been codified.

cation. I heard arguments from the pulpit about the evils of the amendment. It would lead to men and women being forced to use the same restroom, that there would be same-sex marriage, and that women would serve in military combat. I secretly seethed at this outright rejection of equality for women.

As high school students, we attended a daily class called Seminary. We studied the standard works of the church: the Book of Mormon, the New Testament, the Old Testament, The Pearl of Great Price, and the Doctrine and Covenants[5]. These classes took place at our public schools during school hours, and we received high school credit for the New and Old Testament classes. One teacher spoke frequently about the role of women. "Women are here to support their husbands and have babies," he said. When four of us girls rebelled and argued with him, he justified this by saying, "Men are not limiting women. We are putting women on a pedestal." He rubbed it in with pride and glee. All four of us were frustrated by this, but I was the one who was most furious.

Another teacher taught us the law of chastity according to Mormon doctrine[6]. His graph on the board demonstrating the rapid arousal of males and the gradual arousal of females explained why it is the girls' responsibility to make sure the law of chastity is kept. "Boys just can't help

5 Standard works: The volumes of scripture officially accepted by the Mormon church.

6 Law of chastity: The Mormon Law of Chastity is defined as abstaining from sexual relations outside of a legal marriage between a man and a woman.

themselves," he said. How is any of this fair? It's not! I felt truly exasperated.

African American men were not allowed to hold the priesthood at this time. I felt this was clearly wrong. I also wondered why women weren't allowed this privilege. I became less contained and subdued as my feelings of anger, indignation, and rebellion grew. I observed firsthand the power differential between men and women, between husbands and wives. This was evident throughout the entire church structure. All the women's organizations were overseen by men, and men had the ultimate say. I was seeing more and more clearly exactly what was wrong with this picture.

As I approached the end of my high school years, I longed for the freedom and independence that it appeared only men had. I knew I needed to find a way to support myself. I applied to the electronics technology program at a nearby technical school. A few days before classes were to begin, I had not yet received my notice of acceptance. In my conversation with the admissions counselor, he pressed me, "What makes you think you can do this?"

"What?" I thought, but I knew exactly what he meant. Based solely on the fact that I was a woman, he doubted my ability to be successful. I tilted my head, looked him directly in the eye with a slight look of scorn, and said, "What makes you think I can't?" He just looked down and mumbled to himself. The next day, he received my transcripts. I was an A and B student. After that, he fell all over himself trying to ensure that I got enrolled into the program.

I put myself through school by working full time as an operator on the assembly line in a semiconductor manufacturing plant. It was exhausting, but I was determined to have a career that would allow me to be independent and self-supporting. I was adamant that I was NEVER going to get married. No sir, subservience was not for me. I was NOT doing that. And besides, I couldn't imagine that anyone would ever love me in that way. I was not the lady I was supposed to be. I was not marriage material.

I was the first woman in the department to be promoted to a technician. My boss refused to train me, barely spoke to me, and would not look me in the eye. He said, "I will NOT have a woman working for me!" He was okay having women as operators but not as technicians.

Artis, the woman operator who trained me, generously did so because she had learned on her own how to perform the duties of the technician. Without a degree, she was not allowed to bid on the job.

Once I graduated, mid-management tried to convince me to stay on with the company. But I was having nothing more to do with that misogynistic place.

The railroad offered me a union job with the opportunity to relocate. While I was reluctant to move far from home, I was drawn to the opportunity to get away from Mormon culture and start a new adventure. I was given my choice of three locations: Kansas City, Salt Lake City, and Portland, Oregon. I had no desire to move to Kansas City, and I definitely didn't want to go to Salt Lake City, headquarters of the Mormon church. The only thing I knew about Portland was that there were a lot of trees and that possession of marijuana was only a misdemeanor, so it must be a liberal place. I chose Portland!

On October 8, 1979, I started my new job as the first female electronics technician for the Union Pacific Railroad. This time it was different. While the boss was reluctant to have a female technician on his staff, I WAS provided with good on-the-job training. My male co-workers all accepted me and took time to train me. They looked out for me both on and off the job. They WANTED me to succeed. They were all at least 10 years older than me. They called me "kid," and they became my big brothers.

I was hired as a probationary employee, and I worked and studied hard to learn my new job. I already knew that, as a woman in a traditionally male field, I had to work twice as hard and be twice as good just to be considered on par with the men. Being a new technician, I lacked confidence, and I wasn't sure I could cut the mustard. I was afraid of failing, losing my job, and ending up back in Idaho. My faith in God wasn't strong, but I was willing to try anything to succeed at this job, even prayer. Every day before going into my work building, I sat in my car and prayed to God to help me.

With my move away from Mormon culture, I fell into my own natural spirituality. I was deeply connected to nature. I hiked in the forest and rode my bike. I felt that same freedom I had felt as a kid running around the farm. This, and my exploration of something new—kundalini yoga—

started to connect me with my body. Until then, I had felt largely detached from it.

Within a few months, I was shocked to find myself deeply in love with an older man named Richard. My world was spinning. It was as if someone had pulled the rug out from under my feet. At 21 years old, I had never been on a date, and I couldn't imagine that anyone would ever be attracted to me.

I was taught that marriage was preordained by God. If I was in love with Richard, it meant he was the only right one for me. When Richard found out how inexperienced I was, he withdrew from me and started seeing other women. This was extremely painful for me. I began to drink excessively and cycled between binge eating and obsessive dieting and exercise to escape the feelings of heartbreak, confusion, and despair. I was lost.

In my desperation, I sought out counseling. I worked with a young therapist who was pretty and caring, and I developed a crush on her. That didn't surprise me because, even as a young child, I had had crushes on both men and women. I didn't think anything of it. I found it comforting to talk with her, but my depression did not improve. No matter how hard I tried to describe my feelings to her, I didn't feel like she understood how depressed and desperate I was.

A couple of years had passed since my big move to Portland, and this was when the Mormons started knocking on my door. Despite telling them I was not interested in their visits or in attending church, they persisted. I felt pressured and angry. I just wanted to be left alone.

I decided the only way I could get them to leave me alone was to officially leave the church. I didn't believe in Mormonism, and I no longer wanted to be a member. I was done. At that time, my only avenue to terminate my membership was to go through a formal process. I wrote to the local ward[7] bishop and requested excommunication.

It was a long two weeks until their formal response arrived in the mail. It was a summons to attend a court hearing, and it stated that I could bring a witness. I was relieved when my therapist offered to accompany me. Upon our arrival, the bishop wanted to know who my therapist was and why she was there. "She is here to support me," I said. I was told she was not a qualified witness as she was not there to advocate for retention of my church membership. She was relegated to wait in the hallway.

When I entered the large conference room, my startled eyes were met with the sight of more than a dozen men in dark suits, white shirts, and ties who were seated around a large conference table. This was not the three- or four-member local ward council[8] I was expecting. This was the stake high council[9], convened as a disciplinary coun-

7 Ward: A local congregation.

8 Ward Council: The leaders of the local congregation consisting of the bishop and his two counselors.

9 High Council: The twelve highest ranking officials in the stake.

cil, and they would make the decision whether to grant my request for excommunication.

I sat as I was instructed, near the center of the table, with my back to the door. The meeting began with one of the men offering a prayer. Then one of them began to question me. "What sins have you committed that warrant excommunication?" he asked. This took me by surprise. My expectation was that this court would be a simple formality. I would tell them I wanted to be excommunicated, and they would comply. I already told them I wanted out, so why didn't they just do that? It was my choice, right?

"My leaving is a matter of integrity. To be a member of the church is to say I believe all of its doctrines are true, and it is the one and only true church. I don't believe that at all. That's just not how it works," I said. I no longer bought into their black and white thinking. They seemed to be puzzled and confused, like they didn't know what to do with me. They continued to pressure me to confess my sins, but I adamantly refused. I just wanted my freedom. I felt that familiar churning in my stomach. They had to grant my request, didn't they?

They finally realized I was not going to confess anything, and asked me to leave the room while they had a discussion. I sat out in the hall with my therapist for a very long time. My fate was in their hands. When I was called back in, they said they would grant my wish. I would be excommunicated. I was both relieved and pleased. I did it!

Friends asked me why I found it necessary to go through the formal excommunication process. I felt I was in an energetic bind over which I had no control. If I severed my connection with the church, the heavy weight that I carried would be released, and I would be free.

A few weeks later, I received my official letter of excommunication. The process was complete. However, I still felt the heaviness hanging over me. I went to the coast and dunked myself entirely into the Pacific Ocean. Still influenced by my Mormon upbringing, I imagined an "unbaptism by immersion," symbolically washing my pain away. The ritual was effective, but its effect on me soon faded. The heaviness returned. It felt similar to when I was baptized and my sins had not been washed away.

There was also the problem that I had not yet told my parents. This weighed heavily on me. I felt strongly that I should deliver this kind of news in person. Since they lived 700 miles away, it would likely be several months before I could do that. The next time I called them, my dad answered their phone, and I immediately knew something was wrong. My dad *never* answered the phone! My stomach tightened.

Unbeknownst to me, the local bishop had already called my parents and informed them of my excommunication. My dad was livid! He wanted to know why. My stomach churned, and my heart began to beat faster. I told him I didn't believe that all Mormon doctrine was true. He said, "Either it's all true or it's all false. Which is it?" It was a trap that I refused to fall for. Despite his persistent pressure, I held my ground. I told him my leaving was a matter of integrity.

Because he continued to pressure me for a reason, I told him I did not agree with the treatment of women in the church. "Do you think I treat your mother poorly?" he asked. That was a tough one. It was true; I didn't like the way he treated her. I didn't like the way *any* Mormon husbands treated their wives, and I didn't like the way the church as a whole treated women. It just wasn't right. I saw how powerless and subservient Mormon women were. It frustrated and angered me. But in this conversation with my dad, I refused to answer this question.

His next statement hit me in a vulnerable place. He said, "Your mother is crying herself to sleep every night." I was devastated by this. I had been close to my mother as a young child, and I still adored her. When I learned I was the cause of my mother's broken heart, it also broke mine. How could I be so mean? And yet, I had only done what I had to do. Mormons believe worthy families will be together for eternity, but I would not be included. By being excommunicated, I had intentionally broken our eternal bond. I was now "unworthy," all because I had followed my heart. It was an irreconcilable situation; a hurtful rejection to them and a no-win dilemma for me.

The unexpected predicament with my parents was not the only big change brought about by my departure from the church. In what seemed like five minutes after my excommunication, it occurred to me I might be a lesbian. I had had crushes on women ever since I was a kid, but I never connected it with the possibility of being a lesbian. Now I was increasingly aware of my attraction to women. Before I left the church, I could not finish the thought, "I might be a lesbian." It meant I would go to hell. Now it was dawning on me, "Oh, the fact that I am attracted to women ... that's what it means to be a lesbian. I might be a lesbian." A few months prior to this, I had been receiving letters from an old college roommate describing in depth how she felt about me. She went on and on about her strong feelings of caring for me, and it went right over my head. Once I came out as lesbian to myself, I looked at the letters again, and I realized my friend had been writing me love letters! How did I not see that before? Because I just couldn't go there.

I thought once I had officially left the Mormon church my problems would go away. I had worked so hard to feel better and excommunication was the final step. But it wasn't. I didn't feel better. Excommunication did not undo the years of damaging doctrine and practices. I still felt like I was carrying a heavy burden of guilt and shame. And now I was also carrying the pain of knowing that, because I chose integrity and authenticity, I was causing my parents tremendous pain. Therapy was not helping and the feelings became unbearable.

I continued excessive drinking, cycles of overeating and dieting, and exercising compulsively. I worked out twice a day, running and lifting weights. I thought I was too fat, and I hoped that this would fix what was wrong with me.

It was effective at deferring the pain, but only while I was actively engaged in those activities.

On Monday, March 29, 1983, prior to my afternoon therapy appointment, I impulsively drank all the alcohol I had in the house and took leftover painkillers from dental work. I drove all the way to the office, went into the waiting room, and passed out in a chair. Someone woke me and asked me some questions. They called a friend who transported me to the hospital. When I arrived there, they tried to get me to throw up. I didn't want to. I was still drunk. I said, "You're nothin' but a fuckin' intern, and you can't make me!" A threat to pump my stomach brought my quick compliance. When they wanted to admit me to the locked ward, I was taken aback. "Why?" I asked. "When someone makes a suicide attempt, we take it seriously," they replied. This was not a suicide attempt! It was my cry for help. It was as loud as I could scream.

My closest friend, Amanda, came to see me in the hospital with balloons. I was surprised to see that one of them said, "I love you." I could not believe she or anyone else would feel love for me, even the love of a friend. I felt completely broken and not even remotely loveable.

I had fallen into a deep and dark bottomless pit. Amanda reached her hand down into that pit and pulled me up. She cared for me unconditionally as if she were a loving mother and friend. Over time, she convinced me I was loveable. Eventually I could say it out loud, "I am loveable."

A year and a half passed, and Amanda and I were in love. We became partners and purchased a home together.

I kept our relationship a secret from my parents. Coming out as lesbian to them would just be a repetition of the pain they experienced around my excommunication. I was not willing to put them through that again. I held everything inside, obscuring from them all the personal details of my life. This contributed to a massive wall of pain and isolation between us. I continued to suffer from serious depression. I was functioning during the day at work but struggled with even the most basic self-care.

My dad persistently tried to exert his influence. There is a Mormon scripture that was commonly interpreted as, "The sins of the children will be upon the heads of the parents." As my father saw it, when I turned my back on the church, I put his salvation at stake.

I was annoyed by his continued emails and "gift' subscriptions to Mormon magazines. In 1993, he gave me the Book of Mormon with certain scriptures highlighted. "If you will read this and sincerely pray, I KNOW that you will receive confirmation that the church is true," he insisted. My frustration with his arrogance was building, and now I was steaming inside with anger. How can anybody else KNOW what is right for another person?

Partly to prove him wrong and partly to put my own mind at rest, I did as he asked. I read the highlighted passages and prayed to know if the Book of Mormon was true. No confirmation, affirmative or negative, came. If there were a

God, he was not talking to me. I never shared this with my parents, and they never asked. This was the very last time my dad pressured me.

I traveled to Idaho to visit family over the Christmas holidays in 1994 and was staying with my parents. The morning of Christmas Eve it just became too much to hold everything inside. Ten years of hiding the most important thing in my life, being in a relationship with Amanda, was more than I could bear. My tears started leaking out and I couldn't stop them. I cried almost continually all day long as I walked around the small town, asking God to tell me what to do. "Should I come out to them?" No answer. I walked some more, crying and praying. Still no answer. Hours passed. No answer. No answer. No answer.

I decided to confide in my brother-in-law. He knew church doctrine well, and he lived it. I respected and trusted him. "I just don't see how loving another person, even another woman, can be wrong," I said. He gently spoke to me about the different kinds of love. Agape, eros, and philia. Different kinds of love for different situations. When I queried him about coming out to my parents, he said, "I don't think you would be telling them anything they don't already know." "Really?" I thought. I wasn't so sure. Why hadn't they said anything? Couldn't they see how I was struggling so hard to hold it all inside? It would be so much easier if *they* would bring it up. Maybe they didn't want to know, and maybe they *hadn't* figured it out yet. I was still very troubled. How could I find the courage to tell them?

As evening approached, I returned to my parents' home with an extremely puffy face, red swollen eyes, and a throbbing head. I hid out in the spare bedroom and continued to cry until my nose was so plugged up that I couldn't breathe. At this point I had to force myself to stop crying. My mind quieted a bit. I heard my own thought, "Diane, your *body* is trying to tell you something." God wasn't talking to me, but my body was. I finally got it. For my own sake, I needed to come out to them.

Now I was just trying to work up the courage. My older sister came in to check on me, and I told her my secret. She talked with me for a while, helping me to calm down. I asked her to send my parents into the room.

I finally told them I was gay. My brother-in-law was right. They had already figured it out. My mom said two things to me. "Diane, a mom knows these things," and "There is nothing you could ever do that would change the fact that we love you." My whole body lightened, and at the same time I relaxed and sank with relief into the bed I was lying on. I knew it was possible they could have rejected me, as many Mormon families had done just that. My father's response, however, was different. He said, "The only problem I have with the gays is that they have to flaunt it in the streets." I just didn't have it in me to have that conversation. I was completely exhausted.

I was out to my parents, but I still carried guilt and shame for causing them so much pain. At least I now had a skilled and compassionate therapist, and I made continuous progress under her loving guidance.

Six years later, while visiting my family in Idaho, I went with my parents to see my paternal grandmother in her nursing home after her recent stroke. She queried, "Have you received your temple endowments[10] yet?" "No," I said. "Well I guess you'll have to pay your dues in the next world." she scolded me with disgust. That hurt! All I wanted was her love and approval, and instead I felt judged and rejected by her. Choking back my tears, I said, "What matters is that I love you very much, and I'm doing my very best to be a good person." I looked at her for a sign of acceptance or understanding but nothing shifted. My tears welled up again, so I went outside and let myself cry.

A while later my mom joined me. I turned to her and said, "I wouldn't have left the church if I didn't have to, but I had to. I can't believe a loving God would cause us to be eternally separated just because I'm not a Mormon. She looked at me and stated with conviction, " I don't believe that either." Those five words were all I needed! The huge weight I carried for breaking my mother's heart was finally lifted. What a massive relief! My mom was coming to terms with

---

10 Endowment: An ordinance administered to worthy adults in the Mormon temples. It is required in order to reach the highest tier of heaven in the next life. It includes binding covenants to keep the laws of obedience, sacrifice, chastity, and consecration (dedicating one's time, talents, and all that one has been blessed with to building up the church) as well as authorization and the requirement to wear the sacred temple garment at all times throughout your life.

the contradictions in church doctrine, and she was choosing love.

When my dad joined us, he said, "Don't pay any attention to what your grandmother says. She's not in her right mind." Then he added, "Nothing I have ever done for that woman has been good enough!" I realized he, too, had wrestled with the dilemma and was coming to terms with the situation. Their love for me was more powerful than what they had been taught by the church.

Being raised with Mormon doctrine was so painful for me because it purportedly taught unconditional love. Painting the perfect picture of a happy family together for eternity, the Mormon church says, "This unconditional love is for everyone—except for you because you are gay. You are not worthy."

I continued from time to time to be haunted by what I call the "Oh My God! What if They're Right?" moments. I worried, "Had I taken a wrong turn? Did I really promise God in the preexistence that I would come to earth, follow the Mormon path, marry the right man, and raise children?" I felt guilty about what might have happened to those children who were now unable to be born because I had failed to keep my promise. Are those babies up in heaven grieving the lost opportunity to be born into a physical body on this earth? My body filled with a sense of dread when I had these thoughts.

In 2001 I walked into a bookstore looking for a book on depression. When I paused to browse the books in the religion and spirituality section, one stood out to me. It was an older, used book with a dark, blueish-green cover. Opening the back cover, I saw that someone had penciled in www.exmormon.org. I thought my eyes were going to pop out of my head, and I couldn't wait to get home and check it out. The synchronicity of this moment astounded me.

Through that site, I discovered The ExMormon Foundation and a local support group. I delved into early Mormon history and practices. My research led to a much broader perspective on Mormonism, and my thinking shifted. This is how I got *unhooked.* The more I learned, the more the "Oh My God! What if They're Right?" moments dissipated. Those moments soon dissolved and never came back. *I was finally free!*

In 2005, I was single again. I bought a house in a Portland suburb. It was the first time I had lived by myself in more than 20 years. I didn't know the neighborhood well and didn't feel safe. One chilly fall evening, I decided I would dress in a masculine style while working in the yard. "I'll just pretend I'm a man," I thought. I put on my baggy blue jeans, a flannel shirt, a down vest, a baseball cap, and work boots and walked outside. I reached up and tugged my baseball cap lower on my head. With that tug, SOMETHING CLICKED! I felt like a guy, and I liked how it felt!

Ever since I was a young child, I had wished I was a boy and had fantasized extensively about it. But I had no idea what those fantasies really meant or that it was possible to make such a transition and not be seen as a freak by society for the rest of my life.

The idea of transitioning suddenly became a remote possibility in my mind. I searched the internet, discovered the Harry Benjamin Standards of Care[11] and a local support group. Transitioning now felt like a real possibility. I didn't allow myself to think ahead far enough as to how I would tell my family.

Armed with information, I visited my doctor who was very open and accepting. The two of us figured out together how to proceed, and I began transitioning physically and socially.

Not wanting to risk a potentially volatile conversation, I wrote my parents a letter to share the news of this profound shift. I wanted them to have some time to process it before responding. I asked them to call when they were ready to talk. Two weeks passed, and they didn't call. That felt like a very long time. I nervously queried my sisters and discovered that my news had thrown my parents for a loop. The possibility of my being transgender was completely off their radar. They wanted to talk to me, but they just didn't know what to say. So I called them. We had a calm but brief conversation. They asked very few questions but seemed to be somewhat accepting. My family was struggling to rec-

---

11 Harry Benjamin Standards of Care: An international protocol outlining the recommended assessment and treatment for transgender and gender-diverse individuals including social, hormonal, and surgical transition. It is now known as the WPATH (World Professional Association for Transagender Health) Standards of Care.

oncile this with their faith, and two of my sisters expressed their fear that I was making a mistake that I would regret. Over time, seeing how much happier I was put my entire family at ease and their acceptance grew.

By the summer of 2013, my spiritual life was still unsettled. I learned of local spiritual gatherings that were very inclusive. When I attended my first meeting, I saw the familiar face of Rani McLaughlin who was leading the gatherings. Rani and I met back in the 1990s when she taught classes on different religions at the local Unitarian church.

I had transitioned since I last saw her, so she did not know who I was. As I reintroduced myself, I watched the recognition dawning on her face. We were delighted to meet each other again!

In her Sufism[12] class, we did various types of sitting and moving meditation. Rani read poetry and told stories while drumming. We did some Dances of Universal Peace[13], also known as Sufi dancing. “You should come to Sufi Camp this year,” she encouraged. “It’s all about gender.” She was the spiritual director that year. I went!

Camp included an exploration of gender and gender stereotypes, along with spiritual practices from many differ-

12 Sufism: This is a type of Sufism known as Universal Sufism. It sees the Divine as one being and includes traditions from many different religions.

13 Dances of Universal Peace: A form of sacred dance. They are songs and chants from many spiritual traditions and cultures, and they are a blend of simple movements and singing. They are done in unison, and serve to open the heart, and to promote unity, peace and understanding.

ent religions. I was the only person there who identified as transgender. I was welcomed and embraced by most of the attendees and even treated like a guest of honor.

I had known Rani for a long time and had a great admiration for her. I soon asked her to be my teacher/guide, and we have worked together ever since. It is a practice in Universal Sufism for a teacher to give their student a spiritual name. Rani gave me the name Aziz which means purity, gentle strength, and self-worth. Over the years I have grown into my spiritual name. I have come to recognize my worth is inherent. I am a unique expression of Spirit. I am not broken. There is nothing wrong with me.

In 2015, the Mormon church modified their policy on same-sex attraction. Prior policy stated that it was not sinful to *feel* attracted to someone of the same sex, but acting on it was considered apostasy. It was cause for church discipline including possible excommunication for those who were unrepentant. The new policy added the restriction that children of "same-sex" parents were not allowed to be baptized. When the topic came up during a family visit, my dad shrugged his shoulders and raised his hands in the air, saying, "The prophet says..." meaning that church members must obey the prophet without questioning. Dad's mind was closed. Once again, I found his response painful. I began to cry, but rather than leave the room, this time I stayed, and I didn't hold back my tears. I wasn't going to argue with him, but I did speak up. "I love you Dad, but this is hurtful." I wasn't going to hide the painful impact of this policy or his reaction.

Music, an essential part of my path, is the quickest way for me to connect with my emotions and to connect with Spirit. I continue to listen to the traditional Mormon hymns that I sang as a child. It is both comforting and bittersweet. In the Dances of Universal Peace that I participate in, we sing and move in unison like a human mandala. Similar to the feeling I got from singing the hymns in church, they give me a feeling of inclusion and unison.

I now see that my life has been a long spiritual journey. I left the Mormon church, and eventually I also left the 12-step programs because I experienced them as another faith-based institution with overtones of patriarchy, rigidity, and guilt. I discovered a New Thought church, and that felt good for a while. But it became too mainstream, and they wouldn't speak up about the anti-gay ballot measures common in the 1990s. I shifted to Unitarian Universalism and enjoyed their commitment to social justice, but it lacked the heart-centeredness that I was looking for. These experiences informed my spiritual journey, and my current practice includes a non-dualistic view that draws on various elements. I now realize my feelings of hurt, anger, and abandonment were not about God. They were about organized religion and culture.

My family has truly been challenged by me. I rejected the church that defines their lives. With each coming out, whether it was as lesbian, straight transman, or gay transman, my family made it clear that they love me, and they want me to be happy. Their acceptance and their love for me are tangible. I hear it in their words, I see it in their actions, I feel it in my body, and I feel it in my heart. I respect and honor the dedication they have for their chosen religion. But it's not for me. I am deeply pained by the church's sexist, homophobic, and increasingly transphobic policies.

Once I transitioned, I no longer suffered from unrelenting depression. I love the body that I live in with its masculine presentation. My greatest joys are connecting with my family, friends, and spiritual community. Drumming for the Dances of Universal Peace is one way I can share my joy and support others. I am surrounded by people who both embrace and inspire me. I have healed from a deep-seated belief that I was broken. I know that my value is inherent. I am equal to every other human being, and I have the right to take up space in the world. It's okay to have wants and needs. I am a unique expression of the Divine Spirit with my own personal gifts to share with the world. I am just as I was meant to be. It could be no other way. And I am quite loveable!

Author's Note

At the time of my baptism, in my mind, my foot had betrayed me. Now I look at it as a defiant moment. My body was wise. It knew that the Mormon path was not mine, and it was telling me so. "This ... this is not for you. This is not who you are. RUN, KIDDO, RUN! There is a different life for you. You are pure and innocent, sweet and beautiful. You are a gift to the world, and the world is waiting for you. RUN, KIDDO, RUN! Embrace the beauty of your queer, trans self.

Share it with the world. Love yourself. Love everyone. Show the world how to love others. Be authentic. Be free. RUN. KIDDO. RUN!"

I no longer run away from my pain. It's part of the journey, and it is rich with wisdom.

I am running and dancing and drumming and singing with my heart wide open.

I am running towards my own precious authentic self.

So—no matter who you are, and no matter what your age is,

Whether you are 8 or 80,

RUN, KIDDO, RUN!

RUN towards your authentic self.

RUN as if your life depends on it ... because it truly does.

RUN. KIDDO. RUN!

AleX Dean (he/him), raised in Idaho, escaped to the liberal bastion of Portland, Oregon, when he was 21. He now lives in Ridgefield, Washington, with his two cats, Lucy and Fuzzer Butter. Retired from a rewarding career as an electronic technician for railroad and power companies, he now enjoys a well-paced life that includes bicycling, weightlifting,

drumming for the Dances of Universal Peace, inner exploration, and rewarding connections with friends, family, and community. Having experienced life as a straight woman, a lesbian, a straight transman, and a gay transman, he now identifies as "just plain queer."

Aspirations

By Noah Grabeel

"What does it look like outside the car when I am asleep?" I ask my mom, still groggy from the long drive across the Piedmont region of Virginia.

"It looks the same," she answers, rightfully confused as I keep repeating the same question with some urgency. "What do you mean?"

"I mean like when the car is going really, *really* fast," I say.

Soon my mom realizes that in my mind, any routine trip in the car has the potential to become a magical time warp. I get picked up, try to settle into the itchy car seat that has been sitting in the sun for too long, fall asleep, and wake up when the car lurches to a stop in our driveway. It simply makes sense that the car enters a gear shift so powerful that parents can activate it only if the passengers are asleep. What else could shorten a two-hour trip into a split second of absolute nothingness?

And how to reconcile this experience? My anxiety, as much as curiosity, prompts the odd questions and, in turn, my mom's bewilderment. As much as she tries to explain the perception of time to her 3-year-old toddler, my mind only has more questions after each answer. How could we seemingly teleport from one side of Virginia to the other, or how could any parent handle driving those winding Appalachian roads without totaling the car?

Mom sees my concern and exhaustion from so many questions, as they all come back to my continuous fear. Am I safe? She reassures me that, as long as she is able, I will have a safe place to be.

But there are things outside of her control. Maybe it is the regular allergy attacks or rushing to the emergency room in a panic when asthma belabors my breathing at night that stokes these fears. The mundane world is already a source of danger. Pollen from flowers, pet dander, even clean country air from the farm leaves me wheezing. And because my inhaler was left at home, two hours away, I am too embarrassed to say anything about my discomfort. It happens enough that I know the only option is to keep sipping air as

I am able, try not to talk, and count down the hours until I can rush up to my room to breathe again. One more puff counting down to the next refill.

Outside of sleep and that fantastically vibrant dream world, my waking childhood is marked by this dichotomy between apprehension and burnout: the anxiety of everything in my environment, followed by the wheezing exhale of relief in silence, so as not to worry the rest of the family about being able to take care of myself.

The most obvious benefit of quietly keeping this peace is the tedium. Time flies when you're having fun; so soon I realize the inverse is true as well. Visiting extended family creates seemingly never-ending afternoons to share with them. This is what all the songs on the radio and picture books seem to be hinting at to make the most out of the time we get in this life. It seems like a sound plan that pleases the adults who remark on how mature and respectful I am for a child sitting politely through a three-hour brunch at the country club or dutifully attending church every Sunday.

I learn to be thankful when I face adversity and chaos, whether from school bullies or my own father's capricious mood swings. Any time a wave of sadness washes over me, I learn to be grateful for how much longer my time on Earth feels. All discomfort makes sure I squeeze out every last drop of every second of every day.

Therefore, I ration out joy to avoid feeling regret over time wasted. I learn early on the benefit of delaying gratification and saving it for a rainy day. Amidst a largely happy, healthy, and obedient childhood, I still manage to catch my dad's rage for reasons I still do not understand. His discipline in these moments can make time stand dead still. Domineering with a sardonic wit, he can tear me down with a sentence or sometimes just an indifferent sneer, but when his moods give way to physical punishment, he is terrifying. His parenting becomes unrelenting with the goal of correcting any oddness in my behavior. And I am truly an odd one. I learn to hide everything from him unless I am absolutely sure it will make him happy.

Unfortunately, my silence or refusal to answer can be just as dangerous. Ignoring him is not an option, just like he cannot ignore my swishy existence or peculiar mannerisms. As a closeted gay man, he knows what people might say and makes sure I know it too.

"Quit that." He smacks my limp wrists away from my torso. "People will think you're not right in the head."

Keeping my arms tucked into my torso protects me from his unwanted touch, unexpected tickling or roughhousing. I learn to watch his every move, automatically fidgeting and tapping my fingers as I do to release the tension, which he also curbs.

He should know about the stigma of mental illness. He is diagnosed a rapid-cycling bipolar with regular adjustments to his medications, which he claims make him act more erratic. He claims ignorance whenever I bring up his harsh physical punishments or how it feels when he tickles me until I'm wheezing. I wonder when I will be old enough to forget these moments he brushes off, too, or if I will need medication to do so.

He stays closeted until after the divorce, after I start high school. Shortly after the separation, I come out as gay to both of my parents individually. It seems more manageable that way. A year after I make my confession, he comes out with all the vim and vigor appropriate for a recent divorcé, bringing "old college friends" around for visits, and eventually relying on high-risk sexual encounters to survive and feed his addictions. Eventually, these actions would lead to housing insecurity and medical complications, including testing positive for HIV.

But while growing up, he regularly points out my effeminacy without a hint of irony as we bond over reruns of *Golden Girls* and recordings of musicals on VHS. This version of him feels safest. Little calm tide pools of lyricism, levity, and shoulder pads that keep him happy as long as I stay quiet on the other side of the sectional. The dramas play out, and he explains the adult humor or shares an anecdote from his time at the Barter Theater or community productions when he did something similar.

The clouds of his temper still hang low on the horizon, and while his moods shift regularly like the tides, there is no moon or celestial body for me to track them. And yet, I try to keep time by these erratic cycles under a starless sky to savor every moment with him.

* * *

Tidepool 1

There once was a farmhouse in the mountains of Virginia, and inside lived Grumpa and his wife, Nana.

Whenever I visited, Nana taught me the basic components of drawing: how to deconstruct any object you could see and reproduce it as a two-dimensional image. Every day I spent with Nana felt like an infinity of Martha Stewart worthy projects—watercolors, painting rocks, pressing flowers, and baking. Nothing bad ever happened at grandma's house.

One day, I got to sleep over instead of returning home at the end of my parents' workday. There was only one hitch. I had to take a bath in the sulfur-smelling water and pink-tiled tub with a ruffled shower curtain and mobility support for Grumpa. Bathing at home was its own struggle, and this change in location was not helping.

However, since the fear of punishment had never seemed to exist at grandma's house, I flat out refused to bathe that night. I got to say what I wanted, and the truth was that baths were uncomfortable. They felt endless, the water smelled funny, and the sensations of dry to damp, soapy skin were always unpleasant. But not tonight. I took a stand. Here, anything could happen, and I even went as far as taunting my grandmother, saying things like she could never punish me for disobeying or saying no, not like at home. Not like what Dad would do.

Finally, Nana had had enough. Her sweet, serene cooing turned to the harsh tone that must have been necessary back when she was raising three kids and managing Grumpa's foul temper. That's where I had heard this tone before. Sometimes she had to explain to her husband, for the 15 thousandth time, that the doctor had said no more Little Debbies or to mitigate his yowling when she lifted his shirt to expose a doughy lobe of belly while administering his insulin shot. She used this stern tone of voice when there was no alternative, which was enough warning for me to do as I was told and never make her unhappy like that again.

* * *

I am not a morning person. Unbeknownst to my family, I spend most nights fantasizing and scripting out winning arguments with classmates and bullies because I do not want to continue asking them for support. I struggle enough to be well-adjusted and well-liked while managing to be a successful student. School work is easy comparatively, but it seems to take every waking hour and a few borrowed from sleep just to keep up socially and fit into a group. I stare up nightly, tracking the blades of the rainbow ceiling fan illuminated by an orange streetlamp filtering through the blinds. I hope to figure out why I do not fit in, just in case I am interrupted by a drive-by shooter in our quiet Virginia town, because I cannot rule it out.

I always feel like I do not have enough time. The finality of death and the concept of my own morbidity are constant reminders since it is the one problem I cannot solve for me or my family. By the time I am ten, primetime TV is a mainstay of our family ritual bonding, but I am most intrigued by the crime shows dad is not supposed to let me and my sister watch after we have been sent to bed. Unable to sleep anyways, I crouch at the top of the banister to listen and observe what I can. Occasionally, I dare to join him, swearing up and down that the TV will not give me nightmares. Dad seems to sense my desperation to learn from him, even the world's darkest realities. He really knows how to cut loose, too. He pulls out snacks that are just for him: cherry cordials, ice cream, and a Velveeta cheese dip from the microwave which sears my tongue or congeals in the bowl like clay. No middle ground.

These late-night shows are not happy and feel-goody like the sitcoms we enjoy together, which usually focus on eerily similar dysfunctional nuclear families and their histrionics. They do all share one key component, though. The good guys generally catch the bad guys in the end. The live actors bring some validation to the struggle between good and evil, a quality that I love in my cartoons. It's as if forensic science could model realistic heroism for my everyday life. Though Horatio Caine's cool stoicism is a bore on *CSI: Miami*, I immediately fall for Gil Grissom's even demeanor and thorough deductions when solving a mystery in Vegas, which usually resolves in under an hour. After the credits, the TV turns off for the day, and I scurry back to bed to ponder what drove these criminals to acts of depravity or murder. How could they do such things to their friends and neighbors, and most of all, what did their victims do that led to an untimely end?

It is also impossible for me to expect anything in the afterlife, even at 10 years old. I hoped it would be like Halloween Town in Tim Burton's claymation film, *The Nightmare Before Christmas*, but I get the sense that Gil would brush off such a fantastical theory. I toss out any childish notions of Heaven or Paradise and, like all my other nightly ruminations, I try to script it out only to realize scripting nothingness is fundamentally impossible. People say sleep is the closest experience to death, which only makes falling asleep that much harder as I try to actively track my nodding off for any course correction.

Despite willing my brain to turn off, falling asleep becomes another source of anxiety. Surrendering to slumber and dying become synonymous. How would anyone know the difference while experiencing either state? I pray to God my soul to take as I was taught, just to hedge my bets, but that automatic slip into sleep eludes me.

Each of these nights sets me up for a groggy, bleary morning. It never feels like an automatic process to get out of bed. Every step is spurred by its own line of reasoning and catastrophizing as I narrowly avoid my own self-destruction. Just like forensics on an episode of *CSI*, I track out the negative consequences of skipping each step of my morning routine and reluctantly do what I can. After particularly rough and tearful nights, I learn I can run the shower for 10 minutes, allowing me to take a quick nap on the mat without immediate reprimand. I only find the limits of this duping when Mom notices my funk and berates me for not washing properly. I lie to her and promise to wash better next time before skipping breakfast and rushing out the door to catch the bus, lest she remind me of any other skipped steps.

The chaos continues at school. I learned early on that my love of singing garnered a lot of unwanted attention and the label of "gay." Though I have learned to keep to myself, students take any opportunity to poke and jiggle my chubby flanks and bring my weight to my attention. When classes finally start, I am often playing catch up at the beginning of class, scribbling notes on paper to turn in and pass for homework. Education seems like the best way out of the current situation and the only possible chance to be independent like characters in the *Boxcar Children* series or the cavalcade of young adult book runaways on adventures. Those characters never have to worry about times tables or eventually taking care of their parents in their old age, a goal often set by my dad. At any rate, teachers must be appeased to get good grades, but school is nothing like the romantic education I received making art with Nana on the farm.

Except, of course, for art class. Throughout grade school, visual art reminded me of the time spent wearing my Nana's red satin nightgown, sprinkling salt on saturated watercolors of sailboats or finding books about marine life in her library to try tracing and sketching. In school, however, time is severely limited compared to the hours I used to spend filling every blank space of the page. I also know I only have one shot before the next class starts because

I struggle to maintain continuity in my artistic process between attempts. On the off chance I do happen to keep up with a previous draft, I struggle to pick up the momentum again, often tempted away by newer, fresher ideas. My previous attempts repulse me due to all the space left blank and hasty attempts at finishing. As hard as I try to make the most of the 30-to-45-minute period, my body of work does not measure up to any of my favorite picture books.

But if Gil Grissom can solve a murder in one hour, I think, there should be nothing stopping me from tapping into my creativity and making something wonderful, right? My dad tries to bond over my creative frustrations by showing me his costume design portfolio from college—voluminous bustles, structured bodices, and hollow, blank faces. He assures me that talent is in my blood, but I am too undisciplined. I am just not trying hard enough, so I persist while raging at my own inadequacy, hoping all the while to have either more time or more speed for making something truly worthy of his praise.

Someday, I hope I can move at my own pace. Family bonding time in front of the TV does not help with these lofty expectations for my own creativity. On cable, all the conflicts seem to resolve in about 30 minutes or as dictated by the *TV Guide.* Dad responds to the commercial breaks by sneering at a new collectible toy promotion or mocking me about why I didn't think of the latest million-dollar idea so we could live in comfort.

The expectations as a firstborn son spur me through every anxiety-riddled morning. I must be disciplined. I must live up to and try to remember to brush my teeth and bathe and not get picked on by bullies and avoid death and make my family happy and remember to recycle and to stop climate change and also pay back my parents for raising me so that they no longer have to work.

The ruminations bind up pathways in my brain, getting larger and choking out the fantasies played out with sticks, mulch, and leaves. The only time I have to unravel it all is in bed when I am trying to sleep. I am reminded constantly that my every action and every thought of every day could have a lasting, unforeseen, and negative effect. Every moment could be make or break. I try to set aside childish stories about superheroes and magic and start to focus on figuring out what I need to survive.

It is a race against the clock, and it restarts every morning as soon as I wake up.

* * *

Tidepool 2

There was a time I believed in Santa with all my heart.

Every day I was looking for undeniable evidence of magic. Not this new agey, crystal gazing, mindfulness stuff that takes introspection and metaphor to accept. There were enough stories about the existence of magic in the most unlikely of places, and I wanted in on whatever these writers were going on about. Santa was the wishmaker most likely to make that happen. My parents seemed to believe in him, talked about him, and accepted my wish lists without a hint of deception, and as far as I was concerned, his existence meant anything, literally anything, was possible. You need only ask.

But by the time I started grade school and interacting with other students and their traditions, I had to ask whether Santa, with his claims of immortality and warp speed, was really real. I called my parents into the bathroom for a confab. I had been mulling over the question there, on the toilet, bare-ass, when I called Santa into question. Total power move. They gave me one last chance and warned that I needed to be prepared for whatever answer they gave, especially if the answer was no. Big. Hint.

Was this a final test of worthiness? If I said I was ready for any answer, would I be rewarded like the characters from my children's bulletin from church? Was this my Abraham moment, and Santa, like Isaac, set up on the altar facing oblivion? I gave it a fair amount of thought (still on the toilet). If he was real, that meant some system of magic capable of carrying a morbidly obese man and all the hottest new toys around the world in a single night could exist. If that was the case, what else could be possible outside of a strictly Christian model of the universe? However, if Santa was not real, I had just fallen for the biggest prank in history for multiple years.

I made the decision then and there that I wanted to know the whole truth, as I would not be deceived. But still, I was pretty sure magic was real and holding out hope. It just seemed too far-fetched that an entire toy and entertainment industry maintained such a big lie for decades just to make something as mundane as money.

* * *

Spankings or "jerk a knot in your tail" or "smack the tar outta you." Whatever he calls it, the hits seem to last forever. Toward the end of his life, Dad will admit the medications made him crazy. He will apologize for falling into his father's same mistakes and that it is probably best that Dad cannot remember most of my childhood anyways.

But for me the hits are always coming. I do not know when they will come exactly, though, so I start to tense up in anticipation of his downswing.

"Don't brace yourself," he says. "You'll only prolong it. Make it worse for yourself."

I try to let my body go limp across his lap and bury my face in the comforter of my bed. The last thing I want is to be mistaken for backsassing or resisting his correction. Still, I keep flinching and pissing him off even more, even though all I want to do is dissociate from the entire experience, allowing each strike to blur together like a faded memory.

It is the space between the hits that make it worse. He yells. He asks if I have accepted my punishment and retained the lesson. I choke out an apology through snot and tears, but he demands I quit my bellyaching and speak properly. The empty rage in my dad's eyes telegraphs the next hit. I must always be watching for this, even in the quiet times.

Only when he feels he has made his point does he leave me alone in my room to think about what I have done to deserve this throbbing pain. I come to two conclusions.

1. My father's violence is necessary for my development.

2. I learn I can dissociate from any pain or discomfort to distort time.

With Death already established as non-negotiable, I realize that time is much more malleable. A 30-minute lunch at school feels much shorter than a 30-minute appointment at the dentist. Time can change based on the people that are nearby, not to mention the technologies that can capture, record, manipulate, and rewind moments at leisure. Even *Choose Your Own Adventure* books can be cheated by simply holding your place with one surreptitious pinky to take back a fatal mistake.

I reason that the value of a long and fulfilling life is not in uninterrupted bliss. The joy of a long and happy life has to be tempered by discomfort and struggle to carefully curate meaningful moments. Otherwise, my entire life can slip away in one blithely euphoric blip.

* * *

Tidepool 3

When I was around 5 years old, there was a swinging bench hanging under the deck. Dad had painted it teal and mauve.

In the evenings, Dad and I would sit and swing while he sang soothing melodies from the musicals he knew best, like "If I Loved You" from Carousel.

One night, as I was resting my head on his pot belly, he said that things had to change. He had installed the swinging bench under the deck of our new faculty housing on the campus where my parents worked. It was another part of growing up and our recent move to the city. He pointed out the neighbors' windows and yards and said we could not cuddle anymore. It was too childish, and he seemed worried about what people might think.

I suddenly felt anxious about what the neighbors could see from their windows and decks without ever understanding what he was worried about them seeing.

Not just swinging on the bench, but from that point onward, I became hyper aware of every walk I took across campus, who might be watching, and what they could be thinking. I worried about attracting any negative attention. It felt like I was living in a fishbowl within a fishbowl.

Finally, I had to come to terms with a portion of my childhood that seemed to be over for good. Not because I was ready, but because neighbors and my parents seemed to have an opinion on how a male child expresses affection. I realized there was a time and place for everything, and my wants started taking a backseat to what anyone else wanted to see in me.

* * *

For a first grader, freedom can feel like getting wheeled into the operating room for an appendectomy. Novel and alien, but what I cannot deny, while leaving my brave-faced mother behind, is how many possibilities now feel open. At least, anything I could do from a hospital bed and hooked up to an IV feels possible. The doctors and nurses all have a gentle demeanor. They assure me that I will feel better soon and none of them blame me for expressing discomfort about the pain in my body. It is comforting when they ask me about myself, and most of the questions about my interests are easy to answer. As I count backwards and take deep breaths of anesthesia, I wonder how I can feel this calm and secure every time I go to sleep.

Warp speed. I wake up back in my temporary room and need to vomit. The nurse is ready, reminding me about the procedure and explaining I am feeling so nauseous because of the anesthesia. I try to apologize, leaning over the bedside, and again she assures me that none of it, even the vomit, is my fault. I doze back off to sleep until Mom wakes me up. Dad is somewhere behind her beaming with gratitude that I made it through the procedure. He seems charismatic and affectionate, especially vocal when the nurse is in the room, about how nothing went wrong. I wonder how much it costs to stay at the hospital.

Time is much more regimented in this sterile environment. Nurses have regular tasks and charts, and yet I do not feel any rush to fill up my notebooks with writing or drawings. No one expects me to get through any of my homework while recovering, though I have already mostly caught up. This feeling is new. The time is mine to watch cartoons and fill in word puzzles without guilt.

Once I am discharged, the feelings wane at home. The crisis of my appendix had paused our regular routines, but soon my lackadaisical recovery time fades away. I am encouraged back onto the path of productivity and more constructive tasks, the kind of childhood that will set me up for a successful career someday.

Having gotten a taste of so much free time, I do try to run away from home shortly after returning. On one day in particular, Dad has pushed me too far or taunted me one too many times. I want that freedom again, of time and of self, so I pack up my dearest possessions—Dad's hand-me-down brown teddy bear, my favorite blanket, some art supplies, and a desk lamp (like *The Brave Little Toaster*). While he watches TV, I try to sneak into the garage to pack these items into a Radio Flyer wagon. Without breaking his concentration or moving from the couch, he asks what I am doing.

I tell him I am running away. I try to sound aloof but firm, but it is only as close as a first-grader can mimic from reruns of *Designing Women*. Still, I hope that is all it takes for the decision to sting. I hope he calls after me, on his knees, drowning in contrition and remorse. This could be the wakeup call he needs, but it is too late. I want him to feel just awful.

"Really?" He snorts. "Where you off to?"

"Away." Did he not hear me the first time? "I'm running away forever. Goodbye."

"Well, good luck then." He chuckles and continues watching reruns.

Good, I think, attempting to readjust my expectations quickly and without doubt. Just as well. I take his response as permission, as if leaving in a huff was always intended.

But now I have something to prove. I make my way down the steep hill, walk past the neighbor's house, and the first major intersection halts my progress. I grip the curb with my toes through my sneakers as cars zoom by. I am familiar with this corner from the safety of the school bus, but by wagon, the cars seem much faster and more dangerous. I want to cross and start my new adventure, but unlike the operating room, there's not a single adult around to witness me. I am not sure I am allowed to cross the street at this moment. I am sure of nothing and still afraid of what Dad would say when he finds out I could not even run away correctly.

I repeat my dad's question: "So where *are* you going?" When characters ran away from home in books or movies, they packed a lunch, sang a song, and immediately stumbled across a quest or mystery to solve. The rules in suburban Virginia, however, are different. No amount of fighting back tears a few yards from perfectly adequate food and shelter would summon a fairy godmother or eldritch patron for intercession.

I turn back. I trudge up the steep driveway with nothing to show for my grand gesture. No bittersweet anecdotes of high hopes or a powerful life lesson. I think to fib and make up a reason for my return to throw in my dad's smirking face. But what unexpected hurdle would show up just beyond our house's front yard?

"Back so soon?" He turns down the volume as the credits for *Designing Women* roll.

"Yes." I hope this ends the conversation, but it does not. He makes it a teachable moment and points out how unprepared I am for the real world. He reminds me that I do not even know how good I have it and how much worse it is for other children in other homes, if they are lucky to have a home. I am told to enjoy it while it lasts, a roof over my head, three square meals, and clothes on my back.

I know it is better to do as he says.

* * *

Tidepool 4

There once was a family counselor who asked to see all four of us for a session with my father, who had been diagnosed with bipolar.

I believed Mom when she said the appointment might give answers and start to bring peace back to the household, but only if everyone told the truth and was exceptionally open and honest about their feelings. She stressed this part with me as I had lied almost entirely about the pain of my appendicitis so as not to trouble anyone.

Eventually, the day came. I had been scripting and organizing my thoughts the night before, hoping I could finally articulate all of my frustrations with Dad. I even tried to prepare myself for Dad's denials and responses, anything he used to validate his parenting when I complained.

One drawback of the scripting was that I struggled to answer the therapist's questions. I wanted to list out my grievances, but when the therapist asked how I felt, I was not sure how to answer as most of my emotions were negative. And I was taught to be good. The last therapist that tried to help me with these emotions instructed me to yell and hit a pillow, which mostly just made me feel bad for the pillow afterwards.

I became self-conscious during the session. Every time I brought up a complaint, my dad discredited or denied it. Despite the very hopeful beginning, I quickly realized that the therapist's time was short, and I soon would be going home. No matter what I said, my dad's opinion was the one that mattered.

And of course, while I knew it was true that poor behavior was never excusable, a sentiment echoed by the therapist, understanding my dad's mental illness better could help make sense of his outbursts. His diagnosis created a stigma that none of us at the time could acknowledge fully, and so we needed to use more compassion during his manic or depressive episodes. I realized it was my privilege to be mature for a third grader so as to help manage my dad's emotions and join my mom as support. It was the same explanation I got when complaining about bullies, whose mothers started citing ADHD or Autism as explanations for their child's outbursts. Whenever peers saw me as the gentle giant, it seemed I had no choice but to take the verbal and physical abuse without retaliation. It was a privilege of the strong to remain stoic, unbothered, and unmoved.

Hiding the hurt became synonymous with an act of love.

* * *

It is hard to know when the flow of time with Dad starts to deteriorate. Most of my life with him feels as stagnant as the cigarette-laden air in his apartment. He is never without a sardonic comeback or disarming quip that makes me question myself, my core, and my perception of everything. He struggles to remember our shared history. We catch up less and less as it becomes clearer that he does not remember the last conversation or retain details of my life when I move away from Virginia after college. On the occasional phone call, I fall back on old habits and try to say only what will make him happy. I am productive. I am working on multiple degrees. I have a job and pay rent and do not need to ask for money. Whatever he happens to ask about, I am ready to present the most competent version of myself. He need not worry.

So it is easier, as always, to keep quiet and to enjoy the peace. Despite walking this tenuous line in our relationship, I never can be sure what aspects of my life will trigger rage or jealousy in him. It leaves me stuck, ever on-edge, ever-present, on an ever-repetitious loop like waves crashing on the shore. I tense up every time the tide carries the facts of my life across the telephone line and hope for the best.

My only escape is living my life. In that natural process, I come into contact with him hardly at all. I am physically repelled out of his apartment as he picks up smoking again, and my asthma gets triggered. He ushers me out of his house during a visit because one of his "college buddies," his code for a hookup, is coming over soon. The summer before starting college, I plan my own split-custody sleepovers to prove my worth as his son, but this ends when he calls me a "pussy" for not talking to his friends on video chat. I move an hour away for undergrad, audition back-to-back for shows, but still rarely expect him in the audience. I move to New York, get my Master of Fine Arts, join a queer-focused non-profit known for its genesis out of the AIDS crisis. I relay all these details over the phone and once in the middle of an Olive Garden, eliciting very little interest from him: nothing more than a glazed-over expression on his face induced by too many breadsticks, booze, or drugs. It is hard to tell.

I understand that, for most fathers, my life might well seem a bit out there and leave them speechless. However, this didn't feel like shock or an inability to comprehend. He was the same father I interviewed about living positive with HIV. Of course, I missed out on aspects of his life, too: his bouts of homelessness, getting his teeth knocked in while sleeping on the streets, resorting to survival sex, developing an addiction to crystal meth, and so many of his nameless and faceless "college buddies." The only thing I did not miss was looking up his mugshot on Google images.

I wonder if this is somehow my fault as well. If my goal is to maintain his happiness, I feel like a failure with every update. That is, until the final phone call.

It is the day after my 33rd birthday. I get a text, the first in months, to call him. I can feel the tide coming back in. He makes a similar request just about every nine months claiming to want to be part of my life again followed by another few months of silence. Knowing this, I still take the call. I imagine him muttering "pussy" under his breath if I delay.

I am surprised to hear him in such high spirits. In our last conversation, he was in assisted living recovering from Covid and wearing a diaper. This morning, however, he sounds like a cartoon hillbilly, a theatrical voice that I recognize when he is doing a bit. He gets straight to the point of the call. He has prostate cancer, and he only called so I could update my family medical history. The prognosis sounds non-aggressive, but he has chosen to wait and monitor with his doctor.

And that was just the appetizer.

I thank him for the update and tell him to let me know if anything changes. He starts apologizing for falling into his father's bad habits as a parent but mostly blames his prescriptions for wiping out his memory for the last 20 years. When I confirm he is talking about the physical punishment, he "guesses so" but he also adds that it is probably for the best that he does not remember anything that I claim he did.

He also makes sure I know my grandfather has Alzheimer's. I know this from attending my sister's wedding. This seems to remind him, and he apologizes for not making it because no one would give him a ride. He says this to me, one of the people who had offered to give him a ride to the wedding.

He quickly changes the topic. His voice lilts with excitement about my life and what has me busy these days. He asks if I am still doing theater.

I tell him about my 501(c)(3) work and speaking at a vigil for World AIDS Day, but there is no hint of recognition in his voice. It is now my turn to ask him about his life.

He launches into a tirade against his medications making him crazy. However, for the last eight years he has been on a better dose, which is really a shame, because no one has gotten to know the real him. He tells me that he has cut ties with his own father but hopes that we can start having weekly phone calls, though he never gives me a chance to confirm or deny this plan. He runs down the list of catch-up questions. What am I doing for work? Where am I living now? Am I still teaching? Am I still acting? The answers come out automatically. Office work. Portland. No. Not really.

"Do you have anyone special in your life?" he asks.

As many times as he asks this question, I am always surprised by how abruptly it shows up in our conversations. Or maybe I am just acutely aware that school and work have always taken precedence. Every time he asks, I panic like I have forgotten my homework and feel I must produce an acceptable partner to validate my queerness. Usually I do not know what to say in response, but on this call I try to inch closer to the truth.

"Not exactly," I say, "but I'm surrounded by many wonderful people that are special in my life; not just one."

His tone shifts ever so slightly. Even through the phone, he sounds almost haughty.

"So, that's a no," he says, ending the matter. "Well, that's all right."

He tries to tell me I will find someone soon, missing the point of my answer, and I let him think so because it is easier than correcting him. My defiance is tacit. I accept the discord in answering him honestly for once and maintaining my own narrative.

His curiosity peters out. He seems to run out of things to ask, and he looks for the nearest exit to this conversation he demanded of his child.

"Well, it seems like you don't really want to talk to me anymore," he says.

And nothing could be further from the truth. I want to talk to him until I am out of breath. I want to have all the talks. I want to ask what he remembers about the family session with his therapist. I want to bring up every fight we ever had. I want to dig deeper into the things he says he cannot remember, the bad parenting habits from his father's example, the spankings, and the pitiless rage. I have so many more questions, like if he ever considered the impact of watching his downward spiral after the divorce. I want to ask him again why he needed to goad me into talking to his "college buddies" online. I want to talk and talk and talk until we have examined every moment of our lives with the precision of a forensics team. I want to talk until I no longer fear the waning power of his strikes. I want to ask him why he thinks I keep throwing myself at people who are just like him over and over again to prove myself worthy of their love as well.

In a perfect world, I might realize fully that this would be our final conversation. I want to talk about what comes next. I want advice on death or some exclusive preview on how to time everything just right in my life. I want to ask him everything, hoping it will overwrite the critical voice I knew growing up. I want some assurance that confusion and chaos in life is all due to my failure to ask him these tough questions, as if crawling inside his brain would finally give me the perspective to know what is right and wrong in the world.

Instead, this is how our last conversation ended:

"If that's what you want," I say, "then I'll let you go."

He pauses before leaning back into his hillbilly lilt.

"Well," he says, "I don't really understand what you mean by that, but OK. Take care."

"Happy holidays," I say.

I watch the screen as he ends the call.

* * *

Tidepool 5

In a queer place and time, I was a boy and a girl and so much more, all-in-one.

Every day I went out into the world, people would say things like, "You're so mature for your age," or "Your parents must be so proud to have a son like you," or "You remind me so much of your father." And every day I made it my duty to shun all things masculine.

One day I saw the movie The Birdcage *and fell in love with Nathan Lane as Starina. I love how much she struggles to pass as masculine for a single dinner party and how much ease she has expressing herself as a histrionic Miami drag queen and doting mother to her adult son all in one.*

Because masculinity was everything I struggled to be as a child. Masculinity was an unwieldy mask that was supposed to keep me safe.

But because masculinity had the safety of privilege, my true emotions were locked behind a well-guarded, unassuming gate. "I mean," someone said once, "choosing to be female would be like giving up a winning lottery ticket." The comment surprised me as a child, as my mom kept everything afloat. Through my dad's manic spending and chaos, she made sure everyone had what they needed. It seemed laughable to put my dad in charge instead.

So, I rebuilt my foundational knowledge and defied conventional understandings of gender. By the time I found queer theory in college, I could better articulate experiences throughout the rest of my life. There was never another option, I realized. A standardized happily ever after was never going to cut it.

But in all the repetitive linear narratives throughout the world of storytelling, there were many more patterns to be found. There were nuanced dialectics and layered infinities to explore. There were discourses and dialogues that made sense of chaos beyond beginning, middle, and end. Rather than contemplating life experiences as a static, anxiety-riddled series of events, I learned to exist in my histories and reclaim my queer time and space within them. I avoided dissociating from life to survive. I learned to love feeling again.

I remembered the constant ebb and flow of water that narrates our lives.

Noah Grabeel (they/them) grew up in Virginia but moved to Portland, Oregon, in 2017. They received an MFA in Creative Writing from Emerson College, where Noah also taught composition and rhetoric. Their work has been featured in Pulp Factor, Nevermore, *and* The Mystery Box Show. *Outside of storytelling, they volunteer with the Sisters of Perpetual Indulgence and take the stage in various drag and musical performances. Noah's favorite animal is the flamboyant cuttlefish.*

Aspirations

Injustice in Cincinnati: A Personal Reckoning

By Heidi Bruins Green

Cincinnati, Ohio, was a city unraveling in the spring of 2001—frayed by injustice and rage after the police killed yet another unarmed Black man, the fourth in six months, the 15th in six years. A month earlier, the American Civil Liberties Union (ACLU) of Ohio and Cincinnati's Black United Front had filed a lawsuit alleging a decades-long pattern of racial profiling within the Cincinnati Police Department (CPD)[1].

I had lived in Cincinnati for a decade at that point. After days of unrest, I was increasingly angered by the injustice suffered by the Black community, undoubtedly since the city's founding. As a white person, I was an outsider in their sea of grief and defiance, but as a human being, I, too, was grieving deeply. When I stepped into uncomfortable solidarity with the Black community, it became a journey that challenged my convictions, tested where I found "my" community, and pushed me to confront powerful forces—both on the streets and within my world. In the face of my fear and resistance, I learned that standing up for what's right can come with unexpected costs as well as benefits.

The victim of the latest police murder was Timothy Thomas[2], a young man—by all accounts a loving boyfriend and father—who was gunned down in the street for no reason other than being a Black man in a racist community and country. His death shattered the fragile façade that had been patching the city together. The Black community reacted to

1 Clines, F. 2001 (April 23). In Aftershock of Unrest, Cincinnati Seeks Answers. The New York Times, Section A, Page 11. https://www.nytimes.com/2001/04/23/us/in-aftershock-of-unrest-cincinnati-seeks-answers.html; Thompson, K. 2021 (April 16). 20 Years Later: The Death of Timothy Thomas and the Uprising That Followed. Cincinnati Public Library blogs, Library Staff. https://chpl.org/blogs/post/20-years-later-timothy-thomas/

2 Momodu, S. 2017 (October 21). Timothy DeWayne Thomas, Jr. (1981-2001). Black Past. https://www.google.com/url?q=https://www.blackpast.org/african-american-history/thomas-timothy-dewayne-jr-1981-2001/&sa=D&source=docs&ust=1733085766305746&usg=AOvVaw3eB_t5joNP2hSdo6ykt4cN

this latest outrage by heading into the streets and expressing their frustration loudly and with some destruction of property. The Black community called it an uprising, while the all-white city leaders, in their fear, condemned what was happening as riots. I was deeply disturbed by the killing and felt that sitting at home was cowardly. I was safe in my white neighborhood—not surprisingly, Cincinnati was a segregated city—but I could not sit at home and do nothing. My inaction proclaimed a white complacency, which I rejected. I had to be physically present to support the call for justice.

A few days into the uprising, I decided to attend an ad hoc community meeting I heard about on a local Black radio station. That evening I walked into a large tent pitched on the grounds of a city park where hundreds of people vibrated with anger, sorrow, and defiance. As I entered, my discomfort about attending turned into awkwardness and concern that I might be intruding. I was one of just a few white faces in the room. A part of me wondered if I belonged there at all—whether my presence in this space of collective Black grief was helpful or if I was being selfish. But a deep part of me knew that hiding on the sidelines wasn't an option. This meeting wasn't about my self-doubt. It was about standing in solidarity with those who were grieving, angry, and tired of being systematically silenced and murdered. I was not there to lead. I was there to listen. When I figured out how to help, I would offer my support, and I would act.

Looking around the room, I felt the weight of the constant, grinding injustice over so many lifetimes on the people of the Black community. I could feel it in the air; heavy like a storm cloud threatening to break. The people in this room didn't need to tell me their stories of pain and frustration. It was written in their steely eyes, in the restless motion of their bodies, and in the determined way their voices rose and fell as they planned what to do next. They had lived this their entire lives. This was their usual, their reality.

I was far outside my comfort zone, but my comfort was not the point. Fighting against racial injustice had been bred into me since infancy, but I'd never been on the front lines in such a volatile situation. Something about the shooting of Timothy Thomas had pierced through my usual, polite, white distance. I couldn't ignore it. My city had reached a tipping point, and I couldn't pretend it wasn't happening. So, even feeling awkward and unsure, I was determined to stay and to stand with these people.

Two days later, on Saturday, I attended Timothy Thomas's funeral. This time, I dragged a white friend along; a staff member from Stonewall Cincinnati[3], the local

---

3 A now-defunct organization that was primarily focused on the rights of lesbians and gay men. Seen as trying to protect their white, cisgender privilege (though we didn't have those words in the 1980s or 1990s) by many in the community who viewed the group as trying to be a part of the wealthy, white, conservative upper echelon of Cincinnati society, Stonewall Cincinnati did not engage with queer people of color, queer people experiencing poverty, or other intersectional issues. Known primarily for hosting annual dinners sponsored by the Human Rights Commission (HRC), which, at the time, held similar values, nonetheless Stonewall Cincinnati did support the annual Pride parade and similar efforts during its two decades.

LGBTQ+[4] organization, where I served on the board. I knew my friend wasn't comfortable attending, but I needed to share the weight of my feelings. I felt that more white people needed to be visible and supportive. The funeral was somber, with ministers offering comforting words to the grieving crowd and calling for justice. Jesse Jackson and Reverend Al Sharpton were in attendance, making the point that police shooting unarmed Black men was not just a Cincinnati problem but a nationwide one. The Black community's anger simmered just beneath the surface. Still, there was also something else in the air—a powerful resolve, a belief that someday, maybe not today or tomorrow, the Black community and its allies would live in a just city.

One minister spoke about Timothy's life, about how he had been harassed by the police on multiple occasions, including three previous, separate incidents *on the very day he was killed*. He said Timothy may have run simply because he didn't want to be hassled again. The officer who shot him claimed Timothy was reaching for a gun when he was probably just pulling up his sagging pants. The injustice of it all was overwhelming. A young man had been shot in the back in the street for something as trivial as adjusting his clothing. (Newspaper reports would later claim that Thom-

4 The acronym I use for the queer community evolved quite a bit during the 1980s through 2000s, from LG to LGB to LGBT to LGBTQ to what I use now: LGBTQ+ or queer. I use LGBTQ+ throughout this story not to rewrite history, but to honor the evolution of the queer community. When I first came out as a lesbian in 1980, it was called the "gay community." By the mid-1980s, "lesbian and gay community" had become the most often used descriptor. Where an acronym is used in a quote from another source, I have left that acronym as the source wrote it.

as was shot in the chest, implying he was threatening the officer. That was simple whitewashing. The coroner initially reported, and it was widely known, that Thomas was shot in the back *as he ran away*.) It was an indictment of the entire system of a city and a country where Black men are routinely seen as threats and where their very existence is criminalized.

As the service ended, the crowd spilled out onto the streets, hugging one another, offering comfort in a moment where there was so little to be found. Ministers prayed loudly for peace, for justice, and for an end to the violence that had taken yet another life. As my friend and I joined the stream of mourners walking away from the church, we saw signs that read, "Honk if you love justice!" and "Justice for Timothy Thomas!"

It felt like there was a glimmer of hope in the crowd. Maybe it was the easing of the rawness of the murder because beloved national figures recognized this was a nationwide problem. People driving by were honking their horns in support, and for a moment, it felt like this police shooting might change things; that it might be the last one before the country said, "ENOUGH!" Maybe this was the moment when the city would finally reckon with its history of racial violence. But that hope was short-lived.

Just as the crowd approached and crossed a major road, five police cars screeched into the intersection. Officers jumped out, guns drawn. They looked around at the people from the funeral standing on all four street corners. I saw their eyes pause briefly on the corner where my friend and I stood, our white faces visible at the front of the crowd. Then, without so much as a word of warning, the police opened fire on the other three street corners *where there were no white faces*. I watched in horror as people dropped to the ground, some hit, others diving for cover. Not a single officer turned their attention to us. They fired their rubber bullets indiscriminately at the Black mourners. I believe our corner was protected because of the officers' fear of accidentally hitting white people.

It was a surreal and terrifying moment. The sound of gunfire echoed in my ears as the officers jumped back into their cars and sped away as quickly as they had arrived. The street was momentarily still as if everyone was holding their breath. Then, someone in the crowd hurled a soda bottle at the retreating police cars, the bottle exploding harmlessly 50 feet behind the last car. That was all the provocation the police were looking for, and within seconds, the vehicles had raced around the block and back to the intersection. They stayed in their cars this time, daring the crowd to respond, to give them a reason to fire again.

Meanwhile, the ministers on the corners were calling out for calm, for peace in the name of Timothy Thomas. "He didn't deserve to die," they shouted, "and we won't dishonor him with violence." After what felt like an eternity, the police finally left again, aggressively smug in their dominance of the street.

After a few minutes of standing there in shock, my friend was shaken, eager to leave the scene behind. But I couldn't just walk away. I walked into the intersection and picked up some of the rubber bullet cartridges from the street, feeling the weight of them in my hand, a tangible reminder of the violence we had just witnessed. I knew this wasn't over. Something inside me had shifted. I told my friend we needed to align the Stonewall Cincinnati Board with the protesters and stand in solidarity against this blatant oppression. She wasn't convinced. She was frightened, incoherent. I insisted that this was our fight, too. The racism of this city oppresses its Black citizens, its homophobia oppresses its LGBTQ+ ones, and both phobias further oppress those who are Black *and* gay. *How can we not stand with them?* Still, she was hesitant. We agreed to take the discussion to the board.

While driving her home, we listened to a Black radio station in my car, expecting to hear coverage of what had happened after the funeral. By the time I dropped my friend off, I still hadn't heard anything about it. There was no mention of the gunfire or the chaos that had unfolded in the streets. It was as if it hadn't happened. So I called the station and told them everything I knew. Shortly after that, station reporters were on the street talking to the people still there.

Within hours of my call to the radio station, I received a call from the FBI. (As radio stations do with all callers, the station had asked for my contact information to be sure I wasn't a crank caller.) The FBI agent on the other end wanted to know everything I had seen. Over the course of the conversation, I was asked the same questions four or five times in different ways. It felt like an interrogation, not an investigation. They wanted the bullet casings I had picked up at the scene. I agreed, and they sent two agents to my home to pick them up.

That call shook me. Growing up in my activist family, I knew what it meant to have an FBI file, and it wasn't something to take lightly. My mom and dad had considered their files a badge of honor, but it unnerved me. Activism has always been in my blood, but direct contact with the FBI scared me. I felt suddenly thrust into a larger, more dangerous arena—one where my actions were being scrutinized by forces far beyond my control. As a queer woman, the risks were magnified.

I decided to attend the weekly Cincinnati City Council meeting on the Monday following the funeral. I'd never been to one before, but I couldn't sit this out. I needed to speak out against injustice and to make sure those in authority couldn't deny what happened. Speaking out against injustice has always called to me, drawing me out of my introverted shell. I couldn't convince my colleague who attended the funeral with me to go, so again, I was walking in as an outsider alone. To shore up my confidence, I put on what I called "my corporate drag"—a purple skirted power suit with heels, makeup, and statement jewelry. I wore this outfit when presenting to leadership at my company. I wrote my name down for a speaking slot at the meeting.

The room was packed, filled with people who, like me, had witnessed the shootings. They took the floor one by one, each describing their experience. I noticed that all the speakers talking about the police actions as an assault were Black. The white people spoke about other matters or complained about seeing "angry Black mobs" on the street. When my turn came, I stepped up to the microphone, feeling a surge of determination during my three minutes. I described in detail what I saw, finishing with, "I'm from Southern California, and I know what a drive-by shooting looks like. What the police did Saturday was a drive-by shooting[5]."

As soon as the comment period ended, reporters swarmed me. I was taken aback when I realized there were more reporters gathered around me rather than talking to the Black people who had spoken far more eloquently about their much longer experience with the Cincinnati Police Department. The reporters wanted *my* perspective, seeing me as an "objective observer." Disturbingly, my white skin somehow made them see me as neutral and trustworthy compared to those with skin in the game. I was a "corporate executive" to boot, although I was only a second-level manager at the time. Friends had already told me that Cincinnati newspaper reporters interviewing anyone from my global company tended to call the interviewee a "corporate executive." The shiny veneer of the company rubbed off

5 True confessions: While I am from Southern California, and there were at that time an inordinate number of drive-by shootings, I have never witnessed one. I told the City Council it looked like a "drive-by shooting" to call out the outlandishness of the police behavior that Saturday.

on the story and made the speaker, as well as the reporter, more credible. But I knew the truth. My power suit and my skin color had made me relevant to the reporters in a way the Black attendees were not. I felt uncomfortable, and I suggested the reporters talk to the others who had spoken. Mine was not the essential story.

The following day at work, after the papers carried the headlines of the city council meeting and the "corporate executive" who spoke out against the weekend's police action, I received an unexpected call. My company's recently-retired vice president of diversity, a Black man, was on the phone. We'd had a contentious relationship since he created the Office of Diversity in the mid-90s. He was a champion of diversity, but in his mind, diversity meant only Black people and women. He was staunchly against LGBTQ+ people riding the coattails of those "legitimate" groups. He got in the way of our efforts to include the company's LGBTQ+ employees every chance he could.

So it surprised me when this man said, "Heidi, I saw your speech at the city council meeting on TV last night, and I want to thank you for saying what you did. Your standing up for the Black community has gotten people talking and maybe even listening. I realize now that I should have supported you and stood up for your group. I'm sorry I didn't, and I appreciate that you didn't let that stop you from standing up for us." I felt floored by his admission, and affirmed I was doing work that mattered.

The months following Timothy Thomas's death were some of the most challenging I had ever experienced; not just because of the tensions in the city but because they marked a profound shift in how I saw myself and my role in fighting injustice.

After the city council meeting, I realized that I could contribute by gathering allies to stand with the Black community. An obvious choice was the Stonewall Cincinnati organization. But when I approached them, the rest of the board disagreed. "This isn't our fight," they said. I was frustrated by that. Plenty of gay and bisexual people are Black[6]. Was Stonewall saying they would only fight for them if they were being oppressed for being queer, but not if their queer self was being oppressed because they're Black? The white gay community had not yet acknowledged the double oppression in the intersection between racism and homophobia. It's all oppression, I kept insisting. We were all fighting systemic oppression of people who *are seen as "other."*

Even after I spent several months of discussion at board meetings and one-on-one calls with every board

6 According to the Williams Institute, in 2021, 1.2 million U.S. adults self-identify as Black and LGBTQ+. The number of LGBTQ+ adults in the U.S. is between 14 million to 20 million, according to the Williams Institute and the Human Rights Campaign, respectively. That means that Black U.S. adults are somewhere between 6%-9% of the LGBTQ+ community. Nearly one in 10! That doesn't account for people of other races who identify as queer. Stonewall Cincinnati was not the only LGBTQ+ organization dismissing the needs of queer people of color if the problem could be traced to the person's race rather than their queerness. In the 1990s, we were learning about "multiple minorities," the term for being a member of two marginalized groups. Many folks struggled with the concept until they realized there were multiple minorities *they* belonged to.

member, the other board members wouldn't budge. Some of those individual conversations were filled with polite, insistent explanations that I wasn't making sense. They didn't want to alienate me. They wanted me to fall in line. Other conversations became heated, and I was told that everyone else on the board thought I should step down if I wasn't interested in doing the "real" work of the group. They saw me as the one who was out of step. I eventually realized that their unacknowledged racism and desire to protect their privilege made them unwilling to see that we shared a common cause with the Black community. It broke my heart. I had joined the board thinking we were all social justice warriors. I thought we were a community. How could one oppressed community be indifferent to the oppression of another?

Meanwhile, I was finding many queer people in the community who agreed with me. Many from the Black queer and white queer progressive communities in Cincinnati helped put together a coalition. Most tellingly, many had never felt represented by the Stonewall board. We also engaged some activists who had years of organizing experience pushing back against entrenched power. As I lost faith in the board of Stonewall Cincinnati to recognize our dual oppressions, our ad hoc group decided that change was in order. Since an LGBTQ+ group *should* represent *all* LGBTQ+ people, it made sense that Stonewall Cincinnati needed a board with a new vision and a more diverse leadership. We reasoned that many in Stonewall's membership would agree that the oppression of one of us was the oppression of all of us. We came up with a slate of people for each Stonewall board seat. This included seats that had been vacant for years, as Stonewall's bylaws called for three general seats to be held by Black people and another three by women. Ironically, those seats had gone largely unfilled but made the all-white, primarily male board feel they were "doing all they could." We put our names on the ballot.

It all came to a head at our board elections that September—on the night of September 11, 2001. While the world was reeling from the terrorist attacks, we held our board election. Our coalition with its more inclusive vision won. The old board was ousted, and the new board made it our mission to stand with the Black community in the wake of Timothy Thomas's death. As a queer organization in a homophobic city, we didn't wield much power. Still, we were determined to build coalitions that might eventually dent the racism and homophobia in the city. It was a new day in Cincinnati, though I had made enemies in the old-guard, white, gay community.

There was more fallout from my involvement with the investigation into the Timothy Thomas killing. Our new Stonewall board held press conferences supporting the Black community's call for justice at various events. I always dressed in "corporate drag" and mentioned my role as a financial manager at my iconic company when I introduced myself.

One morning, I received a call at work from the son of my company's chief executive officer (CEO). It was completely unexpected as I didn't know him and was unaware that he even knew who I was. He wasn't involved in my part of the business at all. He told me that, during breakfast with his father that morning, my name had come up. He said that his father didn't like hearing that one of their employees' names was associated with something that gave Cincinnati a black eye. His father thought it would be better if I backed off. He implied that my continued involvement could affect the rest of "all" my efforts at the company. It was a clear warning to me that my job and our efforts to secure domestic partner benefits for LGBTQ+ employees could be at risk if I didn't take a step back.

Incredulous, I blurted out, "Are you telling me that your father *doesn't* support racial and social justice for *everyone*?" The company's CEO was, after all, a man who was a long-beloved figure within the company and the community. He equated caring for employees with company success and had been a champion of the company's early diversity, equity, and inclusion (DEI) efforts. I was dumbfounded that he would not champion work against racism. Briefly, the son faltered but then insisted that my role at the company and involvement in "this matter" were incompatible.

It was a bitter pill to swallow. For nine years—longer than I'd been doing racial justice work in Cincinnati—I had meticulously advocated for LGBTQ+ rights within my company. It had been a slow, often frustrating process, but we had gotten many in senior leadership on board and were finally on the verge of getting domestic partner benefits. Losing that ground was unthinkable, yet here I was, facing the possibility that my activism supporting racial justice could unravel all of it.

But could I turn away? I felt connected to this issue at my core. The day Timothy Thomas was killed, something opened up inside me, and I knew I could never go back to being silent. Then, the moment I witnessed the police fire into a crowd of peaceful mourners but not at me, my understanding of privilege and injustice deepened. I was unharmed that day because of the color of my skin, while others had been targeted for the color of theirs. That breaking of trust didn't go away. It clung to me, became a part of me, and demanded that I do something about it. I was heartened remembering the call from the former vice president of diversity, whom the CEO had appointed. I decided to count on the better angels of the CEO's nature if it came down to a choice.

The phone call from the FBI lingered and made me uneasy, too. Later in the year, the FBI completed its investigation and turned the results over to the Department of Justice (DOJ). The DOJ convened a grand jury, and I was called to testify. I was determined to speak the truth even if it came at a cost. As I sat in front of the jury, recounting the events I witnessed, I felt fear of possible consequences but also felt pride in myself. I was overwhelmed by the weight of the moment. One woman on the jury surprised me with her clear bias. After listening to my recounting she asked, "Are you an *activist*?" Her sneering words dripped with disdain, making it clear that if I was an activist, anything I said was suspect.

For a split second, I hesitated. Was I a *racial justice* activist? Until then, my social justice efforts had primarily been centered around LGBTQ+ rights. But was I even an LGBTQ+ activist? I worked *inside* "the system," persuading my employer to make changes rather than boycotting from the outside. I thought of activists as people who took to the streets, chained themselves to gates, and got arrested. I had worked actively for domestic partner benefits at my company but didn't consider myself a political activist in the broader sense. Yet here I was, testifying before a grand jury about police brutality and racial injustice.

I answered her question truthfully, ignoring her implication, "I don't think of myself as an activist, but maybe I am."

It was an honest response. I was still coming to terms with what it meant to be someone who stood up publicly, not just for myself or my community but also for others. The events of that time forced me to confront the reality of my privilege, and with that confrontation came a responsibility I could no longer ignore.

The grand jury investigation eventually led to the Collaborative Agreement[7], an accountability plan designed to transform the relationship between the Cincinnati Police Department and the city's Black community. The agreement was seen as a landmark in police-community relations, a model for other cities dealing with similar issues. It was meant to bring about real change, to address the deep-rooted racism within the department, and to rebuild trust between the police and the people they were supposed to serve.

But even as the Collaborative Agreement was having an impact and holding the police accountable, I couldn't shake the feeling that it wasn't enough. My close friend, Madeline, went on to take a key role in 2003 in the implementation process of the agreement. We met when I was

---

7 After the FBI completed its investigation, the Department of Justice (DOJ) worked with the NAACP, the Cincinnati Police Department (CPD), the mayor's office, and the Black United Front to produce a landmark tool for ensuring accountability between the CPD and the Black community it served, known as the Collaborative Agreement. The agreement, which has achieved sweeping police reform within the CPD by focusing on issues around equity, independent oversight, use of force, and transparency, celebrated 20 years of hard work in 2022. The Collaborative Agreement work continues, and the DOJ checks on their progress every six months.

Almendarez, J. 2022 (April 14). Twenty years after the Collaborative Agreement, a lot has been accomplished. But there's still work to do. *91.7 WVXU News, NPR Network*, Local News. https://www.wvxu.org/local-news/2022-04-14/20-years-after-the-collaborative-agreement-a-lot-has-been-accomplished-but-theres-still-work-to-do

paired with her for a study of racism in the mid-1990s[8]. Madeline's understanding of the history of racial inequities, its impacts, and nuances forever enriched and deepened my understanding of racial justice. She gave me an insider's view of what was and wasn't working with the Collaborative Agreement. The agreement was a step in the right direction, yes, but it wasn't enough. Systemic racism permeated not just the police force but the entire city and beyond. And it certainly didn't stop the killings of unarmed Black people across the country. Cincinnati was just one city in a nation grappling with the same issues. Still, she and I held on to the hope that her work was moving the needle, even slightly.

Back at Stonewall Cincinnati, things were changing, too. The September 11, 2001, board election was a turning point for the organization. The new board members understood that the struggles of the Black community and the LGBTQ+ community were interconnected.

---

8 In 1997, I learned about a project launched by the Intercommunity Justice and Peace Center, or IJPC. They had partnered with a Jewish organization from New York City that had funding to study racism nationwide. The IJPC had agreed to work with community leaders in Cincinnati to create an interactive, experiential museum about the Underground Railroad. (The Ohio River that Cincinnati sits on served as the figurative and literal epicenter of the Underground Railroad, a network of secret routes and safe houses established across the U.S.)

The study was conducted with six groups across the country. I participated in the Cincinnati-based group of ten Black and ten white people, equally divided between men and women. We were split into opposite-sex/race pairs, although I asked to be paired with a Black woman instead of a man as I had had a painful encounter with some Black girls as a child that I felt was holding me back. The facilitators agreed, and I met my lifelong friend, Madeline.

For years, the queer community in Cincinnati had been fighting its own battles—battles against homophobia, against discrimination, against violence. But there had always been a sense of isolation, as though we were fighting alone. The events of 2001 changed that. Some of us realized that our fight was not separate from the battle for racial justice. We were all part of the same struggle for equality and dignity. Our model was the intersectional organization SONG[9], Southerners on New Ground, co-founded by Mandy Carter, a Black lesbian activist and community organizer. SONG's mission was and is to be a home for LGBTQ+ liberation across all lines of race, class, abilities, age, culture, gender, and sexuality in the South.

When I met Mandy in 2001, she was consulting with a group in Kentucky that had built a coalition of Black, brown, poor, disabled, and LGBTQ+ people. They embraced a model

---

9 According to their website: Southerners on New Ground, not surprisingly, focuses its efforts on the unique needs of a wide variety of communities in the southern states in the United States. This is how they describe their work: "SONG builds a beloved community of LGBTQ people in the South who are ready and willing to do our part to challenge oppression to bring about liberation for ALL people.

"SONG develops leadership, builds our membership base, and identifies and carries out community organizing projects and campaigns. All of our work strives to bring together marginalized communities to work towards justice and liberation for all people.

"In particular, we build coalitions and alliances with other People of Color, Immigrant, Working Class, and LGBTQ communities. To make the strengths of our communities and work visible, we amplify stories of LGBTQ Liberation and resistance from our work in the stronghold of the conservative right-wing—the South."

SONG https://southernersonnewground.org/

of "an injustice to one of us is an injustice to all of us." Based in Louisville, Kentucky, they boycotted companies that discriminated against any community the coalition represented. For example, when the new (white) manager of a Taco Bell franchise in the suburbs fired two gay crew members on the slimmest of pretexts, the coalition went into action. The Black and brown organizations, the disability rights group, the local LGBTQ+ group, and all the other groups in the coalition not only boycotted that particular Taco Bell but all the Taco Bells in the area. They wrote letters to the other Taco Bells in the area and to Yum! Brands, the owners of Taco Bell, to explain what they were doing and why. They kept up the pressure, and eventually, Taco Bell stepped up, replacing the franchise owner and giving the two men their jobs back.

That was the type of coalition the new board of Stonewall Cincinnati wanted to build. The challenge was how. We reached out to Black-led organizations. We joined protests, issued statements of support, and worked to build bridges between the queer community and the city's Black activists. It wasn't always easy. There were still years of distrust, missteps, and disagreements to overcome. Previous Stonewall boards had made a show of solidarity for the cameras but repeatedly failed to keep their commitments. But we kept working at it and had some significant successes.

As months passed, I thought about the intersections of race, gender, and sexuality. I had always known, intellectually, that these issues were connected. Still, it wasn't until I was thrust into the heart of the Timothy Thomas murder investigation that I truly understood what that meant. The systems of oppression that sought to silence and marginalize Black people were the same systems that had oppressed LGBTQ+ people. Our struggles were intertwined. Fighting one without fighting the other meant we might win a skirmish but never the war.

The fear I felt when the son of the CEO called me at work lingered in the back of my mind, but it no longer held the same power over me. I had spent years carefully navigating corporate politics, pushing for change from within, and I was constantly aware of the delicate balance I had to maintain. But after witnessing the police violence at Timothy Thomas's funeral, after testifying before the grand jury, and after standing with the Black community in protest, I realized that some things were more important than playing it safe. I was willing to risk my job and my reputation. I was willing to face threats to our progress on LGBTQ+ recognition. I was willing to risk it all because doing the right thing wasn't optional. I also knew I would not stop working for change until the injustices I fought were vanquished. My answer, long after the fact, to that grand jury member now is, "I am and will be an activist as long as there is injustice. Why aren't you?"

In the end, I didn't lose my job. The domestic partner benefits we had fought for were implemented at the end of 2001. My company was one of the early global corporations to offer such benefits to LGBTQ+ employees. It was a victory I personally worked hard for and was proud of. But the events of 2001 left an indelible mark on me, one that went far beyond corporate policies or personal accolades.

More than anything, I learned that justice does not happen without oxygen. It cannot be tackled one issue at a time. True justice requires recognizing intersectionality. Living intersectionally means standing up for others even when their struggles don't seem to impact you directly. It is acknowledging the multiple oppressions that shape marginalized individuals' and groups' experiences and opportunities. Racial and class justice, LGBTQ+ rights, rights for people with disabilities, and gender equality together face a common enemy: entrenched privilege.

Looking back on that year, I can see how much I've changed. I'm no longer the person who attended that first protest meeting, unsure of whether I belonged. I now understand that showing up—awkward, uncomfortable, and imperfect—is the first step in any movement for justice. It's not about being a savior or having all the answers. It's about standing with others, listening, learning, and putting yourself on the line for what's right.

And while Cincinnati still has a long way to go, I know that the work we did in the wake of Timothy Thomas's death made a difference. It wasn't enough to change everything, but it was a start. And sometimes, that's the best we can do at the moment.

Epilogue

The events I witnessed in 2001 in Cincinnati were just one chapter in America's ongoing fight over racial justice. Since then, countless other Black men and women have been killed by police across the country, sparking movements like Black Lives Matter and the George Floyd protests that rippled across the globe, all bringing the epidemic of police violence into the national spotlight. The fight continues, and so does the work of building bridges between communities, recognizing the intersections of race, sexuality, gender, and more, and standing in solidarity with all people who are oppressed.

Out of the Cincinnati protests and boycotts and the Department of Justice investigation that followed, there were two agreements. One, with the Department of Justice, called on the city police department to reform its use-of-force policies and practices. The other, the Collaborative Agreement, was historic in recognizing community members as partners in fighting crime rather than as people who should be viewed as potential criminals. The Collaborative Agreement was implemented in 2002 and to this day continues to be an active element of policing in Cincinnati.

I grew up in a family of activists who always stood up for what was right even when it was hard or unpopular. My mother once told me that my first protest march was in the womb, and while that has always been a family joke, it was actually true. Living in Bakersfield, California, in the 1950s and '60s, there was a LOT of racism and oppression to march about. Living in Cincinnati in the '90s and '00s gave me the opportunity to stand up for those values. When my dad called me the night of the police shooting to make sure I was okay, he reinforced the importance of leading from your values. When I told him about the FBI contacting me, he told me that he was proud of me for standing up against "the man" (in his words) and that "the full force of the Bruins' family trust" was behind me if I got into legal trouble because of actively resisting injustice. We were never a wealthy family, which made his words even more precious. He was telling me that I had his full support, emotionally and financially if I needed it, and that he saw that I was living the values I had grown up with and adopted as my own.

For me, those months in 2001 were a personal reckoning. They forced me to confront my privilege, my assumptions, and my fears. They pushed me out of my comfort zone and into a space where I had to be more than just an ally. I also needed to be—wanted to be—an advocate and co-conspirator in the fight for racial justice. The murder of Timothy Thomas was abhorrent, and I am forever grateful for what I learned about myself and the world from it.

Heidi Bruins Green (she/her) is a social justice advocate who believes that changing hearts and minds involves persuading people to expand their awareness beyond their own stories. She has been a racial justice warrior since birth, having been in her first protest march in the womb. Heidi knows that the oppression of one opens the gate to the oppression of all. In addition, her championship of LGBTQ+ issues in the workplace for the last 40+ years taught her to believe in the magical reciprocity of opening her heart to others. Heidi lives in Vancouver, Washington, with her husband, Jamison Green, and their cat, Squeak.

Infinite Possibilities

By Jamison Green

It's 1975, and I'm 26 years old when I meet Samantha. She has just turned 21, and I'm attracted to her instantly. She's playing hard to get, hanging out with a gaggle of friends, visiting the usual cafes and bars where lesbians meet to chat, cruise, or just relax. There are always women around her. I'm part of the lesbian community at this time because I have a female body and I'm attracted to women, so I feel it's the best place for someone like me to find compatible friends and possible partners. By day, I work at a construction job on a crew of men, and I look—and feel—more like a boy than a woman.

I'm popular on the dance floor in the lesbian bars at night but not always so welcome in more well-lit public spaces by day. I don't know why. Maybe it's because strangers typically interpret me as male or (at best) androgynous. Honestly, being seen with me in public is a risk. I'm either read as a lesbian, or the woman I'm with is read as an available straight woman (one willing to speak with a man). Neither is a desirable position for most lesbians, especially if they hold professional roles. In the second wave of feminism, women are just beginning to understand their personal power and pride as women. Jobs beyond the pink-collar realm are challenging to find, and the prejudice against women who love women threatens those jobs. Yet, for many lesbians, the idea of having to interact with men at all is abhorrent. Due to rampant homophobia, masculine women and feminine men are ridiculed, abused, and shunned. Many people might otherwise enjoy their company if no one were to see them together. People carry their closets everywhere they go.

There's something special about Samantha. Sure, she's beautiful, with laughing, blue eyes and straight, blonde hair that curls inward slightly below her shoulders. She's a few inches taller than me. At five feet, four inches myself, almost every adult I know is taller than me. Samantha is five feet, eight inches tall, slender, graceful, slow-moving, relaxed-seeming, self-possessed. Her laugh is musical, like a low-pitched wind chime with high overtones. Her shyness makes her mysterious. Her friends are in a younger cohort than the women I've been socializing with recently. Right now, my friends are a few law students, an attorney, a physician, a journalist, and an apprentice printer. Her friends are women I don't know, except for the apprentice printer named Carol. Carol, a former lover of Samantha's from when they were attending junior college in Northern California, is our common contact. Our paths now cross in Portland, Oregon. I don't remember how I met Carol, but she's couch-surfing while her apartment undergoes some landlord-initiated repairs. I'd volunteered to host her for a week, which will be coming up soon. Samantha's in town, staying with her aunt in Gresham, just east of Portland's city limit; she doesn't drive, so she takes the bus into Portland and accompanies Carol to work and on outings with Carol's various friends. We keep running into each other in passing, at a restaurant, on a random street downtown in the afternoon, and at night, in the relatively new lesbian bar, the Rising Moon[1], near the foot of West Burnside Street. Then Carol invites me to the home of someone I don't know for a party on a Friday night where Carol is staying that week. I hope Samantha will be there, so I promise to attend.

---

1 Gay and lesbian bars were present in Portland for most of the 20th century, as described in this historical account: https://www.glapn.org/6045walkingtour.html. Although the Rising Moon is listed here as having been located at 413 Burnside, I remember it clearly as being on the opposite side of the street and operating from 1975 through 1977. (I left Portland in January 1978). As I recall, the Rising Moon was popular among young women in their 20s and 30s who wanted a safe space to be together and have fun talking and dancing without men around. The owners and bartenders were lesbians, and any stray men who walked in (even if they were gay themselves) were gently encouraged to leave. It was different from the mixed gay bars where men mostly hung out and from the lesbian bars frequented by "old-style traditional dykes" or the feminist organizers who were actively trying to create exclusive women's communities in the 1970s.

At the party, Samantha has her acoustic guitar—an Ovation, an unusually shaped instrument that is relatively new in the musical field. Its fiberglass back isn't flat like a wooden guitar but curved toward the front of the instrument, so it has no side panel. It promises enhanced tonal quality, which speaks to Samantha's refined musical perfectionism. She also doesn't play too much; even when people beg her to sing some classic folk songs that everyone would know, she resists. At one point, when no one is nearby, I ask Samantha why she isn't playing. She replies: "I take my music seriously. Everybody seems to be having a good time in their conversations, and I don't want to dominate the party. If they want background music, they can put on a record."

"Then why did you bring your guitar?" I ask innocently, not trying to challenge her.

"Carol insisted," she says, smiling. And just then, Carol sits down next to her and asks her to play something—a Joni Mitchell song.

"Play *All I Want*, please, please," Carol implores, leaning against Samantha's shoulder. It's a song that Mitchell released in 1971 when Samantha and Carol were still partners.

Samantha grins and relents. She plays exquisitely and sings like the most unbridled angel I've ever heard. The 20 or so women scattered around the large living room all stop chattering and laughing. They even stop heading for the kitchen for another beer. They just freeze, staring at her. So do I. She's the real thing. I'm hooked. Remembering it now, 50 years later, I can still hear her voice, singing, "Oh, I hate you some, I hate you some, I love you some / Oh, I love you when I forget about me." Such a brilliant observation about young love.

When the song ends and the applause dies down, I say, "Wow! That was spectacular!" And Samantha just gives me a coy smile. She knows how good she is; she doesn't need flattery.

"Jamie," Carol says, "You play something, too!"

"After that?" I protest. "You want me to make a fool of myself?" Samantha offers her guitar to me. I can't stop smiling as I put the strap across my back and my fingers on the strings and strum gently, just to feel the instrument. The roundness of its back panel is surprisingly comfortable, and it vibrates with deep resonance. Its neck is a little narrow for my hand, but the string tension is perfect. Its tone is rich, enticing. The other women start to drift back into their conversations. They don't care about me, which I find encouraging. Maybe they won't listen. I only want to impress Samantha. I stop experimenting with the guitar, give Carol and Samantha a shy smile, as if to say, "Here goes nothing ...," take a deep breath, and launch into *House of the Rising Sun*, the 1964 version by The Animals with Eric Burdon. I sing it hard, bluesy, attracting significant attention from the women remaining in the room, but not much applause, nothing like Samantha's reception. Some give me nods of approval, and one woman says, "Wow, I didn't know you could sing like that," as she passes by me on her way to get another beer.

But the best response comes from Samantha who simply says, "You're really good!"

"Thank you!" I reply with honest gratitude.

"Told you," Carol beams toward Samantha. I decide not to risk anything further and excuse myself from the party, saying I have an early work assignment the next day.

A couple of weeks later, when Carol is crashing at my place for the prescribed week, Samantha visits her. I'm so attracted to her. Her willingness to look me in the eye and include me in her conversation with Carol makes it clear to me that Samantha is interested in something more intimate with me. Within a month, Samantha is living with me.

The first time we make love, Samantha tells me, "I don't know how to tell you this, but I feel like I've just been with a man."

Startled that she sees into me so deeply, I take a long breath and reply, "I don't know how to tell you this, but I think you just were. I think I'm transsexual[2], and I'm scared to death to do anything about it." I hold what breath I have left, anticipating something less than understanding. After all, I hardly understand it myself. But she just says, "Interesting ..." and pulls me closer. She's the first person I've ever shared my secret with.

---

2 Transsexual was a medical term first introduced in the US in the 1940s to describe persons who sought medical interventions to change their sex characteristics so they could live in the gender role most comfortable for them or in which they felt they belonged socially.

We've been together for about a year when Samantha tells me she wants a baby. I'm surprised. In the lesbian world I know, the only way women have children is if they've been with a man. They then forsake him for the superior love of a woman (or for solidarity with other women). Maybe they'd been raped and were unwilling or unable to obtain an abortion[3]. But the very idea of sleeping with a man and being impregnated by him, being dependent on him, and having everything about you and your offspring belonging to him is fundamentally abhorrent to the lesbians I know. When Samantha announces her desire to carry a child, I can only say, "Well, sorry, I can't really help you with that," meaning that I can't help her become pregnant.

"Oh, I know that," she says cheerfully. "I am convinced that one day I will be able to become pregnant without having sex with a man."

I raise my eyebrows. "Really?"

"Yup." She's quite confident. "I don't know how," she admits, "but I know it will be possible before too long."

But before that advancement in reproductive technology becomes available, transsexuality is a topic of discussion among some of the women I know. One of my friends reads an essay by Janice Raymond that appears in the very first issue of a new feminist magazine and shares it with a small group of us. I read it with some interest. I know that

3 The Supreme Court had only ruled on the Roe v. Wade case in January of 1973, legalizing abortion prior to "fetal viability" at 24-28 weeks, and the country was adapting slowly to making the procedure safer and easier for women to access.

feminist thought is opposed to the idea that "biology is destiny," but what I read here is the notion that transsexuality itself is caused by the rigid stereotypes of gender, which are what feminism strives to break down so that both women and men can live fuller lives. I think that's an admirable goal, but trans people are not responsible for reinforcing gender stereotypes any more than any other person. I thought Ms. Raymond missed the boat, too, because she fell for the "born in the wrong body" trope, which is a simple attempt at explaining how trans people feel. I disagree. I think the "gender dissatisfaction" that transsexual people feel is not frustration with the limits of prescribed social roles; it's much deeper and more personal than that. It's a disconnection between the spirit—the sense of self—and the body[4].

4 Raymond, Janice. (1977). "Transsexualism: The Ultimate Homage to Sex-Role Power." *Chrysalis 1* (Fall 1977): 11-23. *Chrysalis* was published out of Los Angeles from 1977 to 1980. The 1977 article appeared to be a "trial run" for the primary arguments in her 1979 book, *The Transsexual Empire: The Making of the She-Male.* Boston: Beacon Press. Ms. Raymond portrayed 'transsexualism' as if the very real and often visible incongruity between a person's sex and their gender expression—that is, the impression of masculinity or femininity an individual displayed that would be perceived or interpreted by another person—was either a masquerade, an ideology, or a belief system rather than an individual's lived experience that they don't choose, but they must learn to live or cope with. Raymond argued that transsexualism should be rejected because it reinforced "socially constructed" sexual stereotypes that damaged women and simultaneously gave male doctors the power to artificially and "superficially" create "women" who conformed to roles and identities that reinforced the social power of men. For her thesis, Raymond relied on the premise that human beings are only two sexes, labeled female and male, and the social and biological functions and capacities of each are separate and distinct. She saw trans women as a threat to women, and trans men as dupes of the patriarchy. All trans people were, therefore, pathetic, confused, deluded, and conformists with gender norms, supporting the systems that constrained and oppressed everyone, and women in particular. She concluded that transsexuals should not change their

My friends who read this article gather at the home of a medical doctor to discuss it. They don't know any transsexual people, and they're sympathetic to Raymond's argument. They also see me as a perfect example of a person who has transcended gender because I live in a female body and don't conform to gender stereotypes. I appear to be doing it successfully and apparently happily. My medical doctor friend has learned of a "sex-change program" at Stanford University[5], and she proposes I apply to the program and go through its evaluation process. Upon my sure acceptance, she proposes I should respond, "Ah HA! I don't need your silly sex change! I'm not transsexual! I am a strong lesbian woman! And gender stereotypes may be for you, but they are not for me!"

There are five or six women present, and we're sitting in the doctor's living room with glasses of wine or bottles of beer. They're all laughing at the thought of my "Dyke Reveal," but I'm not so jovial. I feel like they don't see me at all. Like Janice Raymond, they see what they want to see.

"I don't know about that," I say. "I don't think I'm the right candidate for your demonstration."

---

bodies but should endeavor to prove "both to themselves and to others that persons who experience gender dissatisfaction do not have to transsex in order to live fully in this society." These ideas persist today and are just as problematic and myopic now as they were then. There is much more biological diversity in sex and gender than our simplistic generalizations can acknowledge.

5 The "Sex Reassignment Program," aka the "Gender Dysphoria Program" at Stanford University, was launched in 1968 by psychiatrist Norman Fisk and plastic surgeon Donald M. Laub.

"Why's that?" someone asks.

"I think I would actually appreciate a sex change, whatever that is. I don't even know if it's possible. I love you all, but I don't think of myself as a woman, exactly. I don't think you and I share the same experience of the world."

"Well," says my lawyer friend, "None of us ever really share the same experience, now, do we?"

"Of course, not specifically," I reply, "Not in every sense, but what I mean is, when I walk down the street, other people don't see me or react to me the same way they do to you."

"We can fix that!" another woman says gleefully. "We can dress you up and make you look more feminine."

I bristle: "Oh, you want to treat me the way the girls in my fourth-, sixth-, and eighth-grade classes did! You want to treat me like a doll, like a child you get to manipulate without caring how I feel, huh? That is not happening!"

"If you do that to Jamie," Samantha says, "You'll be just as guilty of erasure as if you exile her from the lesbian world for being too masculine. Either way, you'll be hurting her."

"But we like butch women!" the lawyer protests. "We want her to stay butch."

"Where's the line between butch and not a woman?" I ask. "It's not like I don't like or appreciate or love or admire women; it's that I don't see myself as like you. I'm not better; I'm not worse; I'm just different. And there's no possible way that I could wear a dress, or put on makeup, or do anything with my hair to make me behave or appear more feminine that would make me function in the world like you do. I'm not saying I'm running out to become a man or anything like that. I'm just saying I can't honestly go into a place where they do sex change stuff, and if they say I'm a good candidate, I can't promise that I won't just say, 'Fine, let's get on with it!'"

"That's amazing," the lawyer says. "But what about the argument Janice Raymond is making? She's saying you should persist in breaking the gender boundaries that you are breaking, that you have already broken. You're like the true face of feminism, and you should persist."

"I thought Gloria Steinem[6] was the true face of feminism," I reply. "She was a fashion model. A Playboy Bunny! That makes her acceptable to the world! She can represent women. There's no way I can do that—not in a way that women will believe I share their dreams and experiences. Please don't try to make me the face of feminism. I would feel like an impostor even though I am a feminist."

---

6 Gloria Steinem (born March 25, 1934) was a journalist and political activist who co-founded *Ms. Magazine* in 1972. While working on a story in 1963 about ways in which women are exploited at work, she got a job as a Playboy Bunny in order to truly understand how women were treated in "gentlemen's clubs." By the late 1970s, she was known as a powerful spokeswoman for feminism and women's equality. Her work is wide-ranging, dynamic, and thoughtful, and it deserves greater recognition.

No one speaks for a few seconds, and then Samantha says, "I love Jamie, but I know damn well, if she's promoted as the face of feminism, I'd have to laugh! For the first year we were together, I had to keep reminding myself to use feminine pronouns for her!"

Everyone laughs then, and I feel proud to be with a woman who understands me so well. She struggles to overcome her sense of me as masculine. Or is it her sense of me as male? There is a difference. I'm not sure, in my case, where the dividing line lies. Janice Raymond has her theory; my theory is still slowly forming. It's a combination of internal and external experience and a search for language that is truly descriptive, not just an analogy designed to appeal to others, like the "born in the wrong body" theory. No one's body is "wrong," but some bodies are dysfunctional in various ways. How can I explain what I feel?

It's early 1978; Samantha and I move back to California. Although Samantha was born in Portland, her parents moved to California in 1956 when she was just 2 years old. My parents moved from Portland to Oakland, California, before World War II, and I was born in Oakland in 1948. I attended the University of Oregon in Eugene for six years while Samantha was in junior high and high school in San Lorenzo, California. I earned a Bachelor's in English, and a Master of Fine Arts in short fiction writing before relocating to Portland. Samantha finds herself in Portland because she doesn't want to go home yet after she and Carol split up. They remained close friends, so Samantha followed her. But now, both Samantha and I want to be closer to our families, and we feel there are greater opportunities for work and advancement in the San Francisco Bay Area. We're correct. And the Bay Area is also where the Sperm Bank of Northern California would launch in 1982[7]. But we have to find work and establish ourselves in our communities before we're able to go near any sperm bank.

I say communities because there are several. First, of course, are the communities of our families. Our parents, as couples, meet each other only once during our entire 14-year relationship. Neither of us has spent much time with our families over the past several years; for me it's almost a decade since I'd been at home with my parents for more than a week at a time. For Samantha, it's less of a challenge, so we spend more time with her folks and her two younger brothers. In fact, we live for several months in her parents' garage while I look for work, land a job, and accumulate enough money to rent an apartment for us.

Our second communities are my work environment and Samantha's junior college. She decides to return to school and major in music to develop her innate creative and performance skills to a more professional level. We're living in the East Bay, where Samantha can either take the bus to school or I can drive her if necessary. We're only five or six miles from Chabot College. Samantha hopes to earn her associate degree as soon as possible and transfer to San Jose State University where she can study music seriously. Our

7 The Sperm Bank of Northern California began as a project of the Oakland Feminist Women's Health Center, a family planning clinic. For more information, see: https://www.thespermbankofca.org/about/vision-values-and-history/

apartment is also located within walking distance of a BART light rail station where I can catch a train for downtown San Francisco where I work at the Bank of California. We both also work hard to establish ourselves in the local lesbian community. That's our third community challenge. We balance everything from our centrally-located home base, almost equidistant from my parents in Oakland and Samantha's family in Livermore. And every weekend, we visit one family or the other, alternating between them, keeping secrets while we're still figuring ourselves out.

I land my position at the bank through a referral from my Portland lawyer friend. She knows an attorney at the bank and suggests I call her and arrange a lunch so I can introduce myself. Maybe she'll have a lead on a job somewhere for me. It turns out that this attorney thinks I might find work through the temp pool at the bank. I'm offered a part-time job running the Xerox copier in the bank's legal department, where I meet a legal secretary who is a lesbian writer of romance novels in her spare time. She writes under a pseudonym that, regrettably, I would later forget. She and her partner are very fun to hang out with. Samantha met Kathy in the jazz choir class when some young man spewed a homophobic slur—maybe assuming that no one in the room was gay or lesbian. Both Samantha and Kathy had reacted indignantly, simultaneously telling him (and the entire choir) that he'd better watch his mouth because he had no idea whether anyone around him was gay. He might be insulting someone he respected, and wouldn't that be awkward for him!? Samantha and Kathy become fast friends from that moment on. Kathy is 10 years younger than me, and Kathy's partner, a warehouse worker named Philomena who everyone calls Phil, is around Samantha's age. Phil is a "soft butch" or androgynous-leaning person who looks like a woman in men's clothes. She's pretty comfortable around me, and we become a party of four fairly often.

Another couple of young women also become close friends: Vicky and Beth. We call them "the Fotomates" because one of them works in a Fotomat[8] booth, a drive-up photo processing service that's popular in the late 1970s. We meet when Samantha and I drive up to drop off a roll of film. The young woman is very efficient, issuing me a receipt and saying, "Your prints will be ready on Friday afternoon. My name is Vicky." On Friday, when I hand a different girl my receipt, she looks down at the floor of her booth and says, "They're here!" Up pops Vicky, and the two of them are like enthusiastic puppies, wiggling and jumping and just so excited, as if hoping to be selected from their cage at the dog pound.

"Oh, you're here!!" Vicky beams. "We were hoping to see you! This is Beth!"

"Here are your prints," Beth says, and both she and Vicky lean out the window of the booth toward our car to hand them to me. "We were hoping maybe you two would like to go have ice cream or something with us. We were hoping we could talk with you. We don't know anyone here."

8 See https://en.wikipedia.org/wiki/Fotomat for the story of the Fotomat Corporation and images of Fotomat drive-up kiosks/booths.

Obviously, they recognize us as "family," as lesbians. And, of course, we agree to talk with them. They're just 19 years old and fled their homes in New Jersey when their parents discovered they were lovers. They find their way across the country and almost reach San Francisco when they realize they need to find work and an affordable place to live, so here they are in a small town in the East Bay hills. We're the first couple they've seen who look like family, so they take a chance to reach out to us.

"I could be fired for this," Vicky says. "I hope you won't report me?"

"Of course not," I say.

"You gotta do what you gotta do," Samantha says. "And we're glad you did!"

We become friends.

Mary, a woman we know from Portland, calls out of the blue to tell me she and her partner, Jen, have moved to San Francisco, and they hope we can get together. I'm excited: they're my age and very fun people. Our little community is growing. We keep meeting other women and learning about restaurants, cafes, and bars where women congregate. Samantha is involved with the Wiccan[9] community, and our friendship circle expands to include gay male couples, bi-

9 Wiccans are (loosely) people who shared a spiritual belief in a mother goddess and her consort (a less important father god), and in the natural world, rooted in Celtic traditions but often incorporating Native American and other indigenous spiritual practices and beliefs.

sexual folks, and straight people, too, the latter mostly from my work and Samantha's Wiccan activities. We're settling in, getting our lives together, establishing ourselves.

In October of 1982, the Sperm Bank opens in Oakland. In early 1983, a women's health fair is held at the Women's Building on Valencia Street in San Francisco. Samantha is keen to attend. She and I collect lots of information there from many organizations, including the Sperm Bank. There are hundreds of women at the health fair and scores of booths; I find it a bit overwhelming, and I just follow Samantha around while she gathers pamphlets, information sheets, business cards, and postcard advertisements from every aisle crammed with vendors, healthcare providers, and even a few jewelry makers and other craftswomen. Reproductive healthcare is top of mind for many young and middle-aged women[10]. It's inspiring for both Samantha and me to see hundreds of women engaged in their quests for better understanding and better self-care. Yet so much of what is offered doesn't speak to me. It feels like no one can tell me why none of this resonates with me—not breast health, not

10 Ever since the book *Our Bodies, Ourselves* was published in 1971, women across the United States have been growing ever more conscious of the ignorance of women's actual health within the patriarchal medical system. (See *Our Bodies, Ourselves.* (1971). Feminist Women's Health Collective. Boston, MA: New England Free Press.) In fact, the first comprehensive clinical medical textbook focused exclusively on lesbian health was not published until 2010 (see *Lesbian Health 101: A Clinician's Guide.* (2010). Suzanne L. Dibble and Patricia A. Robinson, Eds. San Francisco: UCSF Nursing Press). So, in the 1980s, much about women's health was still very new for everyone. Women today are still struggling to learn about their bodies and to find reliable healthcare information and resources.

softer skin, not making babies, not even better nutrition to support my menstrual function, or feminine pain relief. None of it speaks to me. I'm proud of Samantha for seeking information and happy I'm there to support her, but nothing at that fair meets my personal needs. I'm not even sure what my personal needs are at this time. I only want Samantha to be healthy and fulfilled.

By April of 1983, I'm working as a publications manager for a computer design and manufacturing company. Samantha has earned her Bachelor's in Music, and we both feel ready to begin raising a family. We go to our first appointment at the Sperm Bank to discuss the insemination process, our expectations, and what our responsibilities will be in any contract with them, should we engage their services. We return a few weeks later to select a donor from the list of available candidates. We select one who resembles me as much as possible and whose medical history doesn't include risk factors that might be compounded when combined with Samantha's genetic history. It's not an easy process. We see only data, no photos, no personality, no sound, just phrases someone wrote. We see circle-the-word options for eye color, hair color, notes on their hobbies, the subjects they had studied in school, and the degrees they had earned (if any). We study the causes of death of their parents and grandparents. What if they aren't telling the truth? We speak with the nurse or social worker who has interviewed them and whose handwriting is on the forms. We ask their impressions of the candidates. They're generally vague and nonjudgmental, not wanting to bias us. When we select one, they brighten and tell us we will have a beautiful baby. Maybe they say that to everyone, but we're hopeful. We take home instructions about monitoring Samantha's peak fertility so we can come back and pick up the sperm at the optimal time. All we have to do is call them the day we need it and bring the money (which is one or two hundred dollars for each vial of sperm.) We can have one per month, on dry ice, in our six-pack-sized Styrofoam cold carrier. The cost is not trivial to us, but we're willing to meet it.

It takes 11 months for Samantha to conceive. Throughout the process, we continue to hang out with our lesbian friends, and we occasionally share about the topics that are slowly consuming our lives: conception, pregnancy, and raising a child. Whenever those words fall out of our mouths, some friends shudder in horror or disgust. Then they laugh at themselves or maybe at us. We don't know. We only know it's an uncomfortable topic for them.

A life without men, the kind of life so many lesbians want in the latter half of the twentieth century, means a life without children. And these women struggle to hide themselves and their relationships with women from their families because to be a lesbian means to be without children. For their parents, that means no grandchildren. And many of these women have heard throughout their own childhoods about their parents' hopes for their grandchildren. The joy they expect in their lives when their daughters provide the next generation to carry on their legacy or their genetic contribution to the world. Those women grow up knowing they will always be a disappointment to their parents, that they will break their mothers' hearts. Some try to tell their mothers they don't plan to have children or hedge a bit as they declare that maybe they don't want children. Their mothers chastise them, saying, "Of course, you'll want children. It's your duty to provide me with at least one grandchild." Sometimes, the conversation becomes an argument, with tears and painful reverberating anger, shaming and frightful, with fears of abandonment or disconnection between mother and daughter. These women carry with them the guilt, anger, and resentment that arises within them whenever they contemplate a visit with their families, knowing the questions will always arise. "When are you going to get married? When are you going to give me some grandchildren?"

And then there are those women who become lesbians in defense against men who've abused them, injured them, violated them. Those women for whom the thought of physical intimacy with a man is abhorrent, completely disempowering, repugnant, infuriating. Their disgust fuels their anger, restoring their power and strengthening their independence.

Some lesbian women who've given birth to children and divorced their husbands have raised their boys to be conscious and respectful of women. They raise their daughters to be conscious and independent thinkers who can care for themselves and stand up for themselves. The dynamics between the sexes and the generations seem more complex than ever now, with technologies, travel, education, and ambition all more accessible than ever before.

As Samantha's womb expands, our lesbian friends gradually drop away. I call our friends who also lived in Portland and invite them over for dinner at our place. They at least have the integrity to be honest: they don't want to be around children. "So, we might as well say goodbye now," Mary says bluntly. I can hear Jen in the distance when she shouts, "Goodbye, breeders!" as Mary breaks the connection.

Our pagan friends stand by us, and so do the Fotomates, and Kathy and Phil, and a gay male couple who become beloved uncles to our daughter, whom we name Morgan. However, I shudder whenever anyone refers to me as our baby's "other mother." Samantha is Mom or Momma, and I'm Jamie, not a mother in any way. Samantha and I are so happy with our little girl, who has green eyes like mine. When she's about 3 years old, we ask the sperm bank if the same donor is available for a second child so our kids will have full siblings. The clinic is able to make that happen for us.

I begin to worry: what if our second child is a boy? How can I continue living in an androgynous state, knowing my pleasure whenever my masculinity is recognized, knowing that I'm infinitely more comfortable whenever people perceive me as male? How can I help my children to understand the discrepancy between my masculine spirit and my female body? Adults might be able to do that, but can my children? Two mommies is one thing, but I'm something else. I can't be a mommy any more than I can honestly be a woman. When Morgan is almost 4 years old, I decide to take that terrifying step and apply to the sex reassignment program at Stanford. Just as my Portland friends anticipated, there is no problem with my acceptance. I walk in looking like I'm already more than halfway through the process. With Samantha's support, I start taking testosterone to begin my physical transformation about six months before our new baby will be born. Yes, Samantha encourages me to do what I need to do, with the caveat that we might not be able to remain together. I know we love each other and that she always knew I was a man in spirit. I'm confident I'm not going to change that much.

By this point, I'd been trying to come to grips with myself around this "gender thing" for over 20 years, without any language to adequately describe my experience of myself in my body in relation to the world. I have no intention of trying to be anything or anyone that I am not. I don't want to be a different person. I want to finally be myself. I don't want to disappear. I've learned more about what it means for me physically, mentally, and socially to engage in this transition; although there's a lot I don't yet know, I'm determined it's the right thing for me to do. I definitely have some concerns about the surgeries that will come later; scarring, for one, and anesthesia is always a risk, but I can choose to stop the process at any time if it doesn't feel right to me. Still, the effect of the hormone over the initial six months makes me feel calm, emotionally balanced, physically solidified, and integrated into my body for the first time in my adult life.

Our second child is a boy. We name him Nick. I severed his umbilical cord, something I was afraid to do for my daughter. The first person Samantha calls from the hospital is not her mother, as she did when Morgan was born. It's Philomena. I ask Samantha what's going on with her and Phil. She just stares at me, silent.

Morgan wanted a little sister, but she is still happy to have a baby of any kind so she can be a big sister. Our two babies are beautiful and sweet. Samantha and I have been together for nearly 14 years. I'm considering buying a larger home. It will only be a few years before our two children will need separate rooms.

Two months later, my "top surgery[11]" is a significant relief for me, freeing me of the softness on my chest that, once perceived, masks my masculinity and causes my integrity to be called into question. I think that's the hardest thing for Samantha to accept. She hates hospitals and the idea of any kind of surgery. She says goodbye to me at the hospital, and she drives me home in silence after my outpatient surgery. I'm still so groggy from the anesthesia that I throw up twice. I'm home for two days, sleeping on the couch in our living room, before I realize she hasn't spoken to me since she said goodbye to me at the hospital. She doesn't say a word when she brings me soup, bread, or water, which she does several times daily. After a week, as I'm becoming more capable of taking care of myself, though I still have some physical restrictions for the next several weeks, Samantha announces she's going out. She leaves Morgan with me, takes Nick, and after several hours, she

11 Top surgery is slang for surgical reconstruction to remove breast tissue and create a masculine chest.

returns with lease documents for an apartment she's found. She wants to move out, but because she's unemployed, she's required to have me sign the lease and take responsibility for her payments if she defaults. I cry. I can't believe she wants to end our relationship without even talking about it. And I can't pay both the mortgage on our house and rent for her apartment. She takes both the children and goes to live at her parents' home. We work out a visitation arrangement, and I gladly pay child support. I cry a lot. My emotions cycle from bereft sadness to anger to elation over the transformation my own body is going through. Then I'm resolute about the practicality of managing selling our home to provide Samantha and the children with financial resources. I perform well at my corporate management job in Silicon Valley and remain cheerful whenever I'm with our children. I cry a lot when I'm alone. And I'm alone a lot. A few months later, during a visitation, Morgan tells me they're living with Phil now. I'm furious, but I don't let on. When she's asleep, I call Kathy to see if she and Phil are still together. Kathy says absolutely not, and good riddance.

One day, I go to the company where Phil works and ask the receptionist to tell Phil I'm in the lobby. It takes Phil about 10 minutes to come out. She's wearing blue jeans and a T-shirt, with her dark hair pulled back in a thick braid.

"Warehouse?" I ask.

"Yeah, supervisor."

"Good for you."

"Thanks. What do you want?"

"I want to know why you did this to my family?"

"All's fair in love and war, Jamie," she says. "There's nothing more to say." And she walks back beyond the security doors. As the door shuts behind her, I say, "I didn't know there was a war. I think it was a coup," although only the receptionist can hear me. She looks away.

It's 1991, and Nick is 2 years old. It's the same month that I go before a judge to get my name and sex legally changed, and I'm served with legal notice that I'm being sued for non-paternity. Not for my daughter, just my son. Samantha wants Phil to be Nick's co-parent. She no longer accepts child support money from me earmarked for him. I have no legal rights. We weren't legally married[12] when both children were born, though I've been listed as their father on both their birth certificates. Because we are not married and we had never established a second-parent adoption together, and because I cannot prove biological paternity, I have no parental rights. I have no option but to agree to Samantha's demands. I continue to have regular weekly visitations with Morgan, but I don't see Nick again for 10 years, except occasionally from a distance, usually by accident. When I pick Morgan up, Phil is feeding him in the kitchen, out of sight of the door, locked into his highchair. Once when Morgan and

12 Same-sex marriage, which would permit trans people who did not have a legally-recognized change of sex to marry a same-sex (though possibly opposite-sex gender) partner, was not legal nationally until 2015. I received legal sex recognition as male in 1991, two years after Samantha and I had broken up.

I are in an Oakland shopping district, we see Nick riding on Phil's shoulders as they walk down the street ahead of us. Morgan shouts, "Hey, Nick!" They both look in our direction. When Nick calls out, "Sister!" Phil runs to get away, lest she or Nick might lay eyes on me. Morgan looks at me with apprehension, wondering what I'll do. I say, "This makes me very sad, you know?" She nods. "But there's nothing I can do because I don't want to upset your mom." Secretly, I want to smash Phil's face in. Sometimes, when I'm alone in my apartment, I act out my frustration and anger, flailing my fists and cursing, whispering furious monologues through my teeth that damn Phil to hell and worse. I never blame Samantha. She lives in my broken heart, and I believe she did the things she did because she was frightened of my transition, the changes in my appearance, and her perception of my new social status as a man, which, to her, would erase her status as a lesbian. I'm sad because she can't see I am the same person she once loved and wanted to build a family with. The Phil who shows herself in my imagination is pulverized by my fists, dissolved into a smear of blood and flesh in the heat of my anger. My anger is not toward women, it's toward people who take advantage of others and undermine others' relationships, who have no capacity to love or respect someone for who they are.

Samantha studies to become an elementary school teacher. She plays her Ovation guitar in her classrooms and is a much-admired educator until breast cancer strikes her in 1996 when Nick is 7 years old and Morgan is 11. Samantha now tries to convince me to relinquish my parental status so that she and Phil can do a co-parent adoption for both kids. If she dies, she wants the kids to stay together and for Phil to have custody of them. I object firmly. I will not give up my parental relationship or responsibilities for my daughter. And no matter where he lives, I will always be present for Nick.

One day, when I pick Morgan up from school, she angrily demands: "How come Nick gets to be adopted, and I don't?"

"Whoa," I say. "Where is that coming from? What did they actually tell you?"

"They said you won't let me be adopted."

I think for a moment. "That's right," I say calmly. "I won't do that. Because if I let you be adopted, then I won't be your parent anymore."

I can see the lightbulb going on over her head. "Oh," she says thoughtfully. "Well, that's a good thing then, Dad."

"I think so, too," I say.

Samantha and Phil separate in 1999. Morgan refuses to attend "family therapy" sessions that include Phil, saying, "That person is not part of my family." And I begin to have occasional, though still rare, visits with Nick because Samantha recognizes it's time for him to get to know me—a little bit. Samantha finally succumbs to cancer in 2008. I adopt my adult son in 2009 at his request so he can have a legal parent. Our children—now aged 40 and 36—live in

Portland, not far from each other, nor far from me and my wife Heidi[13]. I met and fell in love with Heidi in 2001, and we married in 2003, with the kids and Samantha's parents present. We all love each other deeply and recognize the strength and commitment we each possess that has made us who we are and kept us together in defiance of convention and all odds.

People always try to tell us who we are supposed to be and how we are supposed to behave, not to mention what we're supposed to look like to be treated as human beings. But because we are human beings, we have infinite possibilities. We're lucky if we can learn to recognize those possibilities and be true to ourselves and our commitments. I'm one of those lucky people.

Jamison Green (he/him) always knew he would be a writer, a career goal that led to many adventures. He earned his M.F.A. in Creative Writing from the University of Oregon. Since then, he has taught legal writing, skiing, and gender studies. He performed in rock bands, percussion ensembles, and musical theater. He has written for major corporations and led nonprofit organizations. He changed anti-discrimination laws and reformed insurance industry and health-care delivery practice—all while publishing numerous arti-

13 We moved to the greater Portland area at the end of 2017, and the children followed separately during the COVID-19 pandemic: first, Nick, and later, Morgan and her husband.

cles and books on a variety of subjects. His best-known book is Becoming a Visible Man. *Learn more at jamisongreen.com.*

Evolution of a Thought

By Eric Hojka

At first, I thought that this man was trying to play a trick on me. Horrible, mean, and awful, but a trick, nonetheless. I desperately want it to be a practical joke no matter how awful, because that means what I am starting to feel is not reality. As I stagger across the room, I can see the vacant look in his eyes. I immediately feel my body temperature drop, as if in sympathy with the body in front of me. I scream out, "No, no no no no no no!!" This can't be happening. My extremities start shaking as I reach down to touch his skin.

I almost find immediate relief when I discover his skin is still warm. I am about to remove my hand when I realize there IS something different about the texture of his skin. I don't feel the hum and the buzz of his blood flowing. It is silent. I know now my shouts are not going to help. I reach down to shake him gently as if that will wake him. I collapse in grief in front of him. While I know this probably happened in seconds, the moment stretches for hours. I jump up, grab my phone, and call 911 as I start to administer what I remember of CPR.

"911. What's your emergency?"

"I am here ...." I start sobbing as I am trying to give chest compressions while holding the phone to my ear when I realize I can put her on speaker phone. "There's a guy, I don't even know him at all, he came over and he ... I think. I am not sure ...."

"Sir, please take a breath and tell me what happened so I can help you."

I attempt to take a steadying breath, but it hitches as I try to calm down. "I invited this guy over, and now he is not breathing, I think he is using ... err, I mean or used drugs. I see a syringe on the breakfast bar above me and, oh my God, I can't believe this is happening!"

"Ok sir, I understand you have a man there that is not breathing, and he may have used drugs, and you need assistance. Can I have your address?"

"310 Market Street, number 301." The tears are streaming down my face, and I can't think. I feel like I am breaking this man's ribs as I clumsily administer CPR. I realize how hard my heart is beating, feeling the THUD-WOMP, THUD-WOMP, THUD-WOMP inside my chest. I start crying harder as I realize this guy's heart may never beat again.

"It's not working!!" I shout at the operator.

"Sir, what is your name?" The operator asks me in a calm and efficient voice.

"Eric!" I manage to blurt out. I feel like passing out.

"Ok, Eric. I am here with you and will help you as the paramedics are already on their way. Are you doing chest compressions right now?"

"I am, but I am not even sure I am doing it right."

"Eric, I want you to continue doing chest compressions even if you are not sure the technique is right. Where is the gentleman lying?"

"On my couch, but the cushions just keep bouncing him around."

"Ok Eric, I know this will be difficult, but if you can, I need you to move him to a harder surface."

"You want me to do what??! Move him? Oh God, I can't pick up someone who is dead ...."

"Eric, we don't know he is dead, so we continue to give him CPR until the EMTs are there. The compressions you are giving him will be more effective with a harder surface to compress against."

Again, the operator's calm and relaxed voice seems to break through some of my panic. I am sweating profusely, and tears are spilling down my face in deep rivulets, but I manage to take a deep breath. "Ok," I tell the operator. I am going to try and move him now."

The whole world melts before my eyes, becoming distorted by my copious tears. The light from the lamp next to the couch seems to shine brighter and feels more surreal, as if coming from a distant supernova. I shove the coffee table behind me, sending it crashing into the TV. My focus narrows on the man's eyes again, now just dull orbs frozen in time. I put my arms around his head and knees, once again close to him with an intimacy I never wanted. The look on his face is beseeching me to do something ... anything. My mind goes blank, and I think to myself," Is this even real? Am I really here?" I lift him carefully and notice how heavy and unforgiving his weight is. I almost drop him as I move him to the floor. Now I am howling so hard I barely notice the voice coming from the phone.

As my focus shifts back to the voice on the phone I hear, "—ric? Are you still with me? Eric?"

"Yes, yes, I am here."

"Is he on the floor?"

"Yes, please help, are the ambulance guys here?"

"Eric, they are almost there. Continue to do chest compressions. They are entering the building now."

"Ok. Ok. God, his eyes, his eyes." I close my eyes, and it feels like I am drifting away. So far away.

I hear a siren outside, but my mind is so far removed from the present, I can't be sure. I labor through these compressions with my body, but I am not here. My mind goes back there. Somewhere in my past where I am young, and I am safe. I am lying in the sun and shade of my front yard. The summer breeze is blowing on my face, and I am waiting. I am feeling the joy of just being alive. The air smells of possibilities and the excitement of the day lies ahead. Blossoms of hope flowering in my heart, and I am feeling at peace. I am there. I am there.

I am yanked back to the present by a loud knock on the door, as the EMTs burst in. The human being is still not breathing. I have been trying to keep him alive for what seems like eons. I am like an automaton fulfilling a program, and I won't stop. His chest is soaked from my tears.

"I can't stop. I can't stop. I can't stop." I repeat this out loud, copying and pasting my words with every compression. A promise with every thrust. The EMT pulls my arms gently but commandingly away so they can do their work. I am led to a chair, frozen in the moment, my tears building a moat around me. My body is in stasis. My mind on repeat. My eyes darting everywhere. This apartment will never be the same for me. I look across the room at the kitchen, the breakfast bar, the living room. I realize I won't be able to unsee what has happened here. The couch is a memory of my grandparents. It always meant so much to me to have it. Now all I see are cushions with the outline of the body that was resting there. No, not resting, dying. I will never use that couch again. I will throw it out like trash. How did I come to a place in my life where THIS HAPPENS?

The paramedics are now wrapping things up as I hear one of the policemen present ask if I have a name or any information about the man they are rolling out on the gurney. I am consumed with shame that the only thing I know about him is that his name is Chuck. It was a hookup. What did I care about names? Hell, he could have made up a name for as much as this encounter meant to either of us. I relay this information to the cop who gives me his card and says to call if there is anything else I can think of. I stumble to the door to see them out.

I quietly close the door behind them, and I sink to the floor. I feel the sensation of my whole self melting into the floor. I let myself vanish into the moment and allow emotion to flood every cell. Every piece of me is washing away into mental oblivion.

I am not sure how long I sit there becoming part of the floor. I almost have a thought at this point, but my mental energy has all been used up while the paramedics were here. I go on autopilot to my room, reaching for a box on the shelf. I know I should take a shower as I can smell my sweat and fear still clinging to me. I take the box to my bed and open it as I recline back against the headboard. My internal software program is running the show in the background. No conscious thought now, just the code propelling my actions. I take out my meth pipe and lighter, feeling the heat from the lighter work its magic as I slowly inhale. If this subconscious program has a label, it would be "escape hatch." It runs and thinks so I don't have to. It works so I can dissolve into nothing. Getting high is my only modus operandi these days, and I am not in control. My body craves and creates mechanized movements. I am not present.

I fall away and sense that somewhere else my motions continue, but my mind has become separate from my body as I sit there, numb. I drift further, reaching and searching for a time and place that feels safe. The drugs are having their effect, and a superficial and surreal complacency replaces my thoughts. I feel (better?) as I leave the reality of the present.

The past and the present seem to coalesce, and an image appears. I am taken aback by what I see. I see myself at age 7 in a room with one door leading to the world outside. I can see through the beveled glass all the people, places, and things I want to be a part of, but I become stuck every time I try to join the world. I don't fit. Looking behind me, I see that my thoughts about myself are floating around me like small balloons attached to my back, and I can't fit through the door.

I notice in the corner of the room a backpack marked "normal" and it occurs to me that, if I pack these abnormal thoughts away, I can fit through the door easily. I pull these thought balloons closer and see what is written on each: SHAME, SELF-HATRED, FEAR, FEELINGS FOR BOYS, MAMA'S BOY, QUEER, GIRLY. I begin to stuff these into the opening of the backpack, and they disappear into the dark of the bag. The words pull my body down into a hunched position, almost animal-like. It is as if I have transmogrified into the character Eeyore from the classic *Winnie-the-Pooh*. I hear his low voice, "I am ashamed of who I am. Nobody loves me." I close the flap and place the pack on my shoulders, feeling the weight of it. I tell myself this is just a temporary solution and is the way that I survive.

I awake from my vision in the present and realize I must have fallen asleep. Three hours have gone by, and I feel completely wasted. I get up and take a shower to try and move past my awful morning. I take my box of paraphernalia into the bathroom with me as I turn on the shower. Just as I enter the hot jet spray, I hear a loud knock on my door, and I hear someone yell, "OPEN UP!!" I stumble to the door, ask, "Who is it?" and my heart drops to my stomach as they say "Police!" I unlock the door in my towel as several policemen enter my apartment and start shouting at me to sit down. The plain-clothes detective pushes me into a chair, and my towel falls to the floor. I try to recover it, but I am told not to touch anything or move. I am terrified as I sit naked waiting for the next command. I cross my legs for a certain amount of modesty. After years of shoving down my emotions, tears flood my eyes for the second time today. I see the detective is talking to me, but I am not comprehending anything. I am still high and in shock from earlier and now in a state of panic from the authorities bursting in.

The police quickly search my apartment and confiscate my phone and computer from the coffee table. They find my small bag of meth and pipe in the bathroom and start firing questions at me. I don't say much because everything they might want to know is probably on my phone. All I know is that I need a lawyer. I learned at least that much from TV. They keep asking me questions I won't answer. They can't seem to find what they are looking for, which I assume is evidence of me being a drug dealer. I want to scream out, "I am not a dealer!" Then, a quieter voice inside my head says, "You may not be a dealer, but how did you get these drugs you have right now?"

I know that answer easily. My dealer introduced me to his supplier in California, and I did what I always do. I ingratiated myself to the supplier by charming him and seeing if he wanted to meet. I couldn't afford drugs because of my limited income, but I sure knew how to use what I had (my body) to get what I wanted (my drugs). The supplier flew me to California, and I spent a week hanging out with him. He explained he would send the new shipment to my dealer on my return. When it arrived at my dealer's house, he gave me some to take home, and that is what I had on the table when the gentleman arrived earlier. While I will never know for sure if he used the drugs I had on the table or his own, I realize it doesn't matter. What matters is, those of us who are addicts are constantly enabling each other to use illegal drugs, and we never know what the outcome will be. It's a gamble every time. In that way, we help each other destroy ourselves little by little. We don't ever speak of it, of course, but that's the truth. Intentional or not, we don't hold ourselves accountable because we think we are only hurting ourselves. I also think to myself, "How many times have I shared my drugs with others and I didn't bother to dismiss them if they offered some money to me so they could take some with them? How often did I get enough drugs for me and someone else so that I wouldn't have to use alone? That might not be "dealing" in the traditional sense, but I was fully complicit in distributing what I had."

I sit there, shocked and quietly remembering all the other things I have experienced due to my choices while in my addiction over the years. I need to remember HOW I got here.

I remember selling my body for the first time so that I could either get cash or more drugs as part of the package. How many times? Hundreds. Maybe close to a thousand over the years. One time a regular client became a stalker because I left without paying him so that I could get more drugs, which ended up involving the police. Getting arrested with another guy for the first time in my life because we were pulled over, and I had no drugs but my pipe and empty baggies in my backpack. Renting a car for three days and not returning it for a month until the cops finally called and gracefully said that, if I returned it to the rental company, no charges would be pressed. Quitting my job before they would fire me and then taking the corporate card they hadn't canceled yet and buying myself a week in a hotel and then skipping out on payment.

The very first time I tried crystal meth, I ended up in the hospital so dehydrated my speech was slurred and slowed. For days afterward I had so much vertigo I thought I had a brain tumor. So many more hospital visits over the years, ambulance rides, and close calls that I was riding the line. Close to crossing the River Styx each time and not even caring. Thinking that all I had to do was learn how to use it smarter and better. Two years in San Francisco living homeless. Not on the street most nights because of a few other using fellows in the city that would allow me to stay on their couch or in their bed. All this time telling my family and friends that I was fine, not to worry about me, as I walked the aisles of grocery stores and stole food because I had no money to eat. In the middle of the night, walking up a dead-end street, having panic attacks so severe I thought I was having a heart attack but without a phone because I didn't pay the bill. Hanging out with complete strangers in every awful, rundown building in the San Francisco area just so that I didn't have to come down.

These things, ALL these things, are how I am here right now.

The police find my stash in the box in the bathroom and ask me why I am trying to hide the drugs. "Hide them?" I think to myself. "They were in an open box in the bathroom on the sink." They continue to ask the same questions because, I think, they have bigger fish to fry. They do not arrest me but also make sure to let me know they will have further questions and to be available. As they file out, and I close the door, my body once again collapses to the floor. My life has just erupted in a molten flow of lava, and everything is burning. I think about what to do next as the morning burns a scar into my heart and mind.

I feel everything and nothing at the same time, and I just want to escape again. Since they took my remaining drugs as evidence, I now have no way to lose myself and escape. How do I deal with this much pain, emotion, and fear? For almost 20 years, meth has allowed me to escape. Before the drugs, I buried myself in other people's issues so I didn't have to think about mine. I think about my life and the vision I had earlier, and I realize I never really learned who I am. How could I? I packed it all away at age seven and made a choice not to look at any of it. I made that choice. ME.

Standing up, I wobble my way to the kitchen on unsure legs to grab a drink of water. As I gulp down water, I ask myself, "What if this time I make a different choice? What if I decide to actually change and to stop running?" I have made that choice many times before, and it never lasts. I know the drill. Make a good choice. Start down the path to recovery. Relapse. Negative self-talk. Fall into addiction. This time is different. I am at my lowest place. I will not fail.

* * *

With that evolution of thought, my life begins to change.

* * *

I come to a halt, complete an about-face, and finally come to rest in front of the one thing in my house I rarely use. It hangs there, in the hallway directly across from the bathroom door, daring me to look up. I hid the shiny and gleaming surface behind a curtain so I don't have to see myself. With all the energy I have left, I pull the fabric back and away, the mirror begging me to acknowledge its presence. It says, "Here I am. Look. See. Observe." The weight of that voice drills into my heart with a rhythm I am intimately familiar with. With each beat, I hear this tune that has ruled my life. The hum of doubt. The chorded progression of unworthiness. The bass line of fear. The incessant dissonance. I take a breath and look up. The mirror's reflection bounces back from the mirror in the bathroom across the hall. The infinite image it produces creates an illusion of multiple dimensions of myself, split back and back and back. Almost as if I am going back in time. I look at myself but not at my eyes. I am afraid of what I will see there. Mustering up all the courage I have, I finally do look directly into my eyes and notice their puffiness, the red crackled look of the capillaries, and just stare. I recognize for the first time in my life that I don't really know who this person is that is standing before me. I have spent so many years keeping hidden. Pretending. I am a chameleon. I feel a sudden burst of electricity inside me and realize I want to change. I no longer want to be victimized by the emotions that have had so much power over me. I am terrified. I am elated. I fear the unknown so much I stand there one moment longer, and then I see my multidimensional self in the mirror promising to make myself whole.

I throw on some clothes, open my door, and run down the hall. I take the elevator to the first floor and my building's exit. I keep walking, knowing my destination is my friend's house so that I can call my sister. The police took my phone with them. I want to call her and let her know what has happened so I can find a way home to my mom. I have no car; another consequence of never having money for basic things because I used all the cash I had for drugs. I continue walking the two miles, and as I walk I see many faces going about their daily lives. I imagine the smiles on their faces and the happiness they seem to exude could be me again one day. I walk past the quick store I use every day to buy cigarettes. I am suddenly aware that I left my cigarettes at home and realize, of course, I can't buy more because my account is overdrawn. Another casualty of my private war. I continue on, my feet hitting the pavement in a rhythmic fashion, the same words echoing from earlier. "DON'T STOP, DON'T STOP, DON'T STOP." But this time it is to save my own life. I am so tired by the time I reach my friend and ring the doorbell, I collapse inside his front door. My emotions tumble out of me as I ask to use his phone. I can see he is worried and doesn't understand what is going on, but being the friend he is, he allows me to grab his phone to call my sister.

My sister agrees to call my mom and my friend, Jace. This new journey has begun, completely unknown and terrifying, but at least I feel hope and promise for the first time in years. Jace takes me home, and the first thing I notice is how beautiful my mom looks as I enter her ranch-style home in our sleepy hometown. As I cross through the breezeway, she hugs me so ferociously that I am almost certain she will never let me go again. She thanks Jace, and as he pulls out of the driveway, she turns to me. I can see hope and fear in her eyes asking, "Is this the last time, Eric? Will you please now do something different?" Most of all, the thing that kills me through to the heart is that I hear her eyes say, " Can I trust you enough to let myself get close to you again?"

The next two months are filled with so much unrest and chaos that I am sure my heart will burst from all the anxiety. The very day I went home to Mom, I called my social worker at the University Hospital where I had been getting my care for the last eight years. I find the most effective rehabilitation program nearby and enroll in their outpatient program, which is two to three months long. I hire a lawyer with the help of a friend. He tells me after his call to the detective that there is no movement on my case in the last two weeks. He explains that this could be for many reasons, but until he gets more information, I should just hang in there, and he will take care of everything. He said he will call me with any developments as they come. I thank him for his time and help, and in the meantime, I focus solely on my recovery and figuring out what to do about my apartment. I will need to take a trip back there to find out what their decision is regarding my lease because I had broken the rule of no drugs in the building. Being on disability for the last seven years allowed me to live in this complex, but they have very specific rules, of course. My mother agrees to drive me to my apartment, and on the way I am sweating so fiercely I roll the window down. I am aware this is just one of the many ways in which I need to take responsibility for my actions. As we enter the building, the manager gives me a quick look from his office and motions for me to come in. He is on the phone, but I can sense the anger coming from him. I imagine it is because of the danger I put other residents in by having so many people coming in and out of my apartment at all times of day and night to use drugs. He hangs up the phone and says, "You have 30 days to move." That's it. No more. I thank him for his time and scurry out the door like a puppy with its tail between its legs. I also feel a sense of relief in knowing what comes next, and that I can and will move out with expediency so the other residents don't have to continue to worry about my presence there. It is all coming into my mind now just how much my behavior affected others. I am only a week sober and already beginning to see things more clearly. When was the last time I had one full week sober? I assume next to never.

On the way home, the silence is so loud it comes off in waves of energy from my mom. Is she mad? Scared? Furious? Hopeful? Disappointed? I decide I can't take it any longer and ask, "Mom, are you ok? I mean I know that none of this is ok, but how are you doing?" She turns to me briefly, and then back again to driving and says quietly, "Disappointed." I want so badly for this not to be what I heard. I never wanted to disappoint my family, and here it is. More and more of the consequences are revealed of my behavior over the past 20 years. I am confronting my fears and my life for the first time, and it sucks. It sucks so much, and I want to run. I won't though. I am done running.

That night I have a nightmare and wake up to an afterimage of the man who passed away in my apartment that day staring at me with black eyes. My body feels cold. I close my eyes but still see those vacant eyes. My mind feels lost. Every moment of that day comes rushing back. A tsunami attempting to break me apart. It is early, barely 4:30 a.m., but I decide to get up and have some coffee and a few cigarettes out in the garage until my mom gets up. I sit there and stare at the sunrise and exhale a plume of smoke so it creates a hazy smog in front of me and think. It is my first full week at rehab. It will be filled with some in-person groups, activities, and 12-step meetings on Zoom due to the COVID-19 pandemic raging through the country. In between rehab days, I will be going back and forth to my apartment to pack for moving. My mom decides she wants me to temporarily move back to the apartment so I can pack and get out of there as soon as possible. She says she also needs a break from me at home, and I know I have put an enormous strain on her schedule and her emotions. I understand how difficult this is for her, and I agree.

Two weeks into rehab I am actually sleeping through the night. I attend class and group, but because of the pandemic, we are required to have our temperature taken upon arrival and to sit six feet apart in the room. That first night back in the apartment is difficult as I haven't gotten rid of the couch yet, so I try to avoid that part of the living room as

I pack. I decide to get rid of the couch the next day, my heart breaking at the thought.

As the next couple of months roll by, and I am approaching my release date from the rehab program, I am beginning to feel hope that I absolutely can move forward from this and find ways to live a better life. I want to honor the man who died in my apartment by taking whatever responsibility I can in whatever way I can.

I don't know how this will ultimately work, but for now, just staying sober and committing myself to doing better by taking care of myself will do. I do not want to become yet another statistic for my family to mourn over. I realize just how easily it could have been me that morning. It has been almost two months, and still my lawyer states there is not any news on the investigation. At this point, there is not much we can do but wait until they are willing to let us know what is going on, if anything.

One morning I wake to a clear picture and a memory of my friend, Jani, that I left behind about seven years ago during my addiction. She and I have known each other for almost 25 years. The biggest influence she always has had on me is her strength and spiritual eloquence that seems to so easily radiate out from her. She has been a mentor and a friend, until I left her behind like so many other friends, and I feel a rush of love so strong that I call her this very moment.

Jani picks up the phone on the second ring, and I quietly announce, "Jani, it's me Eric." I was ready for her to be caught off guard or disillusioned by my call, but instead she exclaims, "Eric! Oh my gosh, you won't believe this, but I have been thinking a lot about you in the past few weeks. I am so glad to hear from you!" Her compassion and love come across in waves over the phone, and I instantly start to stumble and fall into explaining my years of absence from our friendship and all that has transpired.

She listens with the kind of attention and care she always has, as if no time has lapsed at all. She then begins to tell me about this life-changing program that she has been a part of for several years. She just knows it will help me a great deal in overcoming my difficulties from my addiction and create a new life. I trust her completely and tell her I want to be a part of the next workshop. I feel my mind lighten just a bit and my body stand up a little straighter. I realize I just have taken yet another step toward something beautiful. I can feel it.

As I anticipate the workshop, I have many things to set in motion. By this time, my belongings are all in storage, and I am trying to find a new apartment in a new city nearer my family. In the meantime, I am living in a crappy motel, the kind you might find at any side road in rural towns all across America. Not quite the Bates Motel but close. I am attending my last weeks of rehab. My dad and stepmom agree to help me with the deposit and first month's rent while the income I have is paying for other necessities. I finally find an apartment in nearby Cedar Rapids, Iowa. Synchronistically, I find myself coming full circle with my mom and dad as this townhome complex is the exact same one that they moved into early in the marriage almost 50 years ago. I haven't felt this good in a long time, and I continue to help my own mind heal.

It is moving into winter while November approaches. It is early morning. The leaves shine with dew and the vibrant, warm, multi-colored palette that only fall can produce. The air is crisp. I feel on top of the world. I am about to hit my six-month sobriety and things are moving along so well, I can't believe it.

The end of November comes, and Dr. Joe Dispenza's long-awaited workshop on NeuroChange Solutions is finally here. The focus of the two-day course is learning how to change your mind and create a new personality all through the benefits of neuroscience and meditation practice. My friend, Jani, is facilitating, and it feels great to be in her company again even if it is only by Zoom. It will be Jani and NeuroChange Solutions that will provide me the most strength. I am unwavering in my commitment.

On a clear, winter night, there's a fresh December snowfall and holiday cheer in the air as I put up lights in my apartment and listen to Christmas carols. I am interrupted by a loud knock at the door. It's about 10 o'clock, and I feel a cold shudder pass through my body as I remember the last time I had an unexpected knock at an unusual time of day. I walk to the door and ask who it is. The voice says, "It's Thom," but I don't know anybody by that name, and I say so. There is a pause and then, "It's the Cedar Rapids Police." I break into a cold sweat and slowly open the door.

Three uniformed officers are waiting on my steps, and they verify my full name. I can't find my words, and I can barely move, so I just slightly nod my head. I back away and fall into the chair by the front door. The world around me begins to feel surreal as I hear them say that I am being arrested for a federal indictment for "conspiracy to distribute methamphetamine resulting in death." The tears begin to fall as my new life for myself starts to unravel ... again. This time, however, I have some emotional tools to work with and a realization that I knew something was coming. It had been six months, and my lawyer still had not received any updates on my case, which I now realize they must have been building. I can barely focus, but I need to at least call my mom and let her know. One of the officers is kind enough to let me use their phone. I let the phone ring and voicemail picks up. I leave a message, and my heart aches to think of her listening to it.

Over the next 24 hours, I am processed in the county jail downtown and placed in a maximum-security jail cell as if I were a dangerous and murderous criminal. I look out the small window from the sixth floor and can see all of downtown Cedar Rapids. This view I have seen a thousand times, just not from a jail cell. It all feels like a nightmare. I sleep, I cry, I don't eat, but I use my meditation tools and my mantras, and I wait. I am not allowed contact with anyone yet, and the very next day I am transferred to a county jail in the district where the crime was committed. I continue to meditate on the two-hour drive and attempt to focus on what I can do in this moment and how I can keep my head held high.

I arrive at the new jail by way of an underground parking lot, and as I am processed into this location, I am asked a series of questions. Then the officer finally looks at me to ask one final question.

"Do you consider yourself to be vulnerable to threats and aggression?"

"WHAT?!" I think to myself," Who isn't?" I ask for clarification and realize he is asking me if I want to be in protective custody or general population. I don't really understand either term, so I am relieved when the officer behind him says that I have to go into medical custody because I walk with a cane and can't have a "weapon" like that in the general population. So surreal. "A weapon?!", I think to myself. "What the hell is he talking about?"

Over the next week, I talk with my mom and my sister and try to figure out what I am facing. They are both upset, but my sister says something to me that becomes cemented in my mind. She says, "At least now this part of your journey can begin, and you can face it head-on. No more waiting and worrying. The work you have been doing about not being a victim anymore and taking responsibility in your recovery and life allows you to do this with your head held high." I realize this is the exact same thing I was meditating on the week before on the way to this jail, and it helps me refocus. My sister has been such a rock over the past few months now that I have let her back into my life. I am so grateful for this viewpoint. I take a deep breath and tell her that she is right. I have done too much work on myself to slip back now. I thank her and tell her that I love her as we are cut off by the 20-minute phone time limit.

I look in the mirror after I get back to my cell, and I realize she is right. I can face my fears and my life instead of using escapism at every turn. Again, the unknown is still frightening, but I can feel in my core a sense of power returning. Despite my current environment, I feel a glimmer of hope. I can do this. Whatever this will end up being, I can learn and grow, and I DO have the courage and the strength. I am not a helpless victim. I am strong, and I have people who love and care about me.

The next day I have a court hearing to discuss the possibility of being able to be let out of jail on pretrial release. My sister and brother-in-law are in attendance as I am led into the courtroom in my shackles and orange jumpsuit. My lawyer and the prosecutors do their courtroom dance as the decision is made to allow me to live with my sister and her family for the next six months while I await trial. Tears of joy stream down my sister's cheeks as she and my brother-in-law let me know they will pick me up later that day. I am taken back to my cell, and after the door is shut, I look around and I have to laugh just a bit as I realize that I am in an orange jumpsuit in a cell block, and I kind of feel like a zombie after everything that's happening. Not quite the same experience from Halloween a couple months ago. Life is strange.

Over the next six months, many pieces of my life are still strung about as I try to pick up the pieces of everything that has happened. I am grateful, however, for this time with my sister, Laura, and her family. They are supportive at every turn, and even though they have a house full of four kids, they are loving and kind and have given me my own space to live. My mom also comes to visit several times, which is wonderful. She is 74 years old, and yet she lets me know that she will be the one to pack up my entire apartment to move to storage as I am not allowed to leave the 15-mile radius. I don't have to wear a tracking device, but I know not to test the limit. Everything is on the honor system, and I intend to live by the letter of the law.

I meet with my lawyer, spend the time I have while waiting for trial in another outpatient rehab, take as many drug tests as asked, and attend 12-step meetings on a daily basis. I find a sponsor and a regular meeting online through Zoom, and I like working the 12 steps with him.

My lawyer and I have a few phone conversations as he learns more about the prosecution's case against me. I need to decide if I want to go to trial or to plead guilty. At this point, I am advised that the mandatory minimum sentence for my charges is 20 years. After this phone call, I can barely speak, so Laura and I sit out on the back deck of their home, smoke a few cigarettes, cry and laugh a bit together, and begin the process of unraveling what all this means. I definitely am ready to take responsibility for my actions, but I am disillusioned by the system. I do some research and find out that murderers, who have premeditated actions to hurt someone, get less time for their crimes. As a family, we realize the limitations of the law and what I can achieve by going to trial. My lawyer advises that if I decide to go to trial, I could end up getting more than 20 years if found guilty. By taking responsibility on my own, I am more likely to receive the mandatory minimum.

During the next three weeks, I am meeting with my lawyer and talking with others in my recovery group who have, in the past, gone through similar circumstances. I continue to create a new life by meditating every day. I use the tools and techniques I learned in the workshop and stay in regular and constant contact with my friend, Jani. I am feeling stronger about my decision to choose this route. I am so glad to have her back in my life as I face the toughest part of my life so far. As always, Jani is once again able to help me see things from a different perspective. She says to me, "Are you sure that the hardest part of your life isn't behind you?" She tells me that she loves me before suggesting I take some time to think about that. She never uses the word "should." One of my favorite aphorisms of hers is "If you don't should on me, I won't should on you." I hang up the phone and sit in contemplative silence for a good two to three hours.

As I sit in meditation and resist my old urges to run, hide, and escape the pain and choices of my past, I sit squarely in my mind and observe the past 41 years of my life as an onlooker. Using the lessons from Dr. Dispenza and with an internal high-powered lens, I take an honest and thorough look at myself and see just how much chaos and dysfunction I created for myself and others. Starting at age

7, I feel I have to hide who I really am from the world. I used the drugs and sex to detach from my mind and my body and to affirm this victimized voice that said I am not worth more than this affront to being human. I feel so lost that I disappear almost completely, knowing I am so far down the rabbit hole that I may never get out and maybe don't care to.

By the time I come back from this direct observation of my life, I am sitting in stillness, and I am amazed to look at myself in a new way.

UNLIMITED. For years I have been living a limited life, not believing that I have the capacity to stand on my own. I have already been locked up in a prison for the first half of my life, a prison of my own making. Now, here in this moment, I begin to recognize even more the freedom and the wholeheartedness, the earnestness of making a decision. My cousin, Lisa, said to me recently that a bend in the road is not the end of a road. I am ready to stop running. I refuse to hide in my own shadows any longer. I can take responsibility for my actions and still engage in a life that is meaningful. I created my life then. I can create a new life now. I know my next decision.

I am terrified and relieved at the same time. I look around my sister's house and at all this beauty she has created for herself. The house itself sits on a hill and has an open, airy feel given the high ceilings and floor plan. The acreage is nestled beautifully in the countryside. The deck off the back looks into the forest and onto a natural creek below. The sun is just setting, and I feel the energy and change that comes with the first of the evening. I feel the power in my bones. In my being. While the unknown territory I am entering fills me with apprehension, I know that I am capable of moving forward. It won't be easy, but then nothing worth doing ever is. There will be forks in the road. My emotions will run the gamut from here to there. I will stumble. I will fall. This new life, however, will be mine. Prison might be on the surface, but the one thing this new experience cannot take away from me is the unlimited freedom I feel in my mind.

I pick up the phone, dial the number, and wait. One ring. Two rings. Three rings.

"Hello, Law Offices. How may I direct your call?"

"Yes, this is Eric Hojka, I would like to leave a message for my lawyer. Please tell him that I am choosing to plead guilty to the charges. There will be no need to go to trial."

With those words, my new life begins.

Eric Hojka (he/him) has spent most of his life being a creative. Although this is his first published story, he has been writing poetry and short stories (fiction) as well as performing onstage in musical theater, orchestras, and even under the stage as a pit performer for the last 35 years. He is currently serving a 20-year sentence at Rochester Federal Medical Center and works in the Education department there. He spends his days working with other Adults In Custody (AICs)

to earn their GEDs, teaching Spanish and creative writing courses, and helping AICs find resources to aid in their higher education goals.

Evolution of a Thought

Running Off the Page

By Kane Jesse Howard

Let's play a game. I won't tell you what it is because that's no fun. Your job, however, is to figure out what the game is. Got it? Good. Why don't we get started?

Picture it. Imagine you're *me* and deep into conversation with someone. Then you get one of the following responses to something you've said.

"You are? Wow! I had no clue."

"Honestly, I never would have guessed."

"No way. No way!"

"What did you look like before?"

"I could never tell."

Okay, time's up. Tell me, what game are we playing? You have four minutes. Just kidding. I need an answer now. Oh, fine, I'll give you a hint or two. We could be playing a good-spirited game of "responses to somebody finding out I'm trans." Or we could also be playing a game of "responses to somebody on a college campus finding out that I'm actually in my thirties."

Should I be flattered by either response? Are either of them actually flattering? Maybe we should do a deeper dive.

Many parts of me whisper in constant conversation with one another. I spent at least 10 years of my young life identifying as a lesbian before I got to my early twenties. Then I couldn't run from the rest of my truth any longer. At 23, I decided that I was living only half a life if I didn't decide to transition. Once I made that choice, a lot more fell into place. But for now, let's go a little bit further back.

Part of my background is that I didn't take the traditional school route. I figure it will probably set a more realistic tone to mention that I was home-schooled from fourth grade on. We didn't know yet why I struggled so much academically. I used to tell my mother that the words were simply "running off the page," leaving all of the books from every subject piling up, untouched. It would take a few more years until I'd learn about my ADHD, a part of myself that affects many aspects of my life.

Because my parents wanted me to—thanks, Mom—I tried a few online courses when I was 19. My grades weren't bad. It was simply exhausting to force myself to word-vomit an assignment an hour before the deadline every week. So I quit.

After that, I worked in human services, becoming a Direct Support Professional for eight years. It was supposed to be a trans-friendly job, and I certainly wasn't the only one there. There were two instances where I ended up coming out to coworkers, and both went wrong. Since it was early on in my transition (circa mid- to late 2010s), these bad reactions stick with me much more than the good ones do. For example, one coworker and I were already talking about deep topics when I told him I was trans. Disgust flashed on his face. He brushed me off in a non-verbal way, making it known that this wasn't up for discussion with him ever again. The next several hours of my shift he stared at me, making me feel uncomfortable as I tried to put distance between us. I worried about how he might treat me. From that moment on, I felt a little extra fear sew itself together with the fabric of my coming out.

The next time my transition came up, a well-meaning coworker asked, "Oh, have you had *the* surgery?" Needless to say, that doesn't make me feel *any* better.

Still, I come out in certain situations. I say it, often hiding behind the guise of a screen where I don't have to cross paths daily with anyone or see the reactions on their faces when I say it. I say it on occasion at my book club, though I find myself second-guessing it every time. Even though I feel it's not the fault of the other person, each subsequent time I say it more quietly and with less fanfare. Once I read a poem about being trans at an event through my community college. People are nice to me and tell me they like my work. But my spouse is sitting right there in the front, a constant support I can focus on so that I don't have to navigate this alone.

Seeing the daily news of the world devolving into negative opinions about trans people like *me* goes a long way in my personal "Great Coming Out Reduction." It doesn't help that signs go up in people's yards along my daily commute, blasting their personal transphobic opinions to all who drive by. So I make my socials private, dodge any online groups that are local to my area, and delete years' worth of Facebook profile pictures to hide myself. In a world where my existence is becoming political, I decide it's easier to reduce my visibility.

Even though I can still come out under the *right* conditions, it's a lot easier to walk around and just pretend there's nothing to come out with in the first place.

As far as jobs went, being a Direct Support Professional had an astronomical burnout rate. At 27, that gave me the necessary motivation to go to community college. I also wanted to meet people and make friends. Generally, nobody asked how old I am. Even when they did, I got the usual, "Oh, you look a lot younger than 27!" I'm not sure I believed them, but it wasn't the worst compliment. There's some sort of joke about trans guys and the fountain of youth. Maybe there's something to that—even after eight years of testosterone, I still have a round face.

Unfortunately, starting my degree in January of 2020 during COVID-19 lockdowns meant that I took barely any of said classes in person. That also meant I got very well-versed in Zoom, as well as did most of my classes in my pajamas.

I started community college with a major in music business and changed it to communications with a journalism focus during my second semester. With my academic past, I didn't have big expectations for my success. I told myself, "You know, D is a passing grade; all you have to do is pass," while inserting endless jokes about "getting the D." Funny thing is, I ended up graduating with highest honors and making the dean's list a few times. I attributed it to studying things that I actually felt passionate about. These were things that maybe ran off the page, too, but I ran with them. Also, I learned persistence in teaching myself a variety of ways to cope with ADHD, trying to work with it instead of molding myself to the expectations of others.

Finding a tiny piece of confidence, I jumped feet-first into applying to the only four-year school that mattered to me. I got asked more than once why, as a 30-year-old, I wasn't going for a trade or something Science, Technology, Engineering, and Mathematics (STEM)-related. Why not a healthcare field or building off my time in human services?

That was my first truly defiant moment. I longed to reinvent myself all over again when the world said I shouldn't. And hell, I also got asked why, at "my age," I didn't choose to do the rest of my schooling online. But I craved something I had missed, something the pandemic had taken, something that I never had the confidence to do before: apply to a four-year school.

When it arrived, I cried over my letter of acceptance.

After exploring my financial options, I found that a whole world of merit scholarships opened up for me if I was willing to go full-time and in person. I had no clue if I could do it. I had only ever done one full-time semester at community college, and that was via Zoom. Back then, I felt like I was hanging on by a thread.

To quell my anxiety, I tried my hardest to draw upon my few in-person school experiences. One such past experience sticks out. There I was, sitting in the middle front, trying my best to diligently take notes by hand. My business professor was an older gentleman who wore a lot of button-downs. By far, I wasn't the oldest in the class at 27.

While introducing himself, our professor stated, "Forty years ago, when I used to teach this class, it was all young, white men. Now there's only one!"

Cue the laughter; we all busted up. Until, while driving home and reflecting in the freezing January air, I realized that everyone around me was laughing a different laugh than me. It's because *I* was the young white man in question, the sole one in the room. How striking. The more and more I think about it over time, the stranger it feels.

As a trans person, I feel like I've been exposed to a lot of talk about what medical transitioning was like in the early days. I felt well-prepared for what the testosterone would do to my body. Everybody told me I would stink like sweat, and boy, they weren't wrong. I was prepared for the six weeks off that I'd need after top surgery[1]. Sometimes, I realize I'll never have to wriggle on a cold floor, wrestling myself from the tight grip of a binder on a hot day, ever again. That makes me smile even when I'm all alone. God, it felt like so long since I sat in that frigid courtroom, gripping the inside of my pants pockets, listening to a judge declare that my name was now officially Kane. Still, it takes an extremely long time before I allow myself to accept that when someone calls out, "Sir," I'm the one they're looking for.

After a while, my outsides aligned with the truth I felt inside. What I didn't prepare for, however, was relaying the message back to my insides—my brain, or whatever—about what people outside experience when they see me face-to-face. The adjustment period was so bizarre.

Of course, I'm aware that trans people who pass are more privileged, and there is male privilege in general. I accept those things. Part of the difficulty is in remembering the person actively on display as I navigate the world. When

---

1 In this context, "top surgery" refers to a gender affirming surgery for transmasculine people that involves a double mastectomy with other chest masculinizing effects depending on the individual's preference.

I talk about this, I get either the response of "Well, you were just socialized female" or "Well, if you're trans, you would always have been navigating the world as a man."

Neither of those explanations works for me. I think it's something else entirely. Maybe it's part of being neurodivergent. Or maybe it has something to do with how I walk down the street. Here I am, going down a path in the middle of the day, and I see a guy—who's probably a dozen years younger than me—walking too close behind. My heart hits an extra beat in that moment from an instinctual fear that I can't control. I step aside and let him pass.

I don't hold it against him. I don't think I hold it against men in general either. It's such an automatic habit, and I don't know where it came from. All the way back to wherever I'm going, I have to ask myself, why do I step aside? Does it make sense at all? Is it just an instinct from long ago that never died?

Not every experience I've had has been affected by my identity or my background. However, every single face-to-face experience is now affected by the way the world sees me: as a cis man. Truthfully, passing isn't my total goal. My biggest goal is to feel comfortable in my body, and I've mostly achieved that. Some social situations leave me wondering what my goal is and if I am trying hard enough to be the man that the other person expects.

For example, what should I have said when I was working at a factory and two male co-workers whom I didn't know said something unsettling about women? Hell, I wasn't participating in the conversation, but they laughed and threw a nod in my direction like I got it. As a trans person who wasn't out, my insides felt as gross as my outsides did. I recalled seeing one of those guys aggressively punching cardboard boxes for seemingly no reason, making him a person I didn't want to stand up to. At the end of my shift, I had to go and get changed in the same locker room as them, walk the same dark path to my car close to midnight, and come back the following night to do it all over again.

Anyway, I quit that job pretty early on. Most people agree it was just a bad place to work, but my reasons run a lot deeper. For one, the men's restrooms there didn't have those little trash cans in the stalls. If you know, you *know.* Even on testosterone, some trans guys still need a safe place to discreetly throw things away once a month. The world has been largely constructed without consideration of people like *us,* and from time to time, that reality stings.

On occasion, people ask me if I was "out" at that job. Because life is not a game and I cannot respawn, I certainly was not out. It was the most aggressive workplace environment I'd ever experienced.

It's laughable how in some social settings, I had to figure out how to respond to acknowledgments from male co-workers. I remember thinking, "I figured it out! A fist bump and 'What's up?' isn't a conversation starter, it's a greeting." At least, that's my very fragile understanding, and I'm not sure I can narrow it down any further.

Believe me when I say that I have overthought a million ways of what to do with my legs and feet while I'm sitting. It's trivial. I get it. But it's also unconscious at this point, too. I have a tendency to mimic the behavior of whatever guy is in the room, at least in terms of physical positioning. "How do men *sit*?" was a question I must have asked myself a trillion times, as if one leg positioned in the wrong way would be my undoing.

Some aspects of how I think about passing as a man are painful. When I am leaving a social function with a female friend I've talked to all night, and on the way out, we're still chatting, I feel tense. We both happen to be strolling in the direction of the parking lot, it's dark outside, and we're both parked at the outside edge. On one hand, I look at her and assign what I think she's feeling. See, I feel guilt screaming in my head to stop walking out in that parking lot because I believe I make her feel uncomfortable and that I'm doing something wrong. Despite my internal emotional tornado, she just keeps chatting. It's freezing outside, but I'm sweating. It isn't just her. My brain can find endless ways to insert guilt that I'm bothering every woman I come across for social interactions as simple as "Hey, do you know which aisle instant oatmeal is in?"

Diving deeper, I realize that it's not just the idea of being read as a cis man. I've known plenty of cis guys who don't make me uncomfortable. Rather, it's the psychological effect of living in a society that force-feeds me the idea that trans people are somehow dangerous for existing. Ah, what a time to be alive.

Many times, I avoid exploring those thoughts. Instead, I equate safety with not doing anything that can possibly make *anyone* uncomfortable. Avoiding any situation where I will have to out myself as trans is another thing I do to provide myself with a shield of safety, especially in a country with a stark political view of our existence.

That is the point of my game. Don't interact with anyone who makes you uncomfortable. Don't interact with someone who may be uncomfortable. Don't come out. In fact, sometimes, try to forget what you are if you can, at least in certain circumstances. If you don't forget, you might slip up. When you do come out, do it as safely as humanly possible. If you come out and are doubtful, run away from the situation and never return. Also, remember everything at the same exact time. Simple, right?

Probably not. It's more like someone left the game on advanced mode long before I even arrived.

The mere idea of going to a traditional four-year college in person brought my endless insecurities to the surface. Seeing that through the lens where multiple parts of my identity connect gave me some pretty unique expectations. First of all, this was *not* going to be a community college campus. This was going to be a *lot* bigger. Take that squarely in the context of someone like me who was home-schooled and who had only had a few in-person experiences at junior college.

In fact, I'm not even sure I had ever visited the campus prior to when I first set foot there on Accepted Students

Day. It felt *impossibly* huge. Thank God it was raining that day because it covered up how I was sweating needles, becoming a walking pincushion for anxiety. My mantra became "Don't screw this up." What a silly phrase to try and live by.

We all split up into groups according to our majors, and as I followed at the tail-end of a group, I felt like a panicky fraud. Some ultra-friendly 18-year-old guy popped up next to me with an umbrella. He and I walked and talked along the suburban trek. For one, he wasn't paying attention and kept poking me in the head with that umbrella. But during our talk, I wondered how I was going to fit in at this college. His life sounded so different from mine, so complication-free. I wondered if he would even talk to me if he knew I was 30, if he knew I was trans. Eventually, my deciding factor of inching away from him was that he was about to carelessly poke my eyes out with that umbrella, and I was over it.

We were all led to this big room—a lecture hall, possibly—that looked like a movie theater. I froze in my seat. Then, I looked down at the front, imagining myself having to one day stand up to give presentations in front of a class, and felt a bit faint. How can someone like *me* go up and put myself on display like that? Up in front of a room like that, I imagined that everything about me would somehow be laid bare, obvious for everyone to see.

A little voice in my head told me, "Nod and smile. Look like you know exactly what you're in for. Look like you're not going to pass out."

Part of me wanted to ask how inclusive their bathrooms were, but I didn't want to call attention to myself. Two former friends told me that the campus was very LGBTQ+ friendly. But anybody telling me secondhand about the safety of a particular place wasn't enough to convince me to let my guard down. I had been burned in the past by so-called safe spaces that didn't live up to the hype. All I could say about that is that some places should reconsider waving a trans-inclusive pride flag in front of their buildings if they can't even manage inclusive restrooms. The presence of a pride flag never makes me feel more comfortable by default. A few choice experiences have taught me that it just means the person who put it up wants me to *think* that I should be comfortable.

Everyone throughout the enrollment process was astoundingly nice to me. Part of me wondered if people were really *that* nice? Or was it just me who was highly suspicious?

Before my first day, this massive worry built a home in my head. I didn't know how I was going to handle being an older guy navigating campus among a sea of people under 23. What if I made someone uncomfortable? Did or said the wrong thing? Made myself look like a creep? These thoughts kept me up at night. I didn't want to get into this environment among people so much younger who had the same interests as me, but I couldn't talk to them because I would just be the 31-year-old secretly trans guy who stuck out like a sore thumb. Clearly, the remedy for sticking out seemed to be blending in. Keeping to myself. Not saying a single word for ... how *many* years? However many it took.

Plus, if the news is any indication, it seems like what the world wants is for people like me to stay quiet anyway.

Time ticked away, and soon, that first day was looming over my head. All I knew was a sensation in my chest like wearing a binder all over again, only two sizes too small. I felt so openly exposed, like anyone and everyone who looked at me would know I was 30 going on 31, and that they would judge me negatively for it. Or that anyone who looked at me would know I was trans and do the same. Clearly, the moment I couldn't understand the work and fell behind would be the end of it. ADHD would be the thing to deal the final blow. Caught up in worry, I never wondered why I saw parts of my identity as separate entities conspiring against me.

Trying not to give myself *too* much of a crap talk—the opposite of a pep talk—I arrived at the correct parking lot and removed a piece of paper from my pants pocket. I had written down what time my classes were, what buildings they were in, and what rooms. I looked at the paper probably a hundred times. It was wrinkled and sweaty. The words were running off the page, but only from the terribly smudged ink.

Putting on that backpack and leaving my car, a terrible sense of feeling juvenile struck me. "Oh god," I think.

"Right now, I could be working and making money. Instead, I'm putting on a backpack to go cosplay a 20-year-old."

My apologies now and forever to anyone who looks at me simply because I'm in the path of their vision that day.

Walking amongst a sea of my future classmates, my eyes darted every which way every few seconds. Smells, sounds, and some sights were too overwhelming, drowning me in sensory overload hell. Nervousness heightens everything.

Carefully, I guide myself step-by-step to floor two of the humanities building. To me, it looked *massive*, especially with the enormous glass windows reflecting the campus scenery. Checking and re-checking my mangled paper, I tried to find my class. Round and round I went, walking the halls until a random worker guided me to the correct location. Upon entering the film viewing class, I held my breath. It was *so* big and there were *so* many people. A large, movie-style screen was at the very front of the room. It intimidated me. Pushing my way through the aisle to sit down without brushing up against anyone was an Olympic-level game. I gave up and just said, "Sorry," all along the way, much like I did for just about everything else in life.

Inevitably, I ended up smushed in a seat. After setting up with my notebook and pen, I looked around to see flickers of lights pop up all around me. The vast majority of other students had either laptops or tablets with little keyboards. I was the lone person with a paper notebook. At first, I figured that once class started, the tech would go away, and the notebooks would come out. Nope.

Instead, I was unable to access a website, raise my hand, ask how I could get into it on my phone, and the professor stood there, a little dumbfounded. "Why don't you have a laptop?" she asked.

With a pause, I stuttered, "Um ... I was homeschooled?" It was the only thing I could think of as almost *all* heads turned toward me. The spotlight burned.

"Oh ...," the instructor replied.

Since that day, she and I have laughed about that together. In fact, she has become one of my biggest supporters. I will eventually end up being confident enough to send her some articles on trans allegories in *The Matrix*. In the next class, I sat watching her talk about said allegories to the whole class. I never dreamed that a professor would get up there and say "trans" so respectfully, all without skipping a single beat.

But back to the very first experience of the *first* day, I spent up all of the confidence I had left in reserves with that notebook thing. It wasn't her fault I missed the laptop culture memo. Trying to scope out a "safe" bathroom felt too tedious. So, I wandered into the first men's room I saw. Some guy made eye contact with me, and I felt like he was looking through me. I stayed in that stall on my phone until I saw his shoes disappear.

There were little gaps of time in between my classes. After that first one of the day, I meandered outside and felt everyone's eyes on me whether they were looking in my direction or not. Briefly, I examined the colorful flyers that hung on walls and bulletin boards, and I looked for LGBTQ+ clubs. There were things such as the paranormal club, history club, the student-run radio station, a book club, and more.

Everything looked so fun, and I was unsure if any of it was a space I belonged in.

Wandering further, I remembered that during my tour on Accepted Students Day, I saw a place where I could study quietly if need be. The problem was, no matter how long I walked around, I couldn't find it. Relenting, I decided to ask an office worker. I was pointed in the direction of a quiet place with a computer where I *could* sit and work on getting ready for the three classes that I still had coming that day. It was a quiet, soft space, and I could really settle in with my thoughts.

Exploring the online interface, I peeked at the syllabus for some of my other classes. There, I could familiarize myself in peace. I was taking intro to film, American literature, philosophy, young adult literature, and critical theory. I had *no* idea what critical theory was, and I was prepared to be surprised regardless. Scanning the syllabus, I saw somewhat familiar things such as structuralism, deconstruction, Marxism, and a few more. Surely, queer theory was there, and that's one I was already aware of.

Imagine how jarring it was when I saw the words *"trans theory*[2]*."*

Not only were the words *"trans theory"* right there in front of me, but there was an entire *"trans theory week"* following one about queer theory. It was almost like the universe knew the exact moment I needed to see it.

Somehow I was part of a class that was going to be studying both queer theory *and* trans theory during their own weeks. Leaning forward over that desk, I tried to fathom the experience.

In the past, I learned about multiple theories that we use to examine literature. They always felt like such old, abstract ideas. The realization that there was a trans theory elicited in me this idea that it was something so familiar that I could reach out and touch it. Actually, it felt less like a theory and more like something I was actively part of. In a world where nothing felt like it was made with trans folk in mind, there was something directly inspired by us.

Trans. Theory.

Other students entered the far end of the room and sat down. I eyed them briefly and turned back to my screen. It dawned on me that if I hid myself from the very first day, I'd be setting the tone for how I felt about belonging until I

---

2 In the context of the aforementioned class, "trans theory" primarily refers to Hil Malatino's theories in Side Affects: On Being Trans and Feeling Bad (2022). https://www.upress.umn.edu/9781517912093/side-affects/

graduated. Was it worth it for the perceived comfort of everyone else?

Keeping an eye on the time, I navigated to my American lit class. Sitting at a desk near the wall, I watched the remainder of the class like they were a group of people miles away from me. When I opened my mouth to talk with some guy who was in the same major as me, I scrutinized how high my voice sounded, so I stopped. I just sat there, wondering what it would be like to truly feel like a part of the world around me in such a place.

When the time came, I went toward critical theory class. Getting horribly, awfully lost on the way, I ended up somewhere in the building with a bunch of stairs and *no* idea what was behind *any* of the doors. This wasn't part of my plan. Yet, it *did* end up adding about 500 extra steps to my phone's pedometer, and I couldn't complain about *that.*

I didn't realize it, but I went on to get lost in vastly different ways en route to that class every single day for the first two weeks. I just considered it a sidequest.

Making it somehow on time—despite my first of many unexpected detours—I immediately saw how small the class size was. There were so few of us. And right away, I recognized a few faces that I saw in other classes. I found a seat far from the door.

At first, everything started out like it had in my previous classes. That is, until the time for the obligatory "introduce yourself to the class" ritual. There on the board were our guidelines. Apparently, we would be filling out cards privately first and then telling them to the whole class if we chose to do so. We didn't have to read *everything* out loud.

What was our name? Our pronouns? Our majors? What were our favorite theories?

I was ashamed of that notebook sitting out on my desk. When the professor handed me my notecard, I didn't even think; I looked up and just muttered a weak "thanks." I looked down, wishing it was like one of those movie moments where the wind would sweep it up. It was a 2 o'clock class. I was tired.

Once again, I thought of that future "trans theory" week. Was I really going to sit through a class, as a trans person, where we would be learning all about trans theory, and hide who I was throughout the entire thing? I mean, sure, if that was the way one wanted to play the game, it was within my choice to do that.

Fiddling with that blank notecard, I pondered it. Hiding would be so easy in the moment and harder over the long term. Possibly I was getting a little too philosophical with it. What were the rules for that kind of thing, anyway?

This was already so exhausting.

That felt like a moment of truth—and sure, in contrast to *some* other moments in life, maybe it was a relatively small one. Maybe it wasn't. This wasn't just someplace I was going to go for the next couple years of my life and keep my head down the whole time, never being even a fraction of myself. I mean, I could do that. It was totally an option. I kept my head down and never told anyone who I was at a few different jobs for years. Wouldn't it be better than the coworker I came out to who reacted with disgust?

Or I could stand up and stake my first claim at telling the world who I was going to be during my time at college. I could do that by telling them who I already *was*.

Making up my mind, I scribbled my answers on that note card. Of course, I knew the professor wasn't likely to read them out loud. I second-guessed myself for a split second. But I already turned in the dang card.

Hearing my classmates start to give their introductions, I knew I could still make the choice not to say my piece out loud. My next move was up to nobody but me.

There was a room full of people that I could share the next several months with, for three days a week, giving their answers out loud and telling everybody who they were on day one. I think of that trans theory week again, and I decided to follow through.

"My name is Kane."

"My pronouns are *he* and *they*."

"My major is literary and textual studies."

"My favorite types of theory? Well, I wrote down queer theory and trans theory."

"The reason I wrote that down is because I'm ... queer and ... trans."

Immediately, another student raised their hand, and I braced myself because nobody else's hand went up during anyone else's introduction.

"Oh wow," I thought, "that was pretty a swift response, universe."

She asked me, since we had another class together, if she should only call me *they* in this class because it seemed like more of a safe space and not in the other class? Or did I not mind being called both *he* and *they* in both? It was a good question, I'll admit, but I had just used up my reserve of confidence on what came out of my mouth before.

Honestly, I was stumped at first on what to say. Everybody was looking at me. I glanced down at my desk and responded, telling her she could call me either pronoun in both classes. Somehow, wrapped up in my answer, I used the words, "I prefer *they* but *he* is fine," and that struck me because, while it was true, I didn't often feel confident enough to assert that truth.

Once I finished, class proceeded normally. Nobody reacted negatively to me. Hell, nobody was staring at me in particular. Over the course of that hour, I felt myself relax, contemplating the whole exchange. It took me a while to wrap my head around how I jumped out of my comfort zone and nothing bad happened. Was that really me?

Maybe I don't have to walk around the world apologizing—directly and indirectly, too—for the space I take up. Just maybe I don't have to live my life like one big apology tour, crafting a method to avoid just about everything along the way. I can play the game differently.

There was no turning back after that. A whole class of Gen Zers and that professor knew about my gender identity, and there was no stuffing that truth back inside Pandora's transgender box.

When I walked from my last class of the day all the way across campus and back to my car, I felt like I was standing five feet taller than before. Something about the music on the radio all the way home was brighter, more fun.

Freedom.

I looked out my car windows at people walking by and thought that I could run up to every one of them, shouting joyfully that I'm trans, and totally get away with it. Clearly, I didn't do *that*. But the feeling is alive, strong, fearless.

That feeling needed an identity of its own and now it has one.

Within the first week of class, I sequestered myself away in my bathroom at home and took clippers to my head. My hair had been down to my shoulders when I started the academic year, but something about being bold pushed me to find as many ways as I could to keep being bold. Therefore, the buzz cut made an appearance for the first time in four years. Shaving my head had always been a self-defiant act. It's one that undoubtedly comes with a long string of people asking me a million and one follow-up questions, all to the tune of, *"Why?"*

Because this time marked an era. At the end of it, my hair will be much longer, a visual reminder of how far I've come on this leg of my journey.

Honestly, I didn't expect any of my classmates to notice *me* whatsoever, let alone what I did with my hair. When the new week rolled around, and I strolled back into that critical theory class, two girls gasped. Something about that stuck with me, cementing an idea that I matter. I was *seen*.

Day after day, I found more unexpected pieces of myself in that place. Openly declaring, *"I'm trans,"* in casual conversation happened in just about every class. This included standing up to a philosophy professor face-to-face after an unsavory remark he made about trans people, defiance in my eyes and my words.

"You have trans students in your class," I told him. "And I'm one of them. What you said? It's *harmful*." Honestly, even while I said it, I did everything I could to keep it together.

I was shaking but sure of myself. For the rest of my time in that class, he never repeated his mistake. Part of me hoped that for the rest of his career, he would look out into his class and realize that he can't tell who is trans, who isn't, and decide to show respect.

The old me stood back, smiling, watching the new me I was becoming in that place of higher education.

At the end of the semester, I ended up putting together a final project on queerness in Young Adult lit with another student. He and I spent hours in the library, enthusiastically compiling research on queer stories, and I was completely unafraid. We talked about it at the same volume as everyone else in the library, and nobody blinked an eye.

Even though the timing was only right for me to attend a few meetings of our school's queer group, LAMBDA, I felt immensely seen when I did attend. It was a comfortable sort of being seen, not a glaring type.

School became a place where I wanted to be, a place where I could grow. It became a place where I could take the trial of telling people who I was in order to learn how to keep doing it. It even became a place where I could wear my identity like a badge of honor, feeling secure to be who I was.

Walking from one building to the next with a familiar classmate one sunny day, I actually opened up for once. I told her that I frequently worried that people thought I was some creep or weirdo just by existing and that it was a fear that held me back a lot. Even speaking those words out loud felt like the epitome of forbidden. By saying them, I robbed the fear of its power over me. Also, she told me I didn't seem threatening because I was "very obviously queer." I'm not sure if it was a compliment, but it didn't need to be. What I needed was to keep telling the voice inside of me that it had no power left to threaten me.

One day much later, I found myself at a lunch table with two other students, fearlessly answering the question of "How old are you, again?" Okay, fearlessly might have been a stretch. The fearlessness came *after* I took the plunge, much like that very first stand of declaring my transness.

"I was born in 1992," I say. "So, uh, 31."

"Oh my *God*," one student says. "I had no idea."

Perhaps it was a compliment.

Then again, the name of the game wasn't looking for compliments at all. It was originally looking for permission to exist quietly and safely. I was no longer playing to stay in the background. And I sure as hell didn't need permission.

Living my truth is how I win.

Author's Note

My story portrays my very first semester as an adult student at a four-year college in the fall of 2023. I made the choice to go to York College of Pennsylvania. This was a college that meant a tremendous amount to my very supportive mother, who loved being there yet was unable to continue past junior year due to a permanent disabling event in the

1980s. We joke a lot that she finished the first two years, and I will finish the last two, since I started as a junior. If I inherited a sense of defiance from anyone, look no further than her.

Currently, in 2024, I am still a full-time student at that very same school, yet things have changed radically for me. Earlier this semester, I attended an undergraduate research workshop held by my school. At this time, I found myself standing in front of a room of students and mentors from all over the country, declaring that I was trans to all of them. I spent the weekend refining a research proposal about trans-inclusive language in academic literature texts. Subsequently, I decided to openly pursue this research for my senior seminar class, which will take place in the spring. At this time, I do not fear showing the people around me who I am. My authenticity has become my power.

It's funny because this comes at a time where I'm receiving the message from all sides to be afraid, to hide, to recede back wherever I came from. As a trans person, the crushing blow of November and waiting to see how 2025 will unfold weighs heavy on me. I'm barely prepared for this. Despite the collective anxieties, including my own, I've decided to make my voice louder than ever.

Kane Jesse Howard (he/they) is a writer and Literary & Textual studies major at York College of Pennsylvania. He has won collegiate awards for both flash fiction and screenwrit-

ing. Kane holds an AS in Communications/Journalism from Harrisburg Area Community College. He has been published in Study Breaks *and* The Copper Quill *(HACC), and his work will be found in the 2025 edition of* The York Review. *Kane published the paranormal, sapphic romance* Romeo's Card *in 2022. He lives in Lancaster, Pennsylvania, with his wife and two dogs.*

Running Off the Page

Power Red

By Paul Iarrobino

My first part-time job after school was at a hospital. I escorted new patients to their rooms and delivered mail and flowers to inpatients.

It was the late 1970s, and the private hospital served the uber elite—people like the Kennedys. This hospital sat on top of the rough-around-the-edges Mission Hill neighborhood of Boston. The newest wing, named after its wealthy benefactors, had freshly polished floors leading to exclusive private rooms with the latest new equipment. Each suite offered a million-dollar view of Boston's skyline.

Each day, I took a rickety, old trolley along Boston's winding streets. The trolley conductor tried to avoid the many potholes as we made our way down to the bottom of Parker Hill Avenue. With the energy of a 16-year-old, I barreled up the hill towards the well-maintained hospital, passing worn multifamily buildings in various stages of disrepair. At that age, I was too young in the world to notice or understand how classist this arrangement was. Neighbors weren't admitted if they were in dire straits because the hospital didn't have an emergency room. Locals would need to find another hospital in the area. This hospital's rooms were reserved for the well-coiffed upper crust—those who were connected to Boston's most prestigious surgeons. They enjoyed attentive service and territorial views. Some of them reserved rooms with the best view months in advance for their elective surgeries.

I had delivered newspapers and collected tips in my neighborhood. This new setting at the hospital was a big step up for me. I never knew whom I would meet as I walked the shiny, terrazzo floors. Each day, I made my way around the hospital's labyrinth of floors delivering mail and packages.

One day, while delivering interoffice mail to the blood bank, I heard a man's voice calling out to me. It was one of the phlebotomists. "You have great veins," he said. I was stunned and not sure how to respond. "Have you ever considered donating blood?" he asked. Apparently, the veins on my outstretched arm caught his attention. My brain tried to take this all in. I felt my face flush. I looked down to avoid eye contact and saw his name tag. His name was Jim.

He gently leaned in closer and asked, "May I?" as he motioned for me to display my veins again. This time, I noticed his dark brown eyes behind his spectacles. He had a boyish, playful grin. My heart leaped, and I felt a flow of electricity flooding through my body. His voice was calm and sincere. As he tapped my vein, he asked if I knew my blood type. When I told him I didn't, he pointed to his lab. This was the first time a man showed me this kind of attention, and I reveled in it. At that age, just as I didn't understand the hospital's classism, I was too young in the world to fully understand my attraction to Jim.

Jim sat directly across from me as he carefully explained each step. My mind wandered, at first worrying about my delivery cart and schedule. That quickly vanished when he started rubbing my index finger with a wet sterile wipe. I felt as if my heart would jump out of my chest. In a reassuring voice, he told me that I would feel a little poke in my finger, but it wouldn't be painful.

Jim looked very studious as he applied my blood sample onto small glass slides. A short time later, he looked up at me and smiled. Not only did I have large, healthy veins, but he told me that my blood type was extremely rare. "You are Type B negative. Less than two percent of the population have your blood type. We are always low on B negative. Would you consider donating?" he asked with sincerity. How could I say no to that?!

I decided to donate blood shortly after our first meeting. I would do anything to please Jim. He encouraged me to relax as I sat in the oversized dark green vinyl recliner with a swing arm for easy blood collection. Jim gently ran a few fingers along my vein while I squeezed a nerf-type ball. I thought I would pass out from his touch.

A few years later, while attending college a couple of hours away, I would return to the hospital to work during my school breaks. It was comforting coming back and resuming my role as a helper. As I was making one of my rounds, I found one of the nurses, Charlotte. She was one of the local nuns on the nursing staff. Charlotte was in the hallway. Facing the wall, hunched over, crying. This took me by surprise. I didn't know her well, but we always had good conversations.

I slowly approached her from the side and asked her why she was crying. She turned to face me. Her eyes were reddened, and her tear-stained face had a look of bewilderment. She told me she was just coming back from the morgue and then struggled to find the words before saying, "Something terrible is happening. A lot of young men are coming here sick, and they are dying quickly." Charlotte told me that she went to nursing school to help people, and now she felt powerless and was starting to question her faith. This didn't add up for her. She looked so defeated.

I listened attentively but didn't have much to offer her, other than to let her vent her frustration, before she headed back to work. This interaction haunted me. What was going on?! I considered myself healthy. Would I, too, succumb to some strange death as an otherwise healthy young man?

As time went on, I heard more about some kind of mystery disease that was killing young gay men. I was just coming to terms with my own sexuality as a young gay man. I lived in a little bubble of my own in a supportive college town. The news of these deaths coming from big cities continued making headlines. For the life of me, I couldn't figure out this mystery either. I wondered if Charlotte was witnessing more of these deaths. Would this urban, gay plague come to my small college town? How could I protect myself if it did?

As more information became available, outright panic and hostility took over. I recall one incident that happened to me waiting outside of Buddy's, a popular Boston gay bar on a chilly evening. A carload of men around my age drove by and screamed, "Die fags! Get AIDS and die fags!" That was the first time I heard such hateful words hurled out loud. It scared the bejesus out of me. I was alone as I scanned the crowd waiting to enter the club. They showed no visible signs of distress. I couldn't help but wonder: were they scared too?

I graduated college in 1985. I was working full time that summer at the hospital while actively looking for my first professional job. It was also around that time I learned my rare blood was no longer wanted. As a young gay man, my blood, my lifeline to others, was considered tainted, just like me.

The internalized homophobia I felt had a funny way of messing with my head. To me, it wasn't just that my blood was bad, but somehow, I was too. Self-doubt crept in.

My confidence was undermined by the policies of the Food and Drug Administration (FDA). The FDA quickly banned blood from *all* gay and bisexual men. While this move was necessary at the time to protect our nation's blood supply, it went a long way to make me and others feel "dirty" and unwanted.

Fast forward to the early 2000s. The American Red Cross pulled up with their bloodmobiles in front of our downtown office building. They were actively looking for donors. We formed blood donor teams within our workplace. When coworkers pestered me to join their team, my inner rage bubbled up.

I believed in giving blood ever since my early interactions with Jim as a teenager. Now, decades later, the homophobic rules were still in place! Clearly, I was HIV negative, and I didn't engage in "high risk" behaviors. But I was still considered tainted. I was having none of it!

I signed up. I got the blood donation app and went ahead full throttle. I didn't care about their stupid screener questions. I was making up for lost time, and I now donate blood frequently. I even got text and email pleas from the American Red Cross about the special need for B negative blood like mine. I shelved my rage and replaced it with my conviction to serve others. I told myself those old cronies would not prevent me from donating.

When I told my friends about my decision to donate, their reactions were mixed. While some applauded my efforts, others questioned my lying to the screener. I was not backing down. I felt it was my civic responsibility to help the greater community, like it would be to serve on a jury.

I finally asked the naysayers: if they needed a transfusion, would they accept my blood? Each one immediately responded, "Yes!!" That reinforced my decision and validated my personal campaign of donating blood. I never looked back.

Once I left my job and started working for myself, I donated blood regularly at the local American Red Cross blood bank. That's where I learned about donating "Power Red[1]" from one of the phlebotomists. She explained that since I was so healthy, and I had such rare blood, by donating a "double red" my donation would go a lot further to helping people. I gladly complied and have been consistently donating this way ever since.

While recovering from COVID-19 in 2020, I discovered my "COVID convalescent plasma" could help people who were sick with COVID-19. I started donating plasma at the same blood bank. I was delighted to learn that my first donation helped COVID-19 patients in a North Las Vegas hospital, and that was all the reinforcement I needed. I

---

1 A Power Red (AKA a double red donation) allows you to donate two units of red blood cells during one donation. Power Red is similar to a whole blood donation, except a special machine is used to allow you to donate two units of red blood cells while returning your plasma and platelets to you.

continued to donate plasma until the American Red Cross informed me I didn't have enough COVID-19 antibodies left for my blood to be helpful.

When the FDA finally decided to change their archaic policy of discriminating against gay and bisexual men, I was so underwhelmed. What took them so long? While some people probably disagreed with my approach, I knew there was a need for my blood, and I was determined to help. I simply couldn't follow a policy deeply grounded in fear instead of science.

While donating a "double red" the other day, I found myself wondering about Jim. I hadn't seen him in many years. I never knew for sure if he was gay, but I suspect he was. Regardless of his sexual orientation, I want him to know that his kindness toward me almost 50 years ago resulted in a steady stream of blood donations from me. And, nurse Charlotte, I shed a tear for you. You showed such courage, strength, and resilience during an uncertain and shameful time in our nation's history.

Author's Note

The United States and many other countries started blocking blood donations from gay and bisexual men during the early 1980s AIDS epidemic. They aimed to prevent the spread of HIV through the blood supply. These bans made sense at the time because we didn't have a good way to test blood donations for HIV.

The technology to scan blood has improved dramatically since the early days of the AIDS epidemic. My decision to donate blood was a deeply personal one. Ultimately, I decided that my desire to save lives was more important than standing on the sidelines governed by misguided and outdated policies.

In 2015, the FDA dropped the lifetime ban and replaced it with a one-year abstinence requirement. Then in 2020, the agency shortened the abstinence period to three months. They did this after discovering blood donations plummeted during COVID-19. In my cynical opinion, it was this extreme shortage that caused more rational minds to prevail.

Recently the FDA leveled the playing field with a series of "individual risk-based questions" that are the same for every blood donor regardless of sexual orientation, gender, or sex. While I see this as progress, there's a part of me that is still angry that it took this long.

After my latest blood donation, I received an email that lessened my long-time feelings of anger about the situation. Below is the email from the American Red Cross that read:

Dear Paul,

It is our honor to congratulate you on reaching your 5 gallon milestone. Your 41 lifetime donations have helped make a difference in the lives of many who you may never know.

We are happy to present this digital milestone badge to you as a symbol of your dedication to helping save lives. Share it with pride. Show everyone you're a #DonorForLife. You've earned it.

If you'd like a pin to wear with pride, we're happy to mail one to you. Simply click the button below within the next 30 days to request your pin.

I ordered the pin!

Paul Iarrobino (he/him) is a storyteller, author, husband, and dog dad. He's called Portland, Oregon, his home for over 30 years. He is one of the founding members of Elder Pride Services and received their Lifetime Achievement Award in 2018 for providing leadership during their formative years. Paul is the proud recipient of Oregon Queer History Collective's 2021 Queer Hero Award for his groundbreaking work engaging and inspiring community dialogues during the pandemic. This is Paul's third published anthology. You can follow Paul at www.ourboldvoices.com.

Power Red

Dissecting Daddy

By Kyle Lang

He's up and out of my bed almost immediately. I'm in an Asheville hotel, far from home on my annual trip, and he is a stranger I've met via the apps. We've exchanged a handful of sentences face to face, but we've also exchanged multiple sexual positions. The encounter didn't end in "completion" for either of us, and when I suggest a break due to his waning enthusiasm, he is up and out of the bed in moments.

I get "Asheville" a glass of water, which he drinks in a handful of gulps. He's trembling when he sets the glass down, and I make a quick mental note of it. He begins pulling on his clothes, shoving his underwear in his jeans pocket and his socks in the pocket of his jacket. It's January in North Carolina, and there is a weather advisory in effect. He should be fully dressed when he leaves, and I know this.

I also know he's in some form of distress. His nerves appear to sizzle with electric anxiety, a warning, or high alert, but I can't identify the threat.

I step to him, talking softly. He's not avoiding my gaze, but he's also not holding eye contact. After a moment, he straightens and levels his gaze to mine, and we say our goodbyes. I kiss him softly on the corner of his mouth, an affectionate kiss but not a seductive one, and I pull him into an embrace. He nearly crumbles into me, and I hold him tight. I cup my hand to the base of his skull and run my fingertips through the tight fringe of hair at his neckline. His breath is too quick. He's stressed. Fight or Flight. And I continue to hold him and press soft kisses to the side of his head and temple. It is far more intimate than I'm used to for a hookup, but something compels me to soothe him.

He responds. I feel his shoulders relax a little, and his breath comes back into deeper control.

And it hits me. "Oh, brother, you need touch, don't you? You're starving for it."

He nods, or speaks, I can't remember, but he agrees, and I pull him deeper into an embrace. He meets my energy and squeezes tighter. We stand like this for a couple moments, pressed together, breathing, my fingertips caressing his hair and neck.

"You don't have to go," I say, even as I know it is already later than I planned on being up, but something tells me to make space for this stranger, for Asheville, to hold space by holding him. Something in the experience rings familiar, a shadow of a memory.

"Yeah?" he asks tentatively.

"Sure. Do you want to snuggle? Get back into bed?"

He pauses to consider and asks, "Can I take my clothes off again?"

"Of course," I say, and I crawl naked back onto the bed, setting myself high against the pillows and headboard. He pulls his clothes off again, leaving them in a heap at the foot of the bed, and crawls up to me before nuzzling himself into my chest and neck. I kiss the top of this stranger's head and let my hands wander the open plains of his flesh, his back, shoulders, and neck, and I tease the edge of hair there.

And this is the way it goes for a LONG time.

We revel in our senses, delight in each other, but we don't have sex again. We touch, and we kiss. Our caressing is slow, methodical, and exploratory. But I notice a change in him. I feel his breath bottom out a couple times, shallow for a moment, and I sense he's overwhelmed, not in a bad way but in a vulnerable way. He wants this intimacy, craves it, and now that he has it, if even for a moment, he is flooded.

And the memory surfaces for me of my time with Coach, a gentleman I met in the early days of my coming out. He coached me, thus the nickname. In addition, he mentored me, taught me how to care for myself as a gay man. He taught me where to get free STI testing, about PrEP[1], hygiene, nothing was off limits with Coach. In all of that, in all of the gifts he gave me that would protect me for years to come, the memory that now surfaces is of his tenderness, of his ease of intimacy. I remember how he held me in those anxiety-ridden first days as I discovered my identity, and so I relate to Asheville deeply. I can see him clearly even if he can't see himself.

One Coach session in particular solidified for me a piece of my identity as a gay man. We had finished having sex, it was midafternoon in the midst of a grey Portland fall. Exhilarated by my newfound experiences and spent to a level of exhaustion I had never felt before, I found myself crooked into Coach's shoulder. His hand traced slow circles through the hair at the base of my spine, and I nearly purred at the sensation, but in my drowsiness, it emerged as merely a hum of satisfaction.

"Are you ok?"

"Mmm," I mumbled into his chest.

"Do you need anything?"

"Nuh uh," I mumbled again.

---

1 STI stands for Sexually Transmitted Infection, which replaces the term STD. PrEP stands for Pre-Exposure Prophylaxis and is commonly used by those practicing safer sex. It is a life-saving medication that allows the LGBTQIA2S+ community to enjoy the all-too-human experience of healthy sexuality while minimizing the anxiety-inducing narratives instilled in us by the AIDS crisis.

"How do you feel?" he asked.

"Amazing," I said, and then I sank into a tranquil mindfulness as I checked in with my body, thoughts, and feelings. I was satiated, drowsy, happy, and content. My mind didn't race. Instead, my thoughts and feelings shuffled along languidly to where I could actually keep track of my thought process.

"Daddy's got you," he said, and I immediately bristled.

I bristled because I'm a biological father to an amazing young woman, and Daddy was reserved for her. I knew about the "daddy phenomenon" in gay culture, but I always found it distasteful and a bit creepy. I actively worked against it and told men flat out that I wouldn't tolerate its use toward me. That was my daughter's word, and I wouldn't have it tarnished. In that moment with Coach, I told him all of this in a kind of drowsy haze. As I finished my sleepy diatribe, Coach let out a bemused breath through his nose and stroked my back again. It was sweet, if not a bit condescending, as if he was saying, "You'll learn."

I settled back into the crook of his arm and inhaled his scent. My eyes closed almost immediately. I found myself absolutely present in the moment, pressed into the mattress. I nuzzled my face into Coach's chest, breathing the clean sweat of him like he was fresh from the gym, and listened to my own heartbeat as the corners of my mouth curved inevitably upward.

I knew it then with Coach. I knew when I lay in his arms in a nonsexual way that I was gay. I knew my journey was not about finding a different type of partner to have sex with or about the biology of our coupling. I knew that I craved more from my experiences with men, from my relationships with men. I knew there was something deeper to my desires than simply the male form and its biology. As the memory fades from my immediate recollection, I realize it's true for Asheville too.

How can I possibly know Asheville's truth at the moment?

Because we also talk. He's 53, divorcing his wife, relocated due to work, alone in a new city far from his adult children. He's swimming in the soup of a new sexuality, and only the false intimacy of app hookups has served as a balm for his loneliness. And I am familiar with ALL of that. I can feel in my cells where he's at in his journey.

We talk about his experiences. He's had sex, fucked, gotten fucked, had plenty of orgasms, but he hasn't had intimacy with anyone—male or female—in a long time. I ask him if he's ever slept with a man, like fallen asleep next to another man, if even for a nap.

"I haven't," he replies.

As we talk, he wavers between stoic and the edge of tears. This all feels so familiar, and it takes me to a raw place. I want to give him languid thoughts and personal comfort. I want him to know himself. I want to be a comfort, a resource, a safe place for him. Coach did that for me, and I suddenly understand the importance of having intimacy modeled. Coach helped me understand that I was the worthy recipient of another man's loving attention.

I knew it was ok to accept tenderness from a woman. I'd seen it modeled my whole life, digested thousands of hours of media and literature that showed me what that looked like. But I'd struggled to understand what that meant when it was another man standing in front of me. I was lucky enough to encounter Coach, amongst others, who took the time to show me what that could look like.

Because of those experiences, it dawns on me as I lie with Asheville that this might be the first time I am capable of providing this for another man. I'd grown accustomed to others providing this security for me, but I hadn't even considered providing it to another. I'd been privileged to have played the son role, to have been nurtured along by other men. For I had viewed myself as the newbie, the explorer, the tentative one. As a "late bloomer," a person who recognized his sexuality later in life, I'd come to distrust myself, my thoughts, my feelings, and even my capacities.

Six months prior, I didn't think I even trusted myself or my decision to come out as gay, let alone that I could help another man struggling with his identity and sexuality. Being closeted, denying, or not even realizing my sexuality caused me to distrust my own definition of self, and intimacy is largely predicated on one's ability to give of themselves freely and openly. The closet is not a place of freedom and openness. The realization of how closed off I had been scares me as I lay there comforting Asheville. Terrified of my own emotional capacities, or lack thereof, I recommit to being present for Asheville.

In the moment, it actually makes me think of my other models of intimacy. I'd also been a husband and a father. Under the tutelage of my ex-wife and daughter, I learned softness and intimacy. I held them as they cried, rubbed their backs as they mourned. I've touched their hair and face when they were scared as I whispered reassurances about the goodness that existed in the world. I've known intimacy and tenderness. I've known vulnerability and emotional generosity, but Asheville is my first real opportunity to provide it to a man; the first time I've consciously defied my own expectation that it is improper, or even inexcusable, to give that level of selfless attention to a man.

And so I hold Asheville to my chest. And I rub his back and shoulders. And I play with his hair. And I speak softly to him about his experiences and my own. And I ground him with my energy and my experience and my hands and my voice and my mind and my heart. I give myself willingly to another man, and it has nothing to do with sex, and it is the most intensely connected feeling I've had in a very long time. I truly believe I feel so deeply connected because it is one of the most truly authentic gestures I've made. It's something that expresses my whole and cohesive self in a way I haven't experienced before.

The role of the daddy as I play it for Asheville is the role of the nurturer. It's a role I played in my straight life but ascribed to the feminine and didn't honor even as I knew it was a part of me. Living my closeted life damaged me. It made me think I had to cast off the very traits that made me the person I always wanted to be. I played the gender roles I was taught. I lived with the guilt I inflicted on myself. I denied who I was for years.

And so I played it straight, which is a glib way of saying that I allowed myself to succumb to the gendered narrative. I married, had a child, and wrapped myself in the safety and security of a heterosexual life for over 20 years. At 45 years old, I could no longer live that narrative. I was overflowing with an attraction I was terrified to name. I turned to the people I had built a life with and admitted to them who I truly was. In that moment, I defied the vows I'd made, betrayed the man I'd purported to be. I shed the roles I'd played up until that point. I broke the trust of so many people as I admitted the falsehood I'd maintained for decades.

Those were some of my darkest days. Up until that point, and for many, many days afterward, I couldn't see my inherent worth. I feared my queerness, even as I confessed it. How could I lack so much self-awareness? How could I not see my own value? In that exact moment, a couple of men, especially Coach, came into my life and touched me, both literally and figuratively. Through their gentle ministrations, I saw the beauty in both who I was and in the intimacy I could create with other men. I realize now that the energy of those encounters mostly flowed in a single direction, from them to me, from daddy to son, as they nurtured along my bruised heart.

I've found the strength to resist the narratives that create barriers between me and my connection with other men. I've learned to lean into the role of Daddy. I now stand up and claim my queerness, myself, and my desire for real intimacy with other men, whether it be physical, mental, or emotional. And what I did with Asheville is how I've come to relish the role of Daddy. I see the role of being a daddy as one that leverages knowledge, experience, and compassion toward the "son" in the relationship, and those roles are not exclusively defined by age.

My defiance wasn't directed toward some large external threat that forced me into the situation I found myself in. I had closeted myself. I was so fearful of who I was, I created a labyrinth of rules I had to follow simply to feel I have value, to feel accepted, and to feel loved. The fact that I was still policing the language of others, telling them I wouldn't accept the word daddy was more about my internal homophobia than it was about anything else.

A year later, I return to Asheville, North Carolina, and to "Asheville" the man. Because I lost contact with him, I don't know if we will meet again, but I have my eye out just in case it is meant to be. The experience the previous year was so formidable, I am curious as to what is going on with him now.

It's the first day of my visit, and I'm snowbound in my room. Yet another weather advisory day, and snow and ice threaten. The weather is not my friend in North Carolina. Bored, I open my phone to find a series of pictures of a really handsome man inside my app messages. He's got grey in his hair and beard, more than I remember, and he is slimmer, sharply dressed, and wears a smile that extends to his eyes. I immediately clock him as Asheville, but there is a momentary glimmer of doubt, too. This man exudes confidence and sex appeal. I double- and triple-take the pictures, and while I am confident it is him, I can't tip my hand until I know for sure.

So we chat online for a minute. We share the app essentials, stats, preferences, interests, etc., and I am searching for a way to confirm that this is him. Finally, I come up with this. "Are you native to Asheville?" I remember he relocated from down south somewhere, so this could be my final, definitive clue that this is my guy.

He admits that he moved the year previous, and I tip my hand. I send a message through the app.

Did we meet a year ago? You look REALLY familiar.

You know, I think we did, he writes, *Are you a writer?*

Yep. You came to my hotel on another weather advisory night.

I definitely remember you now. The sex was very good. 😈

After a moment, he adds, *That's crazy.*

This time we exchange names and phone numbers, and we are back and forth and back and forth on text messages, catching up. It sounds like he's doing great, really settling into his new life. His youngest grown son is living with him, work is going well, the divorce is finalized, and he's having some fun exploring. I tell him about the company I bought, about my growing social circles back home, and how my family continues to adjust.

It's too snowy and icy for us to meet, but we make a plan to meet midday the next day when the road conditions are going to improve. And he doesn't disappoint. He's right on time. I meet him outside the hotel so I can chat with him as we walk back to my room, and when he approaches me on the sidewalk, I can tell he's excited.

We catch up briefly, but once we step inside the hotel room, his lips press mine. I receive him and press my kiss back to him, hard. And it isn't long before we are grasping at clothes, pulling on each other, and giving wet open-mouthed kisses up and down each other's body. The sex is passionate and urgent. And we take some time with this, until the moment comes. "I gotta get going," he says suddenly.

"Huh?" I ask a little confused. "You do?"

"Yeah. I gotta get some things going." He rises to the end of the bed and starts putting his clothes back on.

"Oh. Ok," I say, and I'm immediately transported back to a year prior. This was the moment it all really started for me. The anxious moment where I stepped into the daddy role for the first time. I stand up and approach him as he pulls his pants all the way up. I kiss him on the corner of the mouth, seductively this time, and I say, "You know you did this last time, right?"

"What did I do?" he asks, a little confused.

"You got up suddenly from the bed and started pulling your clothes on," I smile at him and level my eyes to his. "Do you remember what happened next?" I ask.

I can tell he is thinking, there's a glimmer of recognition in his eyes, and he smiles coyly at me. "I think so."

"You don't have to go," I say. I turn and crawl back onto the bed, high on the pillows and headboard. Asheville laughs, and sighs, and takes his pants off and joins me on the bed. It is then that I really get to catch up with him. He's in my arms, and we kiss and caress, and I ask him about his kids, about his hopes for a relationship, about his work and his life. And he opens himself to me. He shares with me, and I listen to him and share my own life with him. We while away the afternoon this way.

I played Daddy to Asheville, that full-grown man. I gave him the support he needed to take a risk, to try something new, to make himself vulnerable. I hope I mirrored that vulnerability right back to him. It's not something I'm skilled at, and Asheville taught me that. It's taken everything I have to stand up and accept myself, to accept my place in relationship to other men, to defy the standards of masculinity put upon me. My pathway to strength of identity, to a solid core of security, comes in some small way by mentoring other men, men like Asheville.

I needed to accept myself, to see that intimacy with other men was something of value. It was something beautiful, and tender, and loving, and necessary. I needed to forgive myself for the sin of existing and to defy my own codified way of living in order to finally ... finally ... be whole.

Author's Note

I don't bark at the word daddy anymore when it is bandied about in a bar, or used as an opening salvo in an app message. I've reclaimed the word and given it multiple meanings. My daughter can still use it as a term of endearment for me while my friends and members of the community do too. Being a parent is what taught me some of the very skills I now use to mentor men. Only through my relationships with the special women in my life have I been able to learn what I need to help others, and I would never diminish my ex-wife or daughter's contributions to who I am as a man.

All men—no matter gay, straight or otherwise—are deserving of mentorship. They need it. If I'm honest, I need it. I need to be father AND son. I need to mentor and to be mentored, to grow and evolve and to overcome the stigma of being a gay man in the world. I deserve healthy relationships, and I want to provide opportunities through which other people find their own healthy relationships.

Only by accepting my role as a daddy did I finally understand that I possess this need, too. The need to be comforted, mentored, and led by other men. In a culture of toxic masculinity, it is hard for us to admit we have a weakness or a need—basically, anything we can't handle entirely on our own. I am no different. Asheville gave me such a gift in providing an opportunity to be there for him. And it is important as gay men that we see other men defying the status quo of toxic masculinity and showing us the way forward.

Kyle Lang (he/him) writes from the Portland, Oregon, metro area. He is currently working on nonfiction and poetry addressing identity and culture with a specific focus on LGBTQIA+ intersections, but he has written and published fiction, erotica, and poetry as well. When he isn't writing, he is either parenting his teenage daughter or planning music festivals around the Pacific Northwest. He has published in Story Quarterly, Beyond Queer Words, *and* Flash Fiction Magazine.

Bus to Oakland

By John Lucia

The bus smelled of vomit, diesel fuel, and cigars. The grimy seats and windows looked like they had not been cleaned in several years. There was not a square inch of this vehicle that I would want to touch.

We were on our way to the Oakland Processing Center for our Army examinations. We were potential Vietnam draftees, most of us in our late teens and early twenties. We clutched the necessary documents in our hands that we had been ordered to bring: birth certificates, draft notices, college records. Here, at the end of the 1960s, uncertainty was everywhere.

The bus left from an empty lot south of Market Street in San Francisco. It was a few short blocks to the on-ramp of the Bay Bridge. I fought the urge to open the window and jump out. Of course, I would've probably been seriously hurt or even killed in the process. I felt desperate enough that I might've tried it, but not if I had to touch the filthy window latch.

The draft notice had arrived in the mail three weeks before. I sat and stared at it as though it contained man-eating insects. I couldn't bring myself to open it, even though my mother kept insisting that I do.

I think her past was talking to her. Our family had an uneasy history with the military. Her father served in the First World War, coming back in one piece with no visible signs of damage. He didn't seem to suffer from any lingering mental issues, though he did succumb to colon cancer at the young age of 48. My mother was still in high school when he died. No one wondered whether mustard gas or being doused with gasoline or other wartime hazards could've caused his cancer.

Then the Big Thing happened in 1950. My mother's young brother, Jack, volunteered to join the Army during the Korean War. In an intense confrontation with the enemy, his tank was forced off a North Korean road. It fell over a cliff, killing him and all inside. Years later, I would find the Army's official commendation about my uncle praising his heroism and posthumously promoting him in rank. Before his tank plummeted over that cliff, he had gotten out of the tank, dragged injured soldiers to safety, risking his life, too. He was 18 years old.

This loss was the second large blow to my grandmother's fragile emotions. In the course of four years, she had lost her husband and her only son in war. My father told me about the day that the Army officers arrived with the telegram. My parents had moved in with my grandmother during my first year of life. My father was standing in the garage with the door open when the dull-gray Army coupe pulled up, and two officers got out. My father knew instantly why they were there when he saw the papers in their hands. They asked to speak to my grandmother. He led them up the basement stairs. The news they delivered would change our family forever.

Growing up, Uncle Jack's name was rarely mentioned. His official Army portrait hung on our dining room wall, a silent reminder of his absence. His disembodied image watched over our family gatherings. Christmases came and went, feasts were served, family milestones marked with laughter, cigarette smoke, and platters of food. All the while, Uncle Jack smiled his blank smile.

Our downstairs basement room held a hodgepodge of old furniture and bric-a-brac. Among the jumble of items was Jack's red and white model sailboat that he had sailed on Stow Lake in Golden Gate Park. Over the years, the yellowed canvas sail began to disintegrate, and the boat became covered in a dusty film. It was hard to connect this boat with the handsome man in the portrait hanging in the dining room. Though the reminders were here and there in the house, it was as though he had never been there.

When I learned how to drive, my grandmother and I struck a loosely defined deal. If I drove her around on errands, I could use the car when I needed it. The car was fairly new, and although it was a compact car, it had a powerful engine and was fun to drive.

One errand that would become a regular request was to take her to the National Cemetery in San Bruno. Both her husband and her son, Jack, were buried in the military cemetery. The first visit was burned into my memory.

I had accompanied her to the cemetery a few times over the years, but we had only ever gone to my grandfather's grave. Our routine was to stop at a flower shop in Colma, known as the "City of the Dead" for its abundance of cemeteries, and buy a bunch of flowers. Then we'd stop at the cemetery entrance, place the flowers in one of their metal vases and fill it with water from the outside faucet. We'd climb the hill to Grandpa's grave and stab the vase into the ground in front of his white marble tombstone. Though she was somber on these visits, she didn't cry or otherwise show much outward emotion.

But, on this day of my being a newly-minted driver, the visit routine abruptly changed. We stopped at Grandpa's grave, and she split the flower bouquet in half, placing half in the metal vase. Then she turned around and walked down the hill with the remaining flowers clutched in her hand. She didn't say a word to me. She stepped off the curb where our car was parked and crossed the street, walking further down the hill. I didn't know if I should follow her. I didn't know where she was going. I stood at the top of the slope and watched her. She stopped at a grave. Her shoulders visibly slumped and started heaving up and down. I wasn't sure what she was doing, and then I realized that she was crying. No sound came out of her, but tears silently rolled down her cheeks. She slowly sank to her knees and grabbed the tombstone for support, still holding the forgotten flowers in her hand. I went over to her and put my hand on her shoulder, feeling it rise and fall. She didn't flinch or acknowledge me in any way. I knew whose name would be on that tombstone: Jack's. It was the first time I had ever seen my grandmother express grief for her son.

My Uncle Jack's death left my mother with a strong streak of patriotism. She was proud of her brother for protecting us from Korea and the threat of Communism. She thought it was a good idea that I join the Army. I couldn't believe my ears. I was her teenage son, only a little older than Uncle Jack had been when he went to Korea.

Every day, she asked me to open the envelope. On the third day, I did. The government draft notice demanded that I report for a physical exam in Oakland. It gave the designated place to meet an Army transport bus that would take me there.

* * *

The bus pulled up in front of a faded three-story building. Sitting on a piece of ground by itself. It might've been plopped there with a crane. There were no bushes, flowers, or plantings of any kind anywhere around the blank, barren lot. We were instructed to walk into the building in single file. One by one, we took lockers and stripped to our underwear. I was even more embarrassed and nervous than I usually felt in high school gym class.

Documents in hand, we lined up to be poked and examined. Expressionless soldiers took our temperatures, listened to our heartbeats, and asked us to do various things: breathe in and out, show the soles of our feet, submit to scalp and ear exams. I tried not to ogle some of the hunkier young guys walking around in their underwear. Though I was somewhat interested in my fellow draftees, I was far too worried about what might happen.

Then we sat down to complete the form we were given. It looked like an employment application. We were asked about school, work, and health history.

One of the question boxes asked, “Do you, or have you ever had, homosexual thoughts or tendencies?” I froze, wondering what would happen if I told the truth. I'd read articles about men who were excused from serving because of their positive answer to this question. I decided that I would not lie. I answered “yes.” The next question was, “Do you still have these thoughts?” Again, “yes.” I took a deep breath, thinking that I might have to tell one of these dullards all about my sex life; a horrifying thought.

I finished filling out the form and handed it in. We were ordered to get dressed and line up to board the bus back to San Francisco. I had a moment of panic. Had they seen those answers I gave about homosexuality? Was I going to speak to someone about it before we left? Would we just board the bus and cross over the bridge?

As we passed a young soldier near the door, I quietly asked him if I could speak to someone about some of my answers on the form. He looked at me quizzically and said, "What do you mean?" I timidly told him about the boxes about homosexuality, and he said, "I wouldn't worry about that."

I wondered what that meant and asked, "Don't I have to speak to someone now?" He said, with a smart-ass expression on his face, "No. Now get on the bus." My obedient Catholic schoolboy sense of compliance was about to kick in, and I began to climb the stairs onto the bus—but then I stopped.

To this day, I don't know how I raised the courage to say to him, in a firm voice that sounded like someone else, "No, I'd like to speak to someone about it *now*." His half grin disappeared, replaced by a menacing curl of his upper lip. He turned and disappeared. I was now in full panic mode. I turned and looked at my fellow travelers, sitting in their bus seats, staring at me through the window. I was delaying their departure from this awful place for the comfort of home. I was now everyone's enemy. But something in me told me to hold my ground or I'd be chewed up, spat out, and shoved into an Army transport plane bound for Vietnam.

A rather large, imposing man in a uniform approached, the smart-ass doorman in tow. He said in a booming voice, "I need your name." I gave it to him, and he turned and left. Was I supposed to stand here? Meanwhile, Mr. Smirky just glared at me, his half smile back on his face. I could almost read his expression: *NOW you're gonna be sorry, Fruitcake.*

The uniformed man returned, my papers clutched in his hand. "Follow me," he barked as he took off for a row of glass cubicles along the back wall. He stopped short at one of them, ordered me to take a seat, and left. I could see in the distance the guys sitting on the bus, glaring at me. The bus engine suddenly roared to life, and I panicked. Were they going to leave me here? How would I get back home? Was I *going* back home at all? I watched the bus pull away. Oh great.

Another uniformed officer appeared, his dangling medals decorating his jacket. I swallowed loudly. Though he looked very officious, he had kind eyes. I mentally memorized his nametag. I later learned that he was an Army psychiatrist. He sat down at the desk and said, "Are your answers on this form true?" I answered, "Yes, sir." He avoided my eyes and spoke to the form rather than to me. "Son, do you have sex with other men?" he asked. I thought, well here goes. I looked right at him and said, "Yes, sir." "Well then, we will review your answers and make a determination about your service. You may wait for the next bus going back to San Francisco, though it will be about an hour." Without looking at me again, he stood up and walked away.

New dread bloomed in me. My service? "Wait. I won't find out today if I am eligible to be drafted?" I asked. He turned back halfway in my direction, an impatient scowl on his face and said, "No, you won't. It will likely be several weeks before you hear from us." I felt like I had just been hit by a bowling ball.

I walked out to the outdoor bench in a fog and sat down heavily. What would happen to me? What if they ignored my admissions?

I saw no signs about not smoking, so I lit a cigarette and waited for the bus.

I started skipping college classes in the mornings, staying home and waiting for our mail to arrive. Days ticked by, producing only shopping flyers, bills, and useless catalogs to our mailbox. My mother noticed my constant presence and my obsession with the mail but said nothing.

On Day Five after the exam, an official-looking envelope from the Selective Service arrived. It contained a small card stating in blunt, tactless terms that I was eligible for military service and that I would be informed of a date to report for duty. My stomach clenched tightly, and I felt like passing out. I dropped into a nearby chair as thoughts raced through my head. Didn't the officer say it would be weeks before I'd get a determination? How did this happen so quickly?

My friend, Danny, told me about a legal group downtown that helped people with draft issues. I ran to the phone, pulled it into the bathroom, and called him at work. He gave me the name of the group. I thanked him, hung up, and called immediately. A kindly woman's voice asked me how she might help me. I blurted out an abbreviated version of the events, and before I knew what had happened, she had booked an appointment for me to see an attorney the following afternoon.

I hadn't had time to process what the notice card meant. How could they ignore what I had told them? Didn't they care? What if they wouldn't listen? I guess they hadn't since I was now a 1-A classification[1]. That night I tossed and turned, getting very little sleep. I wasn't sure what this attorney could do for me. What if it was hopeless? Would I die in a foreign land far from home like my Uncle Jack?

The next morning passed with glacial speed. I was sure that the hands on the clock were not moving. I left long before the appointment time, determined to be there and ready to act, whatever that meant. I parked in a garage downtown and walked the crowded streets for almost an hour, looking at department store windows and into shops but not really seeing anything.

1 1-A registrants are Available for Military Service.

I walked into the busy legal office, giving my name to the receptionist and taking a seat. The office had a casual air about it. The furniture was all basic metal, the floor was not carpeted, covered only with worn linoleum. I was beginning to think that I might've made a mistake to come here.

I had brought a book but couldn't concentrate on reading. The wait felt like it lasted a week. Finally, a short, well-dressed man came out of an office behind the reception desk. He introduced himself as Martin Caulfield, using a slow, languid Southern drawl. His twinkling blue eyes looked kind and warm. I followed him to his tiny office.

After we sat down, he said "Well, John, tell me your story." I recapped the events of the day of the exam, watching him take notes. He didn't register a reaction about the homosexual questions. No facial expressions or remarks. All business. When I had finished, he said in his hypnotic drawl, "This is not an uncommon occurrence. I've already spoken to countless young men who have had the same issue. The Army is playing a game of pretending not to hear you. In cases like this, we need to force their hand."

"What does that mean?" As soon as I asked the question, I was afraid that it sounded childish and whiny. Martin explained, "You'll need to be seen by a psychiatric professional, and he'll prepare a report, and that report will be submitted by me to the Army for review. If the case is presented convincingly, the Army will dismiss you from service." I stared blankly at him, not knowing whether this was an indictment of me, and wondered if he was on my side.

He must've read my thoughts because he said, "Don't worry. We need to make the case that you shouldn't serve, but that doesn't mean you're a bad person. It's a report that will not likely paint you in the best light, but we know that the Army needs to justify your disqualification. I have faith in the man I'd like you to see." I asked a few more questions and then agreed to visit the psychiatrist that Martin recommended. He gave me the contact information. He urged me to make an appointment with the man as soon as possible since the draft clock was ticking.

* * *

The doctor, a stern German man with a clipped manner of speech, sat in front of me, legal pad and pen in front of him. He was large and rather dour looking, though I didn't think he was much more than 40. His disheveled suit, vest, and shirt were dotted with ash from his pipe, and he looked like he had slept in them for more than one night. The pipe smelled of smoky pine, and he absentmindedly kept tapping it against the ashtray, which was distracting and noisy. I forced myself to concentrate on his questions and my answers. He asked me about my job, my home life, my sex life, and my feelings about these things. I felt a vague uneasiness, as though he was passing judgment on me. The questions about my sexual activity seemed rather personal and probing, and I wondered if they were necessary.

Like Martin before him, he was all business and no fraternizing. Unlike Martin, he exhibited little warmth or empathy. A few of my answers emitted a strange noise from him akin to a grunting burp. He offered no opinions or conclusions, though he did say that the Army would view some of my actions as likely unacceptable. I got the impression that this would work in my favor.

At the end of the hour, he told me that he had enough material to write a report for Martin to submit to the Army, and he shook hands with me and showed me to the door of his inner office. Out at his secretary's desk, I wrote a check for the $60 fee. She handed me a handwritten receipt for the payment. I walked out into the hall and wondered what would come next. I was in a daze. In the past several days, I had been through an examination, a denial of my being gay by the Army, a categorization as ready for service, a consultation with a legal aid attorney, and now a psychological evaluation. I had just turned 20, the same age my father had been when he landed on Omaha Beach in Normandy in 1944.

Martin submitted an opinion letter along with the report by the psychiatrist to the Army. I attended classes and went to my after-school job for weeks as though I were sleepwalking. I couldn't concentrate on anything for very long. Television programs came and went, though I couldn't have told you what they were about. My mother kept me in her peripheral vision when I was nearby, as if I were a dangerous mountain lion that had walked in the front door and set up residency. I had not told my parents about the attorney, the psychiatrist, or even WHY I was challenging the draft board.

But my mother knew something was up. I caught her looking at me like I was a hungry mountain lion.

The first thing that finally straggled in by mail weeks later was a reclassification to 1-Y[2]. I quickly called Martin at home, reaching another man who told me that Martin was not there. He agreed to have Martin call me back. Who was THAT?

It was late the next day when Martin finally called. By then, I was in full-scale hysteria. I had paced the floor, chain smoking and casting glances at the idle phone. In his cool Southern accent, he asked me to read him everything on the 1-Y notice. He said, "They're processing your rejection for service. I can just feel it. This isn't the last notice you'll get. Hang tight." I tried to think of a way to ask him about the mystery man who had answered his home phone, but I couldn't come up with anything. I promised to call him upon the arrival of the next notice. Martin made sympathetic cooing sounds of reassurance, and then he hung up.

We didn't have to wait long. An official notice arrived from the draft board only four days later, and I almost cried when I saw it. I was now officially classified as 4-F[3]. I knew what this meant, so I quickly called Martin's office. When he picked up, I started to tell him about the notice, but I

---

2 1-Y registrants are qualified for service only in time of war or national emergency. (This classification was abolished December 10, 1971. Local boards were subsequently instructed to reclassify all 1-Y registrants by administrative action.)

3 4-F registrants are Not Qualified for Military Service.

couldn't get the words out. I was crying, and he could hear me. In his wonderful calm voice he said, "It's 4-F, isn't it? Don't you cry now. God has other plans for you. I'm so happy for you. I'm going to take you out to lunch. There's someone I want you to meet." We made arrangements to meet downtown near his office the following week. I sat on the hallway floor, the phone receiver clutched in my hand. I was in shock and would stay that way for over a week. It was almost over. I now had to figure out a way to tell my parents.

The previous year, I had had a bad argument with my parents that culminated in my coming out as gay. I had been living with a man, and my parents guessed the nature of the relationship. I was sure they noticed there was only one bed in our one-bedroom apartment. Angry words followed, and I didn't speak to my parents for almost a month. We eventually patched it up, and then my boyfriend and I split up, and I moved back home. Now, on top of being a homosexual, my mother would see me as a draft dodger.

At the dinner table the next night, I chose to drop the bomb. My siblings would be there, and it might help the atmosphere. "Mom and Dad, I decided to appeal my draft notice. I just learned that the Army has decided to not draft me. I'll tell you more about it later." I said, glancing sideways at my brother and sister.

Right after dinner, my mother uncharacteristically left the dirty dishes in the sink, grabbed my father, and steered the three of us into their bedroom at the back of the house. She slammed the door, and before I could say anything, she shouted angrily "What did you TELL them?!" I didn't bother to ask what she meant because the three of us all knew what she meant. I closed my eyes and said quietly, "I told them that I'm a homosexual." Both of my parents let out a disgusted sigh, and my mother said, "So, now the whole world knows that you're a queer?" My heart sank at that horrible word, but I stood my ground. I raised my voice and said, "Would you rather that I get killed in Vietnam!? And I don't want to lie about this anymore to anyone!" She sneered back, and said, "And what did you have to do to get them to believe you?!" At that point, my father said in a very soft voice, "June, stop it. It's not your decision." Both of us turned and looked at my father in disbelief. I had never heard him say anything even close to that to my mother. He always just passively agreed with her. It was part of their script. She was the boss. His job was to defer to her ... always.

Though she kept a frown on her face, she let it go. Something clicked in her, like a switch being thrown. Her expression changed, softened. I've wondered over the years if she was thinking of her brother, Jack, at that moment. Weeks later, she would apologize to me, something else that rarely happened with my mother. "I don't want to lose you to this stupid war. This family has lost enough to their country. Let them find someone else to send off." What had happened to her patriotic demeanor? I hoped that my Uncle Jack was whispering in her ear.

At noon on the following Tuesday, I met Martin in front of the agreed restaurant. There was a very handsome young man with him who looked to be at least 10 years younger than him. He was tall, blond and tanned, looking like he spent a lot of time on the beach in Santa Cruz. Martin said, "John, this is my lover, Bernard." He beamed as he spoke the word, just as Bernard extended his hand to me. I was in complete shock because he had said "lover." The thought had occurred to me more than once that Martin might be gay. But here was the real deal standing in front of me.

Bernard was a lively character, full of stories about law school and his life growing up in Santa Barbara. I would look at Martin occasionally and see him staring at Bernard. Their story was an interesting one. Martin had met Bernard a few years before on a tour of the law school that Bernard attended. Though it took courage to ask, Martin had made a date to come back to the school the following week to take Bernard to lunch. He wasn't sure if Bernard was interested in him. At the end of the meal, Bernard had taken Martin's hand and held it.

They recounted the early days of their dating phase. They traveled back and forth between northern and southern California to be together. While Bernard was still in law school, he moved up to San Francisco to be with Martin, and he stayed in Santa Barbara during the week. Bernard returned to their home every Friday night. He had just graduated from law school a few weeks before our lunch. We toasted my new 4-F status and Bernard's life change. No more traveling back and forth between law school and Martin anymore.

The meal went by quickly, and I bid them goodbye, walking down to Market Street to catch the streetcar back home. How nice it would have been to have a romance like theirs. Maybe that would be the next step for me. I was so relieved to have the draft issue behind me.

My mother would go on to join a group of Korean War veterans' families who petitioned the War Department to erect a Korean War Memorial section at Arlington National Cemetery. She wrote several letters, including to her congresspeople, imploring them to remember the soldiers who gave their lives for our country. The group also requested that the government stop calling that war a "conflict" and rename it as the Korean War. The government did eventually make the change. My parents lived to see the memorial after it opened at Arlington.

After my father died, my siblings and I were cleaning out my parents' house and found a mildewed box under his bed. It belonged to my mother who died eight years before. I knew this because of what I found inside. It was the rest of Uncle Jack's life. The life that neither my mother nor grandmother wanted to remember.

Inside the box were years of Mother's Day cards to my grandmother from Jack. His Boy Scout medals. Grammar school class pictures. Report cards. His Scout neckerchief. A newspaper article about Jack and the other Scout honor guards who attended the first United Nations meeting in San Francisco. Birthday cards to him. Baby cards received when he was born. The silk material he sent home from Hawaii on his last trip before shipping out to Korea.

In the basement I found his personal photo album. It covered the period right up until he left for Korea. A particular pretty girl showed up in many of the pictures, including a final one on New Year's Eve before Jack left for basic training. There were humorous shots of Jack and his friends, taking turns wearing a strange diving helmet they had acquired from somewhere. I had a vague memory of that diving helmet from when I was little. It used to sit outside the back door into our yard. It was there for years, then it vanished. I took the album home with me.

We eventually donated the red boat to the model boat club at Golden Gate Park. I always hoped that someone got great pleasure from having that vintage boat. I pictured it with a new, crisp sail, gliding silently on the glassy surface of the lake.

I sometimes feel guilty for the decision to challenge the draft. But I really can't imagine what life would have been like for me in the Army. The Vietnam War always seemed tainted to me. There didn't seem to be a way to win that war. Among my friends who did serve, few came back without serious, lingering mental and emotional issues.

I do wish that Uncle Jack had survived and returned to people who loved him. He never had a chance to marry the pretty girl in those photos or watch his kids grow up or buy a house or die of old age. He will forever be a war hero and an enigma to me. Whenever I recall his Army portrait hanging on the wall of my childhood home, I am reminded again that he died while I got to live.

Born in San Francisco, John Lucia (he/him) moved to Portland, Oregon, in 1994. He traveled the country by RV for 10 years, working remotely at times. He's worked mostly in accounting management, having had some early forays into floristry, secretarial and property management. After spending over 10 years in Tucson, he came back to the Pacific Northwest to enjoy the beauty of the area. This is John's second published story. His first was part of the Defining Moments *anthology in 2023.*

Bus to Oakland

Graduations

By Natasha Nunn

It's 1989, I am 14 years old, and every morning I have an hour-long bus ride to school. The bus is empty when I get on but fills up quickly as we travel down Range Road 11 and circle through Treasure Island Estates. We stop at almost every house in the estates—from the half-finished ski chalet, to a couple of newly built McMansions, to Emily's small brown bungalow.

The bus is a microcosm of all the uncertainties of junior high school. Each year, we move another row away from the front of the bus. In grade nine, I am only two seats away from the prize of the back seat. Except that's where Emily sits—on the days that her stepdad doesn't drive her to school. She's the queen in that coveted seat, backcombing her hair as high as it will go, smearing bright pink lipstick on her full pouty lips. She swears a lot, using words I've never heard of, even though I thought I knew every bad word there is to know. People at school whisper that she's a slut.

Once she invited me to sit with her in that back seat. She did my hair—yanking and teasing my bangs till my eyes watered. She told me I had a nice forehead. Every day after that, I hope she'll be on the bus, and if she is, I try to catch her eye, ever hopeful she'll invite me to sit with her again.

Emily never acknowledges me when we are at school, but one day she stops me in the hall.

"Doug thinks you're cute." She catches her lip between her teeth for a second as she relays the news.

I know who Doug is, but only in passing. He's one of a group of guys—including Emily's on and off boyfriend, Mark—who move through the school with impunity, the hallway river parting as they hunch along or bang on the lockers. The thought of Doug noticing me without me knowing seems like a failure of my warning system. My cheeks redden, but to say that I'm blushing does no service to what I'm actually feeling. Heat is rushing through me and charging up to my cheeks to blotch my neck red.

"Well." Emily steps close to me as if she's a messenger taking important news back to the king. "Do you like him back?"

I stand frozen in the mess of the school hallway, half-open lockers, brown-bag lunches spilled on the floor, the smell of rotten apples and bleach. All I want is to get away, to retreat to some other place, a bathroom stall, home. But at the same time, the energy pulsing through me is new and brilliant, and I want it even if it's scary.

"Yeah. Yes. I like him."

My answer is relayed. At lunch Doug and I meet outside and walk through the wide field across the road that rings the school. There's a frozen pond in the distance where, in the summer, old men cast their lines for fish they've stocked themselves. Doug doesn't hold my hand. He talks about his truck, about how his dad bought it for him, and how he's refurbishing it in his garage so that, as soon as he gets his license, he'll be able to drive me around town, maybe even into the city. He says the truck is red and that I should come to his house and see it. I walk at the same pace as him. I don't say anything except yeah and hmmm. In my head, a stream of questions. Is it really a conversation if only one person talks? Has he ever had sex? If we drive his truck out onto the iced-over pond, would the ice break, would we sink?

At the end of our walk, he leans down and presses his lips against mine. I wonder if he's my boyfriend.

Over the next couple of months, as we approach the end of the school year, there aren't many interactions between Doug and me. Emily and I go to his house and watch him and Mark play Mario Brothers. I sit in his red truck up on jacks in the garage, one wheel missing. We kiss in his basement while listening to *Bizarre Love Triangle* by New Order.

On the night of the ninth-grade graduation party, my best friend, Angie, and I pool our money and ask someone's older brother to bootleg for us. We know nothing about alcohol, so we ask for a two-six of cherry whiskey. We start drinking in her room as we get ready, wincing as we chug the burning saccharine liquid straight from the bottle. We finish the entire bottle by the time we get to the party.

I wander around looking for Doug, but what I'm really looking for is my balance; what I'm really looking for is a way to hold on as everything slides off the face of the party and down into a sickening wave. I'm so drunk that the bonfire spins out over and up into the streetlights and the stars. I trip and fall against Mark.

"Da know whar Doug ish?" My slurring words sound like a dog drinking water.

Mark has a thin, black mustache, a long rat face. He is taller than me and wears a hoodie with a white clown face on it. The clown is sticking out his tongue.

"Let's go look for Doug." Around the fire, the faces of the other kids float in the black sky. Bile in my throat. I swallow, shake my head to clear it, which only makes everything spin and settle and spin again. I hold onto Mark's arm as he leads me away from the fire. Down a hill. The firelight fades. Trees loom. He holds tightly onto my arm. He spins me around. Or is that the whiskey? I'm on the ground. Leaves in my hair. Or am I standing? I open my mouth to say no, but he's talking over me. Mean words. Something about sluts. Something about what I am that I hadn't known till now. Then pressure. Dead weight on my bones.

I wake up at home in my single bed. My head feels sawed open and raw to the sunlight streaming through my bedroom window. My ears are ringing as if I'd been listening to loud music all night. My body speaks in a way I've never heard before. It's a quiet message, but it swells like tears, blooms like blood in water. I'm not me anymore. Before this, I had known who I was by not having to know, by simply inhabiting what I had always been. But this thing that happened split me in two: a body and a witness. A body I could not protect and a powerless witness.

My mom had picked me up at the party, stopped twice to let me puke on the side of the road. She strong-armed me up the stairs and into bed. She didn't notice the blood on my pants. When I come down from my bedroom, she gives me a firm talking-to about the dangers of alcohol. Boys will take advantage. I don't know how to tell her it already happened.

On Monday, on the bus home from school, Emily invites me to sit with her in the back seat of the bus. She tells me Mark told her that I'm a slut. I seal my mouth. I can see the word rolling off of her and onto me. It's a naming, a naming by someone who is already named and knows exactly what it means. I've heard she'd slept with her stepdad—that her mom had offered her to him. The bus smells of gasoline and hairspray; the windows smudged with handprints and fogged with the exhales of bored kids. The seat is torn, and I pick at the fluff underneath. We lurch down the long gravel roads. The dust picks up behind us like a cyclone.

"He's a dick. Don't listen to him," Emily says in her husky voice. With those words the sun cuts through the dust. She squeezes my hand, and I want to kiss her. All the painful electricity that's been running through me since waking up from the party dissipates, and I hold my head high. Slut that I am.

Two years later, it is Emily's grade 12 graduation, and I am at that party too. I have been invited by a boy I hardly know. I'm getting used to boys liking me. I've had an older long-term boyfriend who taught me everything he knew about sex. I think I'm a grown-up in the way only a 16-year-old thinks they're grown up. The graduation dance and banquet are at a hotel on the edge of the city. We drive there in a cave-like limo. Emily and Mark are in the limo—they're back together for something like the 10th time. He doesn't look at me, doesn't even seem to notice I exist. Chris, a joker I know from biology class, sticks his head out the sunroof of the limo and yells some exuberant swears onto the freeway. He's wearing a silver tuxedo and has his hair cut to make him look like Spock from *Star Trek*. The limo driver rolls down the partition glass to tell him to shut up. Chris makes me laugh. I've been to his house once—a group of us went to watch MTV in his basement. His mother came in with a plate of snacks. She asked him to clean up the glasses off the table. He rolled his eyes, but also said thank you for the food, and took the plates and glasses upstairs. I heard his mother tell him she loved him, and he said, "I love you too, Mom."

The boy I came with hands me a glass of champagne. It tastes rotten. I squirm in my pantyhose, which feel like plastic bags wrapped around my thighs. I'm wearing my sister's red dress, but being in that limo with rat-faced Mark makes me wish I was wearing pants and a hoodie, makes me wish that my hair was pulled back in a simple ponytail instead of piled on my head like an elaborate wedding cake.

The graduation dinner is in the basement of the hotel in a large convention room. The round tables are decorated with pink plastic flowers. Most of the waiters are only a few years older than us, and they pour all of us wine even if we don't ask for it. I eat the chicken breast in white sauce too quickly. It's dry and turns into a thick paste in my mouth that I swallow down in small batches. As the night wears on, the waiters look annoyed at the mess they'll have to clean up, the cigarettes put out on the plates of food, and the napkins pushed under the tables.

After the food is cleared, the waiters move the tables to the side, revealing a round dance floor surrounded by carpet. There's no DJ, just music pouring in from some speakers. A set of blue lights focus on a disco ball while a smoke machine spews noxious fumes. I dance with the guy I came with. He's tall and uncoordinated. Emily and Mark dance beside us. Emily's wearing a black and gold dress that clings to her curves. The slow song ends and Madonna's *Like a Prayer* comes on loud over the speakers. Emily and I start dancing together. She moves like a goddess, all slow hips and smooth lines. I keep up. I can also turn my body into a serpent, a moving stream of light. We don't touch but dance in unison. I see, from the corner of my eye, people standing and watching, but I block them out, focusing only on the movement of her body, the way her knees and hips and shoulders move one after another like a slow morning dream. She comes closer, puts her hand onto the swell of my hip. I keep my snake-like rhythm. She matches me. I lean into her. She moves back so my face comes close to her neck. She smells warm and smoky. I lean away, and she comes towards me. She is pressed fully against me now. We kiss. Her lips, her breasts, her tongue, all impossibly soft and firm, alive, overwhelming, like the squeeze of a boa constrictor.

"Fffwwwwwwhhhhhhheeeeeeeeeeeeeeeeee." A loud obnoxious whistle. The kind made by sticking your fingers into your mouth. I break away from Emily and come back into the room like plunging into a cold pool. The smoke machine hisses, and I wish the smoke would obscure me completely. Emily is grinning. She doesn't seem worried by the whistle or by the girls holding their hands over their mouths as if in some primordial shock, whispering, "*Lesbians. Dykes.*" This is 1991, years before it's considered cool for two girls to kiss, years before Katy Perry croons, "I kissed a girl and I liked it." Maybe we are on the cusp of those changes. Maybe we are canaries in the coal mine. I step back from Emily and try to keep dancing as if nothing is happening. I look around for an ally, but none of my friends are there. But I do see Mark. He isn't hollering or whispering. He's looking at Emily and me with hungry rodent eyes that make the tops of my feet hot. Those eyes flash a memory of that night two years ago—the hulking trees, the spinning.

I head to the bathroom to hide. I sit in a stall and look at the graffiti—a few names, a couple of hearts. There's a run in my stockings, thin at the knee and widening up my thigh. My skin is translucent and plump under the ladder of the run. I wish I could beam myself home like *Star Trek*, but I'm supposed to stay in a hotel room with some other girls so no one has to drive. After sitting in that stall for almost an hour, I skirt the dancing and take the elevator up to the third floor where our rooms are. The elevator smells of stale smoke.

I'm fairly certain I'm supposed to be staying in room 304, but I have no key. I knock, hoping one of the other girls has already come up. Mark opens the door. His face in the shadows. He smiles menacingly, grabs my arm, and pulls me into the room. There are six or seven guys in there, hulking on the beds and the floor and the worn hotel chairs. The air is thick with smoke and the smell of alcohol passed in sharp sweat through the skin of teenage boys.

"Well look who we have here—now we just have to find Emily, and we can have ourselves a show." My belly goes hollow. The room is too full, the many male bodies speak to me of terrible things. I turn to leave but Mark steps between me and the door.

"Stay. Hang out with us. We won't bite."

I want to bite Mark, tear his lips off with my teeth.

"Let me out of here."

He grins, reaches his hand out towards me. I slap it away.

"Oh feisty." He isn't talking to me.

"I like that." He has a pimple on his cheek that's so close to bursting you can see the pus under the skin. "You weren't so hard to get last time."

The other boys in the room are very still as if they haven't figured out what is going on, as if they are frozen in place. One of them has a slight cock to his head like he's asking a question. The air conditioner kicks on and blows the curtains up like ghosts. I look around for allies for the second time that night, and I see Chris sitting behind another boy on the bed furthest from the door.

"Chris?" I hate how my voice trembles when I say his name.

"Mark let her go." Chris stands up. His face knitted with worry but also with a quiet strength beneath his ridiculous, black bangs.

Mark seems shocked that Chris dares to confront him, shocked enough that I'm able to duck around him and out the door. I fly down the long hotel hallway, my claustrophobia increasing with each identical door I pass. Behind me the laughter of the boys bounces off the walls like the braying of donkeys. I push open the door at the end of the hallway and tear down three flights of stairs and out into the side parking lot.

The moon is a silver ball illuminating the dull gray concrete. Directly ahead of me cars sweep past endlessly on the wide freeway. I sit down on a curb and look down at my legs. The run in my pantyhose is now huge. I stick my finger into the run and pull, pull so hard that the run rips down my leg. I kick off my shoes and wiggle the stockings off. The coolness of the concrete on the backs of my legs is shocking, but I don't move. I let the cold come right into me.

I decide that I'm not going back to that hotel. When he'd dropped me off, my dad had said, "Remember. You can always call us." So, I walk to the gas station and call him. I don't tell him what happened. He asks if I am drinking, and I say, "Not much, and please can you just come pick me up?" He sighs and says, "Of course."

At home I open my bedroom window and crawl out onto the roof. The view spreads far out to the south; the fields like a silver wash of paint under the blue-black sky. I light one of my dad's cigarettes, which I'd managed to sneak after he'd left the truck and lay back onto the scratchy shingles. I let my mind drift back to that hotel room, to what Mark wanted, to what could have happened. I think of dancing with Emily, of how she and I had created a golden bubble in that hotel basement. I try to memorize her soft lips, the feeling of her skin, her body moving against me. Her smell. We were a shining treasure surrounded by hoarding dragons.

We are something to be coveted. I can imagine being one of those desperate rats, how I would salivate and want, how I would put us in a cage and keep us forever.

Natasha Nunn (she/her) is an academic librarian and writer based in Northern Alberta, Canada. Her work explores the intersections of identity, family, trauma, and resilience. Passionate about the transformative power of literature, she believes the stories we tell shape how we understand the world. Natasha is currently working on a memoir. You can learn more about Natasha at nnunn.ca.

Graduations

Pride Is Resistance

by Brandy Penner

From birth, I was defiant. I was born to a 22-year-old mother who weighed 125 pounds when all six-and-a-half pounds of me came into this world—breech, ass first. Three years later, I was diagnosed with ITP, an immunodeficiency blood disorder. After one spinal tap, months of steroids, and weekly blood draws, I was given a clean bill of health. As an only child, latchkey kid of divorced parents, I became adept at being independent at an early age.

Along with that independence came a strong sense of self and a clear sense of right and wrong. As a young feminist with a burgeoning understanding of the world's injustices, I became a social worker. Social work trained me in pragmatism, and I quickly understood that helping others would never solve the world's problems. But my work would be worth it if I could help one person a day.

My first job out of undergraduate school was at a confidential domestic violence shelter in Eastern Washington State. I supported women and their children who had fled from violence and were hiding from their abusers. Many were from distant states and landed here through various connections and organizations.

Many of the women suffered through addiction and untreated mental health issues due to lifetimes of trauma and violence. Many had never been safe, and while they were safe at our nondescript house in a blue-collar neighborhood, we all knew what the statistics said. Most people go back to their abusers several times before they leave for good. Some are never able to leave.

Yet here they were, trying to find safety. Many came to us, leaving their old lives behind, with only the clothes on their back. They were simply trying to save themselves and their children. This is defiance.

In graduate school, I worked with HIV/AIDS patients at New York Presbyterian Hospital's Center for Special Studies on the Upper East Side of Manhattan. Did you notice how the name of the clinic gives no mention of HIV/AIDS? Of course, you did, and so did the founders who started the program in the mid-1980s at the height of the epidemic. The name reflects the intense stigma that caused the virus to go unaddressed and untreated for an inhumane amount of time. I met men who had been infected for decades and who were the first group to have lived with the disease. They were the early survivors who were now passing. They lived lives that defiantly spanned 20-plus years after their diagnosis.

One patient exuded a calm confidence, having outfoxed the virus far longer than expected, and had a twinkle in his eye even as he lay in his final hospital bed. I am certain that he spent many days deep in grief, anger, and sadness. In the end, he was boldly defiant in transitioning to death, just as he was defiant in how he lived his life.

Professionally, I took a break when my partner, Miles, and I began having children. We had met unexpectedly at a university alumni event in Portland, and while I wasn't looking for a relationship, he was such a catch I couldn't say no. He was the first person I had dated who was stable, fun, and up for adventure. Little did he know that his best pickup line was, "Yes, I have a job and my own house."

When we decided to have children, I wanted to stay home and throw myself entirely into figuring out these tiny humans. We had Olivia, followed three years later by Elliott, and two years later Phoebe boldly arrived to finish our family. After five years of newborns, babies, toddlers, and preschoolers, I finally had a child in school and a little more breathing space.

I quickly volunteered to support the classroom at my child's school, mostly because I was anxious that my precious 5-year-old was in a huge school. I wanted to get to know her teacher and classmates. At my first parent group meeting, I was met with a tray of samples of cauliflower "popcorn" from the onsite garden teacher and chef, a position funded exclusively through the very active parent group.

I was stepping into a well-oiled machine that raised six figures annually to pay for everything from full-time staff to technology. I hadn't participated in this level of organizing before, and it only took one fundraiser to realize that these groups were raising hundreds of thousands of dollars and creating a rich experience for public school students.

A decade into domestic life, I had perfected my freezer sauce recipe, learned how to grow and can just about anything, and decorated and redecorated our house too many times to count. In the fall of 2015, I found our next family project: an uninhabitable 4000-square-foot house on 20 acres in Willamette Valley's Wine Country. Miles and I looked at the house on a cold, rainy October afternoon. Our real estate agent thought we were nuts, making her drive up the steep, half-mile, seven switchback, gravel driveway in the middle of what felt like nowhere. While ominous, even the deer carcass on the road out front could not stop me.

At the top of the hill stood a dark, overgrown, Pacific Northwest, lodge-style house. It had been built in 1980 and never touched again—everything was original, down to the interior paint, which had yellowed over time from cigarette smoke. While the real estate ad mentioned views, all photos featured an outdated, uninhabited monstrosity of a house slowly being overtaken by the surrounding forest.

The house had been empty for two years since the previous renters moved out due to its deteriorating conditions. They were having a baby, and the incessant buzzing from the thousands of honey bees in the rafters and the other creatures beginning to take over was an issue. A roof leak fed the slime mold growing on the living room carpet, which was prone to shoot out a cloud of spores when the front door was opened. One closet mysteriously had a light fixture full of water that would slosh around when the switch was flipped. The house smelled like a combination specific to the rain forests of the Pacific Northwest, the competition between decay and growth.

Once outside, we took one look at the view, and we were sold. Though the house was being reclaimed by nature, the view was breathtaking and magical. Set up on a hill facing west, it had an unobstructed view of the horizon over the Coast Range, guaranteeing a year of stunning sunsets. To the north, neighboring vineyards lined up their neat rows, growing world-renowned Pinot Noir. Facing east and south, the views offered pristine forests of Douglas fir, noble, and maple trees. The house could be fixed; the view was priceless.

We spent the next nine months tearing everything down to the studs. We kept the sweeping beams of the vaulted ceilings and towering three-story Timberline rock fireplace, and that was it. Everything else had to go.

I designed the space and chose all of the materials. Miles and I dove into learning about HVAC systems, sprinkler systems, and cabinet pullouts. From the clearances needed around toilets to window trim types, we rebuilt, replaced, or removed everything in that house. The project became all-encompassing and dominated all aspects of life.

We spent the final summer months camping in the front meadow. A combination of optimism and idiocy drove me to purchase a 1995 pop-up tent trailer on Craigslist. It served as our home once we sold our perfectly lovely house in Portland until the farm was completed. While using the contractor's port-a-potty, as it was our only bathroom at the time, I did question my life choices. In September 2016, we finally moved into our mostly finished dream home. Then came November 2016.

After the 2016 election, I immediately questioned our decision to move our family to a rural area. My idyllic dreams of raising free-range children came crashing down. Now my concern was about a possible reality in which we were raising them in a red county surrounded by people who were sure to hate us.

Desperation drove me to gather friends and travel to the Women's March in Washington, DC. I had never been to a proper march before and was a bit nervous about what to expect. Well, I wasn't nervous until my grandmother told me to be careful and stay close to exit routes. What hadn't she told me about her life?

As I gathered with hundreds of thousands of women from across the nation on that cold, grey January day, I knew this was a life-changing experience for me. I had never been around so many people. Women climbed onto trees and on top of walls to see the speakers, women in their 80s, and young girls marching together.

We were there to share our collective outrage, fear, and sadness. To visibly show our courage and defiance in the face of an unapologetic, misogynistic, hateful man becoming our president. History has shown that our crowd was much larger than the sparsely-attended inauguration and our collective outrage more powerful.

I took away one message from that experience: run for local office in your community. Now was the time to serve your nation by serving your community. I returned to my new home full of enthusiasm. I immediately realized I knew nothing about elected office. I had no idea what I could do in this isolated place where I knew only the grumpy neighbors next door. So I turned to what I did know: volunteering.

Soon, I became the local elementary parent group president because, if you show up, you will be given a job in schools. I enjoyed the small country school and made friends with other parents. But that message to "be the change" nagged at me. I remembered Michael Moore's message at the DC march: "You have to run for office. You! Yes, you!"

In the spring of 2017, I saw a small notice that the school board needed a representative from Zone 2. Digging a bit further, I learned I was living in Zone 2. I met with the board chair to learn more about board service and submitted my application that week.

A public interview at the next board meeting was scheduled, and I showed up, having never been to a school board meeting. I was the only member of the public there and the only person who had applied. Left with no alternatives, they voted unanimously to appoint me to the Newberg, Oregon, school board.

Over the next two years, I dove into the district policies, starting with the dress code. I became the chair and was elected to represent 11 area school boards at the state association. I enjoyed getting into the weeds of detailed policies and budgets and loved visiting classrooms and forming relationships with district staff. It was the best small-town living: easy civic engagement, a strong sense of community, and gorgeous rural living. We were living the dream.

In May 2019, two new members were elected to the board. Dave was a long-time resident and high school coach, married to a teacher, and known around town. The other newly elected member, Brian, was new to the community and ran on a fiscally conservative platform with a vanilla voter pamphlet statement. No one knew him, but based on his benign photo and middle-of-the-road platform, he easily beat the incumbent who was a young woman.

With the election of these two new members, the seven-member board was split between two progressives, three moderate members, and two extremists. While the new board member's true colors and intentions were not yet known, what was clear was that they were there to stir things up.

I was elected chair of the board in what was a contentious process that was a preview of the sexism to come. I served as a vice chair, taking the traditional route to the chair, and I had the support of the majority of the board. It was apparent that Brian had other ideas, as he nominated every man on the board, and he was shot down each time. As every male declined the nomination, I was the only remaining nominee and won the chair position. The cards were now shown.

In March 2020, public schools became ground zero in handling a contagious pandemic in a large public space. Would we be taking the temperature of every child as they enter the building? Could we mandate that everyone wear masks? How will the one nurse in the entire district implement a public health campaign?

We were deep in the process of determining how to conduct schools safely during COVID-19 when everything was ordered closed by the governor. Suddenly, every teacher, staff member, and child was ordered to stay home. In a district of 4,500 students, we now had an entirely different education system—one that none of us had experienced before. Questions now became how do we feed kids, how do we get internet access to our rural students and staff, and how long will this all last?

Systems to deliver education in this new reality were developed at lightning speed. The district IT department became the center of everything, as every student and staff internet connection was vital. School buses delivered food to students' houses, and the previously lightly-enrolled online school option became increasingly popular as parents juggled kids and classrooms in living rooms.

As the 2019-20 school year wrapped, we breathed a sigh of relief. We had completed and survived 12 weeks of virtual learning and were looking forward to a fresh start in the fall. As the 2020-21 school year approached, it was clear that students would not be allowed back into the hallways and that classrooms would remain empty.

Most system decisions regarding public education were made at the state level, and local school boards had little sway during the pandemic years. Tensions continued to rise on the board nonetheless, and as chair, I was confronted with the reality of how Brian and Dave were treating me. Staff and community members asked how I planned to address Brian's overtly sexist behavior toward me. Even on a Zoom screen, there was a palpable tension and dislike from all sides.

I attempted to take the high road and not comment on the poor treatment. When confronted with continued attempts to derail meetings and asked to add socially explosive topics to the agenda, I turned to procedure and policy.

Referring Brian and Dave to policy became a drinking game for those watching as people made bingo cards to follow along with the board meetings. How many times could Brian demand an outrageous ask, and how many times could I shut him down? It wasn't pleasant, but I saw it as my responsibility to ensure meetings were conducted according to legally-required public meeting standards and that the board's business should not be shut down or derailed onto tangents.

After all, there were only two extremist members and five moderate-to-progressive members to keep it all on track.

May of 2021 was an election year for three of the seven board seats. Incumbents ran for two seats; a third seat had two new candidates. When the polls closed, extremist candidates won two of the three seats. This would be the election that drastically changed the direction of the school board and district.

Of course, they didn't campaign as extremists. Both were white, middle-aged residents with no children in the schools and no experience in governing a school board. They campaigned on benign promises of fiscal conservation and parental engagement. Once on the board, their intentions became clear.

They were recruited to run by a group of political extremists explicitly because of their conservative views, not based on any interest in public schools or governance. They immediately focused on dismantling the school-based mental health center at the one high school in town.

This had been a years-long partnership between the school district and a local, large-scale healthcare provider. They regurgitated conspiracy theories about nefarious mental health practices and that parents should be the ultimate counselors for their children.

The focus on parental engagement and policing of classrooms would be a theme throughout the ensuing years. Of course, the hypocrisy was that, out of the seven school board members, I was the only one with children in the public schools.

This disengagement from public schools was again intentional. The members with school-age children either had wives that homeschooled or sent them to one of the Christian private schools in town. Private schools that denied admission to students had appalling test scores and were so focused on propagating faith that they couldn't meet basic state standards.

A narrative became clear. These public school board members wouldn't send *their* kids to public school until public schools stopped indoctrinating students by exposing them to new ideas and critical thinking skills. At this point, I lost count of the hypocrisies.

Over that summer, a new school board chair was elected. Now that the seven-member board had four extremists and three progressives, Dave was elected board chair. I made my objections clear in the public meeting, knowing that my arguments would find no footing or sway the direction of the chair election. I knew his tenure would be marked by flagrant dismissal of public meeting laws and chaos, but I wanted the public record to reflect his genuine threat to the school district's operations.

A school board has three jobs: fiscal responsibility for the school district, serving as a final judicial body in case of personnel or student issues, and hiring, supervising, and firing the superintendent. Those are significant responsibilities. However, the superintendent's purview extends to the district's daily operations.

Due to this structure, the relationship between board members, and especially between the chair and the superintendent, is vital. That relationship is in jeopardy if a board doesn't align with its superintendent or vice versa. I knew that the relationship between the board and superintendent would turn contentious with Dave as chair.

The first shots were fired in August of 2021 when the majority members of the board introduced a policy to ban Black Lives Matter and pride flags in all school classrooms. Their arguments ranged from the BLM movement being a terroristic organization to pride flags turning kids gay on sight.

Censorship is dangerous in the best of circumstances, but when introduced into an educational system, it can quickly turn learning into fear. Curiosity is replaced by fear, and learning is replaced with indoctrination. The very thing guaranteed to all students in Oregon—a free and appropriate education—is denied based on political ideology.

This was happening in my town. To my children. I had to stop it or, at the very least, go down kicking and screaming. Hundreds of people attended that virtual August board meeting, including the media.

As I sat in a hotel business center in Montana on vacation with my family, I joined the meeting on Zoom and read the following statement.

In the last few weeks, the board has seen engagement like never before. Students, staff, parents, and community members have shared their experiences in often deeply personal and heartbreaking detail. Thank you to everyone who has spent precious time to help inform the board in tonight's decisions.

Pride is resistance. There should be pride in a culture that has thrived despite violence, pain, and cruelty. Creativity and beauty thrive despite. Artists and poets brought the pain and beauty of Black and LGBTQ+ experiences to the forefront of our culture. Powerful voices like Audre Lorde, Nina Simone, and Mary Oliver. Powerful cultural influences like music, art, writing, cuisine, and fashion. Amazing and powerful forces that are changing our world. John Lewis, Martin Luther King Jr., and Harvey Milk elevated oppressed voices. Billie Holiday sang, "Southern trees bear a strange fruit, Blood on the leaves and blood at the root, Black body swinging in the Southern breeze, Strange fruit hanging from the poplar trees ...."

There is pride despite the brutal enforcement of oppressive laws and policies. Laws and policies that people like us create. Beatings and death for simply daring to be who you are. For being unapologetically out and proud. To be fully themselves always.

I am proud to be leading in a time when I have the opportunity and the privilege to be an ally. And right now, that means acknowledging that you matter. Don't ever stop showing your pride in who you are, what you are, or why you are. Never let someone else determine your worth. Be unapologetic and proud of who you are.

To my fellow board members, now you are in the position to create policies that will uphold a system of oppression and are attempting to eliminate policies that uplift and support students. You are attempting to create a system that will have to be enforced with no regard for student or staff well-being. You are forcing teachers and educators to remove signs of pride. Why? Because it makes you uncomfortable?

Ask yourself why it makes you uncomfortable, angry, and fearful? Why does the idea that someone other than you could be proud make you uncomfortable, angry, fearful? The idea that someone other than you, that someone who doesn't look like you or love like you could be proud, is problematic for only you. *This isn't about politics or other people. This is about you. You are leading, and you can choose to build or you can choose to destroy.*

Attempt to destroy, that is. Resistance subverts oppression, always. From the underground railroad to the Stonewall riots and the already newly designed signs of pride in our community, you can not oppress pride. What side of history will you be on?

To the staff and students in our community, you are amazing because you are you. All of you, not despite of but because you are you. What you may see tonight is not because of you. It is a misguided attempt to lessen the amazing you.

For every child, student, and staff member who is hurt, scared, and angry, regardless of the hate you see around you, stay bright. Remember, you are the best you that will ever be, so be unapologetically you always. All of you, loud and proud.

This is one more battle that has been forced upon you, and unfortunately, my friends, you have got to resist. We have all got to resist. You have got to fight for your basic inherent human dignity, and it's unfair, and it's hard, but this is the reality of your existence. As long as I am here, I will be in service to every student and staff member. I will stand up and support your right to walk the halls of your schools safely and proudly. Open and honest in who you are and in your hard-fought, rightful pride.

The majority members passed the policy during the board meeting. The battle lines were drawn.

By November, the relationship between the majority board members and the superintendent had devolved. The superintendent refused to uphold or enforce the flag ban policy and was fired by the majority of members in yet another contentious meeting. As the three minority board members stood by, the majority members fired the district leader two months into the school year with no interim in place and no plan. The wheels began to fly off, and chaos replaced governance.

The repercussions were felt in town and classrooms. Parent volunteers I had worked with on middle school fun runs were now asking the principal to check children's genitalia before they entered bathrooms. Dads who ran bounce houses at the school carnivals were now harassing the superintendent with dozens of drunken, rambling, abusive phone calls. Pride flags were being torn off of houses, and Nazi salutes were being captured on doorbell cams.

A month later, my oldest child wanted to begin cross-dressing, including in the halls of the high school. Our child was a freshman then and was known as Director Penner's son. "You know, the school board member, the one who is always on the news about the school board stuff." Even the most casual of civically-engaged citizens knew what was happening by now. Friends from around the world were reporting that their parents saw me on the local news. A friend on the East Coast who was responsible for closed captioning typed my name on a news broadcast in Ohio. Russian state media approached me, and I began to screen my calls.

Suddenly, this intense fight for human dignity came to my home. This was no longer even slightly theoretical; this was my baby. These hateful, broken people in power had their sights set on my kid and everyone like her.

We went shopping over winter break and bought feminine outfits that I knew would bring unwanted attention—cute dresses, boots, tights, and skirts. My child knew more than I did what walking down those school halls now as Penner's daughter in a dress would mean. This would be one of the hardest things she had done in her short life, and she did it.

At that moment, she was the bravest, most defiant human I had ever met. Here I was locked in a very public battle, and here she was in a dress, defiantly thundering through the halls of a high school that did not want her in a town trying to erase her existence. She was having none of it.

I was terrified for her. We knew the safe people in the school, her friends, and a lesbian counselor who continued to cover her office in pride flags. Yet I knew it only took a moment, one person, to hurt her and change our lives forever. I saw her trying to bloom in an environment with very little sunlight. She was using her dead name[1] at the time, isolated with few resources in rural Oregon and with a mother screaming from the rooftops. To say it was challenging is an understatement.

Yet she persisted. As time went on, she continued to transition and became more upset when people misgendered her. Since she was using her dead name, we asked if she had thought about changing it since names are often gender cues. She replied that girls could be named anything, and

---

1 Dead name is a term used to describe the birth name of a transgender person who has changed their name as part of their gender transition.

that was it. Her defiance in the face of intense social pressure did not surprise us. She was born screaming and rarely stopped, but it was a signal to us as parents that she was unapologetically growing into the woman she was always meant to be.

Immediately, my intense focus on the school board took a back seat to the development and support of my child. I had never had a trans friend or co-worker. No one in my family was out, and while they had grown used to my feminist rants, I had no idea what family would do with this new iteration of gender expression.

Sharing the news with family went as we expected. Elliott and Phoebe accepted it as nothing groundbreaking. Grandparents had many questions. Some worked to learn more, and all began using her pronouns and, eventually, her feminine name. Distant conservative aunts and uncles have never been disrespectful, but neither have they been curious or supportive. All our close and important relationships remained intact, and we collectively breathed a sigh of relief that the battle for visibility, love, and acceptance would not have to be fought in our home.

As the 2021-22 school year marched on, the rhetoric and dysfunction of the school board continued. Now, without a superintendent, a hasty search for one began. The majority of board members already had a candidate in mind: a disgraced superintendent from a tiny rural district under investigation for various issues related to student safety and bad management practices. He was a board favorite due to his conservative social stances, not because of his ability to run a school district successfully. He had left his previous two districts in disgrace and had no experience leading a large district. But none of that mattered.

In the shortened interview process, it became apparent that no other candidate stood a chance. The next superintendent had been chosen, not in a public setting but behind closed doors. The superintendent's firing and the subsequent sweetened deal they offered the replacement would cost the school district hundreds of thousands of dollars.

Compounding this financial hardship for the district were the mounting lawsuits brought against the majority of the board by parents, staff, and community members. Staff lawsuits claiming unfair hiring and firing practices, favoritism, and parent and community lawsuits for breaking public meeting laws were just the start of a prolonged financial downturn. While I was not named in any of the lawsuits, I knew the road ahead would be paved with legal and financial woes that I was powerless to stop.

By then, the board began to meet again in person, and the verbal bullying had ramped up. I was told that no one liked me, no one wanted me there, and no one wanted to sit by me. This happened in a boardroom of elected officials, not an elementary school cafeteria. It was laughable at the time to think that any of that would deter me from speaking out against their hate, but what it did do was show me that this was a broken group of humans. I had no hope that the ship could be righted, and all was lost.

Seeing the writing on the wall, I and the remaining progressive board members made a pact to step down together in the summer of 2022. We couldn't leave the other behind, and we couldn't stand being there alone.

By then, my family had decided to leave our home and our town. Seeing the dysfunction, the disregard for humanity, and the mounting legal and financial repercussions of the board's actions, I knew the school district would be in dire straits for years to come. I was not willing to sacrifice my children's education to these people's ideology.

We loaded a moving van three weeks after my resignation and returned to Portland. Leaving behind our farm, the beautiful home we had created, and the idyllic pastoral life we had dreamed of for our children, we returned to the city we knew would love us not for what we weren't but for what we were.

Leaving everything I loved professionally to save what I loved personally was not a hard decision. Turning my back on all of those kids and the beautiful community of supporters and change-makers was a tough choice. I was left with a sense of defeat and failure because I couldn't save everyone. Knowing that as hard as I had tried, I couldn't stop all of the ugliness that would now continue undeterred. The fact that the queer kid in an unsupportive home, facing homophobic slurs at school, would not have anyone in that boardroom to fight for them was gut-wrenching.

In May of 2023, with the support of statewide organizations like Basic Rights Oregon[2], the five-member majority was broken. Five new moderate and progressive members were elected, and the hold over the district would soon end. In November of 2023, the five members who illegally fired the superintendent were found financially liable for the cost. Including legal fees, each member owes tens of thousands of dollars to the school district and community[3].

Defiance isn't without consequences. When we take a stand, we do so without knowing how it will end. I stood up because I was driven to bring attention to unacceptable action. It was an easy choice to be on the right side of history. I'm proud of my work, my public defiance of hate, and that my children had the opportunity to see their mother fight for them. What wasn't easy was the personal toll, the stinging defeat, and my inability to end the hate and attempted erasure. The enthusiastic energy in which we enter a battle for good is only matched by the crushing blow when we don't achieve what we aim for. And yet...maybe the greater

---

2 Basic Rights Oregon is a nonprofit LGBT rights organization based in Portland, Oregon. It is the largest advocacy, education, and political organization working in Oregon to end discrimination based on sexual orientation and gender identity.

3 In May of 2024, it came to light that the district was facing a $14 million budget shortfall due to the gross mismanagement of the incompetent superintendent and his staff. Not long after, he went on leave and, as of 2024, remains a paid staff member, although he has no formal role in the district. He has since filed a lawsuit against the district, asking for $2.3 million in damages. That legal battle continues, as do the financial repercussions of these five board members. But if the past teaches us anything, it is that while justice may not be swift, we can hope it is thorough.

lesson is in losing. Taking the unpopular or minority stance, even when we know we can't change the trajectory, is defiance. If it were easy, we wouldn't call it resistance.

Author's Note

It's been two years since our lives took an unexpected detour back to Portland. When we purchased the farm and embarked on a rural journey, Miles wanted me to promise this would be our last house. Knowing myself and my wanderlust, I couldn't promise him that. But I promised to stay there until our kids were grown and out of the house. When the decision was made to leave, it felt devastating.

The disruption to our daily lives and children's lives cannot be overstated. We moved from this large house with loads of outdoor roaming space to a small apartment in a city that was experiencing an unprecedented level of homelessness and mired in a drug crisis. And it was the best decision we could have made.

I visited the elementary school where our youngest, Phoebe, would be enrolling as a fifth grader, feeling guilty that I was asking her to leave the small rural school she had attended since she was 5, just to have that followed the next year by the dreaded middle school transition. We were greeted by her new teacher, a gay man, in a classroom full of pride imagery. He was familiar with my work on the school board and thanked me for my advocacy. The classroom was warm and welcoming and embodied all of the reasons we were returning to Portland. It took everything in me not to burst into tears and hug this stranger! She had a great year and is now enjoying middle school, surrounded by friends and caring educators.

Elliott, our middle child, had to start seventh grade in a school where he knew no one. The counselors were on edge, sharing that the seventh grade is a particularly tough year to transfer. He jumped into his new setting and discovered his love of performing arts. He quickly joined the drama kids and finally found a good use for his booming voice. That summer, he also started sailing and is now a proud member of the high school sailing team. He would have never had the opportunity to experience this joy in his life if we hadn't relocated.

Our oldest, Olivia, is a thriving senior looking forward to starting classes at Portland State University next year. Relocating meant that we are now close to her medical team, and she has had easy access to gender-affirming care, something that most kids in the state cannot say. Moving into the city also meant that she could get her first job, have the freedom to walk to her favorite bookstore, and become a more independent teen. She loves Portland, the affirming LGBTQ+ culture, and the freedom to be herself.

When I think back to her life just three years ago, I can't even recognize that person. Before she came out, she was depressed, suicidal, and angry. Had we not been able to change her path forward, I fear she wouldn't be here with us today. It is because of the team of medical and mental health practitioners, a supportive and loving family, and her tenacity that she is thriving today.

I took a year to get everyone settled into our new home and schools and to mourn what was lost. Going from a massive, all-encompassing experience to a more normally-paced life was a considerable challenge. I fluctuate between relief, depression, and uncertainty. Remnants of my school board service keep rearing up. I was called to testify in one of the lawsuits against the five board members and realized that I couldn't remember large portions of events in some of the most contentious meetings. I could remember how I felt: the anger and disbelief that this group of people were tearing apart a community and, in the process, upending my life. I've come to better understand what traumatic events do to memory and nervous systems. We often downplay our trauma and fail to recognize the very real emotional and physical impacts.

While the kids were all adjusting to their new lives, I was unsure what was next for me professionally. Eventually, I found my way to a small nonprofit and began working full-time advocating for LGBTQ+ older adults. I don't miss the frantic pace of public service, but I do miss the significant impact that I had, and I hope to continue advocating on a large scale as we navigate what will be tumultuous years.

Brandy Penner (she/her) is a social justice advocate who currently works with LGBTQ+ older adults and draws

experience from supporting her transgender lesbian daughter. She holds a BA in Sociology/Social Work and has experience in public service as an elected official, campaign manager, people organizer, and program manager. Her favorite things are a love for travel, adventure, the outdoors, and a comforting cup of black tea with honey.

Sometimes Your Heart Needs a Break

By Stacey Rice

After laying on a hospital gurney for the last few hours, I was finally rolled out of the emergency room and down a hallway by a patient transporter. As a single row of fluorescent lights leisurely passed above me, I wasn't sure what was worse at the moment—finding out a short time before that I had suffered a heart attack or that my transgender self was in this hospital. My dilemma followed me down the hall and through the opening elevator doors with the anxiety about having a heart attack winning out over my gender identity for the time being.

A couple of nights before, I was aroused from a deep sleep with a sharp pain in my upper stomach. It felt like a huge knot had taken over a space that was way too small for its size. What had I eaten during the day that would have caused this indigestion? I couldn't think of a thing. After a few minutes, I couldn't bear lying in the bed with the pain any longer, so I grabbed a bottle of Tums from the bathroom and headed down the stairs to my darkened living room.

I reached out for the blanket I had thrown over the back of the sofa before I went to bed, wrapped it around my body, and sat down in my favorite chair—the one whose fabric design reminded me of spinning galaxies of red and turquoise planets following orbital paths made up of intermittent yellow rectangles. As I sat there in my newly-made cocoon, I shoved a handful of Tums in my mouth hoping that the high concentration of ingredients embedded within would dissolve the strong and consistent discomfort emanating from what seemed like an expanding knot. Fifteen minutes spun by. Thirty minutes came and went with no relief. A couple of hours later, the pain slowly began to ease, and I fell asleep in the chair.

When I woke up, the discomfort was gone, but I was left with an odd feeling of detachment from my body—like my spirit had decided to take a break from the pain. Had my galaxy chair heard my pleas for pain relief and flung me into another dimension? I carefully got up from the chair, walked upstairs, and got in bed. Before falling asleep, I promised myself that if I felt any pain when I woke up, I would go to urgent care.

A couple of hours later, my alarm went off, and I drowsily wondered if I had dreamed the whole episode from the night before. I recalled my promise and made a quick scan of my body to see how I felt. "Okay, there is no pain, and I think I feel better. Sure, I do!" As quickly as that thought flashed through my mind, I felt a single sharp pain in my upper stomach. The universe was saying, "For goodness sakes, go to urgent care. You promised."

I drove 15 minutes to urgent care. As I sat in the quiet waiting room, I anxiously looked around, trying to guess why everyone else was here. Anything to take my mind off of the fact that I was sitting here. A nurse appeared, called my name and led me into a treatment room. I shared with her what had happened the night before. And after a few more minutes of questions and vitals taken, she left. Soon, a doctor walked in and said, "Describe the pain you were feeling last night." With all the casualness I could muster, I replied, "Oh, I had a bout of indigestion that seemed stronger than usual, but it's gone now. It was probably just my gallbladder acting up." She replied, "I want to listen to your heart." Her stethoscope slowly wandered around my chest and back. She stopped and looked up at me and then started another round of listening. When finished, she stood up and asked, "Do you feel any pressure in your chest or discomfort in your arms, neck, or shoulders?" I shrugged. "No, I don't, and I didn't feel any of those things last night either." She thought about what I had said for a moment, then said, "Well, we are going to run an EKG to check on your heart and to see if there is anything going on there." Going on there. That felt like it could mean anything, which heightened the anxiety I was already feeling.

The nurse came in a few moments later, pushing a cart that held the EKG machine. As she attached the machine's leads to my chest, I took a couple of deep breaths that were constricted by my apprehension. She finished attaching the leads and turned on the machine. I watched as a reddish-orange paper tape, slowly being imprinted with jerky, black ink pen strokes, poured out of the machine. Whatever was triggered by the electrodes and sent through the cables that snaked from my chest emitted some type of information that deeply held my fate.

After a minute or two, the machine stopped, and the nurse tore the tape off and said, "I am going to give this to the doctor." It wasn't long before the doctor came back in with a troubled look on her face and said, "A heart abnormality is showing up on your EKG, and you need to go to the hospital emergency room." She continued, "You can't drive yourself to the hospital in case something more serious occurs. You can either go by ambulance or call a friend to take you." Taking an ambulance seemed extreme. That's only for people who have experienced a major health crisis, not gallbladder issues. I told the doctor, "I will call a friend."

I left the emergency room and went outside to call one of my best friends. When she answered, I said, "I need your help. I'm at urgent care and need to be taken to the hospital emergency room." She was confused. "What happened? Why are you having to go to the emergency room?" I shared what happened the night before, the EKG results, and what the doctor said, and added, "I don't know what is happening, but I am starting to get really worried." I gave her the address and hung up. I sat down on the curb. It was a Sunday afternoon, and the drop-off lane was deserted. I waited, desperately trying to figure out how I had gotten here.

She picked me up, and 20 minutes later, we pulled up in front of the hospital's emergency room. I hopped out of the car, and she went to find a parking place. I walked through the giant automatic sliding doors into a large waiting room that was eerily empty but filled with blinding light from the summer sun. Weren't all emergency rooms jammed with people in some state of chaos? I spotted the only person in the room, who was at the check-in desk studying a pile of papers. As I approached, she looked up, deliberately slid over to her computer, and asked me for my name. "My name is Stacey Rice, and I was sent here from urgent care with maybe a problem?" Her head immediately jerked upwards like someone had violently yanked it from behind with an attached rope. She replied with seriousness, "Urgent care called and told us you were coming. You have to get into a treatment room. Now." She picked up the phone to call someone in the back to come out and get me. My friend had shown up by now, and before we could even sit down, a nurse appeared and took us back.

She led me towards a set of closed curtains, which she pulled back to reveal a treatment room, and asked me to lie down on the gurney that was centered in the middle of the room. As I settled in, she bombarded me with a rapid-fire list of questions. What happened, what prescriptions are you taking, and how are you feeling right now? The questions ended, and the ER doctor walked in and asked, "Stacey, what has been going on with you?" One last time, I tried to convince someone that it was just my gallbladder. I said, "I woke up last night feeling pain in my gallbladder area. It probably came from something I ate." In hindsight, I realized he felt sympathy towards me. He knew I was running from the truth. "Stacey, I will give you this: one of your symptoms does indicate possible gallbladder issues, but we are going to run a few blood tests to see if anything is going on with your heart."

An hour or two later, the ER doctor came back in with the test results and said, "Stacey, I wish I could tell you it's your gallbladder, but there is a heart muscle protein showing up in your blood work. Normally, the protein stays inside of the muscle, but if there has been any damage to your heart, it shows up in your bloodstream. The test we ran shows you have high levels of this protein. This means you had a heart attack and possibly an earlier one—maybe a month or two ago. I am very glad that you came in because if you hadn't and experienced another heart attack, you wouldn't have made it through that one." At a loss for words, I could only spit out, "But I didn't have any typical heart attack symptoms." He said in seriousness, "If I had a dime for every woman that comes into the emergency room with your symptoms and thinking it is their gallbladder, I would be able to retire. Women can have different symptoms than what is assumed to be typical." Why had I never heard this before? Was there a link between being a transgender woman and having these atypical symptoms? He added, "We will be moving you up to the cardiac floor for further treatment."

When the elevator doors opened, a nurse was there to greet us. "Follow me," she said. Once we got to the room, the gurney was lowered, and the nurse helped me move into my new bed. I was quickly attached to an IV, which started dripping a magical liquid into my left arm that the nurse explained was a medication to prevent me from having another heart attack. My room eventually quieted down, and through my bewilderment, I thought about all the things that had happened over the last eight hours. But then the thought I had dismissed earlier came roaring back: I am a transgender woman in this hospital.

Navigating any medical environment as a trans person is full of potential calamities. Each appointment, lab test, or procedure that I experienced filled me with dread. Would I be on the receiving end of transphobia this time? Would I have to out myself because my course of treatment was going to be affected by the remnants of my male body? I always assumed there would be some kind of issue that would arise from my gender identity and the interactions I had. Very early in my transition, I came up with a plan to combat this. I greeted everyone I came across with a big smile and an over-the-top friendliness that would hopefully win them over before they studied the computer and found the word transgender in my medical record. I hoped that all of these actions would soften up whoever was in front of me. I tried to make them think, "Oh Stacey is such a nice person," and hopefully blunt any transphobic tendencies welling up inside of them. I even exaggerated my Southern accent as there had been times that people I met were charmed by an accent they rarely heard in the Pacific Northwest.

But now I am in this hospital. One where a trans nurse friend of mine had worked and transitioned on the job while working in the hospital's ICU. Just a year or two ago, he had shared stories of transphobia that patients experienced here and what he had experienced himself when he transitioned. They were horrific. ICU nurses called trans patients "it" when they were out of earshot of the patient and also made fun of who they were. My friend's coworkers refused to use his correct pronouns during and after transitioning and belittled him every chance they got. He reached out to hospital administration for help with these issues but was given a happy talk, "Yes, that is a problem. We are working on it." Nothing was ever done to correct the issues. Now I was here—in this environment where trans people were neither respected nor valued.

First thing the next morning, the attending physician on my floor stopped by to introduce himself and to check in on me. After some initial conversation about my treatment, he said, "One thing we will have to do is pause your estrogen prescription because of the risk of blood clots with this medication. If you do have surgery, we will have to see how you are progressing afterwards and then decide when you can start it back up again." I began to panic. "I can't stop it. It is as necessary to me as the air I breathe. I can't, I just can't," was all I could say. He patiently explained how serious the medical risks were if I didn't stop taking the estrogen, especially with my heart's weakened state.

I barely heard him as I tried to comprehend what this meant. I had been on estrogen for sixteen years – what would happen if they took it away? Would I go through menopause? The estrogen had softened and feminized my facial features – would that be reversed? What about my body changes? It felt so cruel. The one thing I needed to live as my true self was also the thing that needed to be taken away to give me a better chance to live in this moment[1]. There was silence between us as I quietly weighed what felt like an impossible choice. After some time, I decided that I needed to live in this moment, so I quietly told him, "Okay, let's stop it."

I was still concerned about being transgender in this hospital, but my confidence in being treated well cautiously

1 After my surgery, I was sent home with my estrogen prescription still paused. I was told that when I came back in six weeks for my follow-up cardiology appointment, they would evaluate whether I could start it again. Almost every day during those six weeks, I would stare for a few moments at myself in the mirror to see if I noticed any facial changes. Some days I thought I saw the beginnings of my male face coming back. I also braced myself for any menopause symptoms that might show up, but none appeared, and I finally gave up looking at my face in the mirror. My estrogen was started back up at my appointment.

grew with each positive and affirming interaction I had with the parade of nurses, doctors, and lab technicians that came through my room. Some nurses were inquisitive and asked questions like, "What has your transgender journey been like?" More than a few people asked, "What do you think of Caitlin Jenner?" Caitlin had just come out the year before, in 2015, and I explained that her journey as a trans child was like many in the trans community, but before I could finish my sentence, they would jump in and say, "But she has a lot of privilege, doesn't she?" My only reply was, "Yes, she does."

* * *

The imaging done earlier had picked up blockages in two of my heart's arteries, but it wasn't clear how blocked they were. My doctor explained that performing an angioplasty would allow them to find out exactly how blocked the arteries were and to possibly clear and open them back up. He explained to me that angioplasty is a procedure that uses an inflated miniature balloon to push a blockage against the artery wall to make enough space for a tiny expandable metal mesh coil to be inserted to keep the artery open. The hope was that if my angioplasty worked, I wouldn't have to go through open heart surgery.

I agreed to this procedure, and a few hours later, I was taken to the operating room. Even through the haze of receding anesthesia, it felt like a very short time later that I woke up in the recovery room. A nurse came in, and I asked, "How did the surgery go?" All she would say was, "Your heart surgeon will explain what's next."

I was eventually rolled back up to my room on the cardiac floor where a small handful of friends and coworkers had stopped by to check on me. Soon, a doctor, one that I had not met before, walked through the door. He introduced himself to me and my friends in the room as my heart surgeon. He confirmed the short time I was in the angioplasty operating room by saying, "They attempted to unblock your arteries, but both of them were so blocked—one at 60 percent and one at 100 percent—that they couldn't continue with the procedure. That means we will have to do open heart surgery so we can bypass those blockages."

In his somewhat detached, unemotional voice, he shared the details on what my surgery would involve. I would be given anesthesia, and a large vein would be taken from my inner thigh to be cut up and used as bypass veins. My breastbone would be surgically sawn in half to expose my heart for the surgery. Then my heart would be stopped and attached to a heart and lung bypass machine that would do the work of those organs during my surgery. In the end, my heart would be restarted, and my chest would be sewn back up with metal wire.

He stopped and asked if there were any questions. One of my friends asked, "What will Stacey's recovery look like after she is out of the hospital?" The surgeon began, "Well, 'he' will not be able to drive for six weeks. 'He' will also need someone to be with 'him' around the clock for two weeks after surgery." I was puzzled. Why was he saying "he" and addressing the only male-identifying person in the room? Why was he even talking to my coworker?" As

I struggled trying to figure out what was happening, one of my other coworkers said loudly, "Her pronouns are 'she,' not 'he.'" The surgeon paused for a second, said, "Oh," and then started right back up where he left off with the pronouns. "He" will have to come in for a check-up a month after "his" surgery. Yes, there will probably be changes to "his" diet. And so on. It dawned on me that he was using "he" to talk about me. When I finally found my voice, I nearly shouted, "Stop, please stop! My pronouns are 'she,' and you know you are messing up, right?" He looked at me with a stunned and flustered look and stammered out, "Well, maybe I am not the surgeon for you." With that, he turned and walked out of my room into the hallway.

Oh my god, what had just happened? I quickly glanced around the room to see if anyone else knew. From the looks on their faces, I could see they were as puzzled as I was. Then it hit me. Oh no, this surgeon has a problem with someone who is transgender. With that realization, my wounded heart sank below the floor only to be replaced with a terrifying rush of vulnerability and anxiety that I had not felt since realizing at 5 years old that I was transgender. "Why did this have to happen now?" I whispered. I was already at a deeply vulnerable place, and now this?

Surely, he had seen my pronouns on my medical record. But I also knew in my heart he had seen I was transgender. Even as a trans woman, I can mess up pronouns. It always horrifies me, but I quickly apologize to the person and work as hard as I can so that it doesn't happen again. But this doctor didn't make any effort to use my pronouns even after he was corrected. It was like he said to himself, "I am not going to change what I think about this person and, for sure, I am not going to acknowledge who they think they are."

I said to no one in particular, "Where are my clothes? I am going home because it's not safe for me to be here." One of my friends said, "Stacey, you can't do that. You had a heart attack, and you need to have an operation." I replied, "Oh yes, I can leave. I am not afraid of dying, but it's not going to be at the hands of this guy." All I could envision was being on the operating table as he performed this delicate surgery on me while holding a hateful attitude. Maybe his mind would not be totally present during my surgery, and he would make a mistake—maybe a major one that took my life. I said once again, "Where are my clothes? I am getting out of here." The same friend pleaded quietly, "Stacey, you can't. Your heart needs repairing." My heart had just been broken again, now into a million pieces, not by another heart attack but by what had just occurred. I wasn't sure it could be repaired. However, the looks on my friends' faces convinced me. "Okay, I will stay, but it's against my better judgment."

* * *

Someone ran out to grab a nurse. Quickly the nurse came rushing in with a panicked and concerned look on her face and asked, "Stacey, what just happened?" I told her, and she replied, "Oh no, oh no. What do you want me to do?" All

I could think of was, "Please find someone who can help me with this," and she left the room to find help.

One of my other coworkers spoke up and said, "Stacey, I just gave a Trans 101 workshop to the staff in this hospital two weeks ago, and none of the surgeons showed up—said they were too busy. Would it help if I reached out to some of the people I know here?" "Some of the people" my friend knew happened to be the president of the healthcare organization that owned this hospital and a number of other people in higher positions. I replied, "Oh my gosh yes, can you do that?" "Of course I can."

It wasn't long before the fallout from my friend's phone calls started to materialize. The director of Diversity, Equity, and Inclusion stopped by my room, profusely apologized, and said, "We have been working on the issue of transphobia in the hospital and system, but it is obvious we have not done enough." Next, the head of the cardiology department showed up and said the heart surgeon had walked into his office and said, "I think I am going to be fired." I replied "Well, maybe." He continued, "You know he only used the wrong pronouns a couple of times." I angrily replied, "That's bullshit. He misgendered me multiple times—way beyond just two—and he wouldn't stop even after being corrected. There are no excuses for what he did." The department head looked at me and unconvincingly said, "I am sorry."

When he left, I was taken downstairs for more imaging, and while I was gone, the director of medical operations at the hospital had shown up wanting to talk to me. Since I wasn't there, he told the nurses to bring me to his office if that was possible. As soon as I got back to my room, the nurse rolled my wheelchair over to his office. He welcomed me and immediately said, "I am so very sorry that this happened to you. What happened is unacceptable and has no place in this hospital. We have fallen short, and I guarantee you that we will fix this. The surgeon you interacted with has been taken off your surgery, and a new surgeon will be assigned to you, and we will make doubly sure to treat you with the respect you deserve." I thanked him but also said, "Even before I showed up in this hospital, I heard stories of transphobic behavior here and the struggles that your trans employees were having in being accepted. The trans issues you have are systemic, and you need to do something about it. As part of that, you need to promise me that all the staff at this hospital, including the surgeons who say they are too busy to be bothered, will attend mandatory transgender competency training so this doesn't happen again. So what are you going to do?" He answered, "We will do better, I promise, and we will have those trainings." As I left, he gave me his business card with his direct phone number and said, "Please call me any time."[2]

When I got back to my room, the nurse asked, "How did it go?" I shared the conversation with her. When I got to the part about getting a new surgeon, she interrupted me to say, "Yes, your new surgeon has already been assigned, and he is the best heart surgeon that we have." She added, "I think you also need to know that the news of what happened to you has spread throughout the hospital and caused quite the commotion."

I soon was occupied with getting ready for surgery. I did get a new surgeon, and during our first conversation, he assured me, "I don't want you to worry, especially with what has already happened, but we will make sure to take very good care of you." And they did. I came through my surgery without any issues and was discharged a few days later.

2 When I got out of the hospital and back to work, I started calling the director of medical operations every two to three months to ask, "How are the trainings going? What have you been doing after the fallout from what happened to me?" His reply was always, "Well, we haven't done those trainings yet, but we hope to." And my reply every time was, "But you promised to do them." I called for a solid year and his answer never changed, and as a result, the trainings were never done. My frustration with his lack of interest in effecting change in his organization led me to start my own consulting business focused on advocating for the transgender community. Over time, I have led a number of workshops and trainings where I educate people on what the transgender journey is all about and the issues that the transgender community faces. And you can bet that when I get to the pronoun section of my workshops, I tell the story of what happened to me.

The next six weeks I spent at home, slowly recuperating. I wasn't allowed to drive during that time. If I did by chance drive, get into an accident, and receive any trauma to my chest before it had the chance to heal, it would greatly impair my recovery. I had visits from friends, family, social workers, and physical therapists. Everyone, including the new cardiologist I saw for a checkup four weeks after my surgery, said they couldn't believe how quickly I was healing and recuperating.

I spent an inordinate amount of time thinking about what I had just gone through. My heart had just given out, and it was a profound experience. I was lucky to still be alive. I realized that I had found the strength and courage to confront and face the never-ending stream of important and life-altering decisions that I was presented with. However, I was still puzzled with the "why" when it came to the interaction between myself and the transphobic surgeon.

Maybe my experience with him and the aftermath might help make things better for the trans people who would follow after me in that hospital, cardiac floor, or system? I was so very lucky that I had allies in the room who could stand up and advocate for me. If most trans people were like me, they would usually be alone in the treatment room when problematic things were said. A few times, I didn't say a word as I was fearful that speaking up might have made matters worse. A few months after my surgery, I went for my yearly checkup at my provider. When my doctor came in, I asked, "Did you hear about the kerfuffle that happened concerning me when I was in the hospital for my heart attack?" She looked at me with wide eyes and said, "Oh, I heard. Everyone in the entire system heard about what happened." Maybe, just maybe, other trans people will be treated better when they access services at this organization.

Were there any lessons for the surgeon? Hopefully, he now understands the importance of pronouns, but maybe it was for his growth as a human being to learn lessons about acceptance, compassion, and arrogance. If nothing else, he intimately knows now that karma is a hell of a thing.

However, the biggest reason eventually revealed itself to me, and it wasn't what I expected. It was that I realized my chest had to be cracked open so my heart could release the trauma it had been holding—starting at 5 years old when I found the little girl hiding inside of me. My heart was saying, "Okay, we need to take a break now. If we are ever going to get rid of this trauma, I need to take matters into my own hands." With the surgical saw that the surgeon used to open my chest, there was no longer a physical barrier between my heart and the outside world. The loneliness, vulnerability, stress, fear, anxiety, and lack of self-esteem and self-love came pouring out of me. My heart could finally launch all of my hard emotions out into the universe to be healed. I wish there had been an easier way to do this. But there wasn't.

After the launch, there were a few scraps of trauma left behind. One was the struggle I had accepting compliments as a result of my low sense of self-esteem. But a year or so after my surgery, I was at a large town-hall-type meeting in the LGBTQ+ community center where I worked. During the meeting, one of the attendees stood up, pointed at me, and started praising me for the work I had done at the center. With all eyes focused on me, I defaulted to giving my usual outward impression of, "Aw shucks, who me? I was just doing my job." This time, I caught myself when out of nowhere, an image of a small door frame containing two closed doors planted itself right in the middle of my chest. As the speaker continued and for some reason—maybe a divine one—in my mind's eye, I reached up to the small doors, grabbed their knobs, and swung the doors outward and wide open for my heart to take in the beautiful gift that was being sent my way. I could feel the warmth of my co-worker's compliments filling my heart and taking away the subconscious feelings of unworthiness. I have almost worn the hinges off those doors since then, but they are still hanging in there.

To this day, I still have visible reminders of my heart attack and surgery—a long scar down the middle of my chest and one that runs along the whole length of my inside thigh. I am proud of those scars. They are a constant reminder to me of what I went through and that I found more strength and courage than I could have ever imagined. The other reminder is a pillow that sits on my galaxy-spinning living room chair. When I woke up in the ICU after surgery, there was a very large heart-shaped pillow, covered in a light green fabric with pink seashells, lying on my lap. At first, I thought I was seeing things after the anesthesia, so I asked the nurse, "What is this pillow for?" He replied, "We give this to every open-heart patient. When you cough, hold it very tightly against your chest to keep the wire and stitches in your chest from coming undone. It wouldn't be a good thing if that happens, so use the pillow." I picked it up and marveled at what a beautiful reminder it was of my repaired heart and that maybe my heart was a bit bigger with the increased flow of blood coursing through it. As I continued to look at the pillow, he added, "There is a group of women who make these, and it is their gift for the heart patients. There is also a tag on the bottom that tells you who they are." I turned my new heart over, and there, on a cream-colored piece of satin stitched on the heart, were the words, "Stuffed With Love. Piecemakers of Milwaukie Lutheran Church."

I held that heart pillow tightly for the next couple of days while the coughing came fast and furious as my lungs tried to clear the fluid that had accumulated. But it became more than just that. I held it while thinking about the ultrasound machine that was rolled into my room early in my hospital stay. The doctors wanted to get information on the extent of damage my heart might have experienced due to my heart attacks. After the technician hooked me up, he turned on the machine and asked, "Do you want to watch? I am getting ready to insert a medication in your IV that will light up in rainbow colors as it passes through your heart and is picked up by the ultrasound." Oh, my goodness, rainbow colors! I replied, "You bet I do." As he turned the ultrasound screen towards me and before he injected the medication, I caught my first-ever glimpse of my heart. It was violently pumping in and out, and it looked like it was going to jump right out of my chest. I slightly panicked and asked the technician, "Is that normal, and is my heart supposed to be working that hard?" He looked at me with a smile and said, "Yes, always."

Stacey Rice (she/her) is a speaker, educator, consultant, and community leader on transgender issues. She has been recognized as a Queer Hero by the Gay & Lesbian Archives of the Pacific NW and is the former Executive Co-Director of Portland's Q Center. She is one of the stars of the documentary Who's on Top? LGBTQs Summit Mt. Hood. *The documentary profiles the lives of four LGBTQ+ community members and how they overcame the obstacles that stood like mountains in their lives. She was also a recipient of a 2023 Oregon Humanities Community Storytelling Fellowship. You can find her at www.staceyrice.com.*

The Improbable Advocate

By Scott Strickland

It was 1981, and I was a shy 20-something who had spent the previous two decades avoiding attention and hiding in the shadows. I was comfortable living in Minnesota, which was generally a progressive place even with some conservative elements that would occasionally rise up to bite me. A complicated childhood had left me with poor social skills. Fear defined me, whether it was heights, water, speed, strangers, and certainly the unknown.

I received a stern directive from the administrator of my internal medicine graduate program informing me that I was required to give an educational presentation to the medical staff. I was terrified. The administrator was not a sympathetic mentor to me. I knew there would be no compromise and no offer of support from him or the unfriendly medical staff. Conversing with one person was difficult for me. The thought of giving a presentation to the medical staff nearly paralyzed me with fear. What do you educate people about when they all know more than you do? These people could eviscerate me with one sentence. I wasn't sure I wanted to stay in graduate school. Quitting felt like a reasonable escape from this onerous task. Somehow, I decided to stay. It was the most courageous decision I ever made up to that point. It informed much of what happened over the next two years.

I considered myself to be openly gay, but all that meant was that I went to one of the local gay clubs on Saturday night and danced with other men. I was not part of the pre-AIDS gay culture and had no gay friends, although I chatted with other guys at the club. One Saturday, I overheard a conversation between two gay men. They were swearing off sex with others outside of their relationship because of the "gay cancer" that was being reported in New York and Los Angeles. I finished my drink and trailed off to my apartment wondering about this "gay cancer."

I went to the medical library the next day and read everything that I could find about "gay cancer" but came up empty-handed. A stack of new magazines was piled high on a table, and I thumbed through them. A small pamphlet had a lead article about a few cases of an odd disease showing up in homosexual (in the nomenclature of the day) men. They were developing unusual infections and cancer—the "gay cancer." The bibliography led me to the only other articles that had been written on the subject, which I quickly located and read. After reading all six, I had just studied everything that was known about what we would eventually call AIDS. It was time to start searching for a subject for my presentation to the medical staff next month, so I pushed all the magazines to the side. I started reading through the tedious text of medical publications for something but kept being drawn back to the magazine articles. At first I was concerned about my personal risk, but soon I chose it as the subject for my dreaded lecture. Maybe I could tell this bunch of old coots about something that nobody had heard of, and they wouldn't ask me too many questions.

I was a hot mess for the next month as I prepared for the presentation. The week before my presentation, I found my name emblazoned on the bulletin board outside the lecture hall. I walked by that room every morning and hyperventilated. On the day of my presentation, I shuffled into the room and slumped into a seat in the first row. The room was packed, and people were standing in the aisles. Normally, these lectures were not well-attended. What were all of these people doing here? My name was called, and I ascended to the stage. I turned to look at that room full of people and developed tunnel vision. I could only see one person in the room. I have no memory of what happened during the next 45 minutes, but as I finished, that one person visible in my "tunnel" raised his hand and asked a question. I knew the answer! Slowly, more of the room became visible to me as I relaxed and took a few deep breaths. The following 15 minutes were full of answerable questions and an enthusiastic round of applause as the ending time arrived. As everyone filed out, a friendly face approached me and asked, "That was interesting. Would you be available to speak at my hospital?" I assumed that he was talking to someone else but realized no one else was standing near, so I whispered "sure" through my bone-dry mouth. I had no idea what had just happened, but after 20 years of spinning my personal compass, it had just stopped and found a direction.

The next few months dragged on as I returned to my uninteresting job and my awkward social life. I never approached looking for work with any kind of intention. I had internalized the social expectation that I had to work, and I toiled at whatever came along. Enjoying my work was a total oxymoron. My current job was no exception. I was in an inner-city county hospital working with indigent patients who rarely wanted to be there and were often abusive. The other workers were also overworked and tired like me. Most were trying to get out of work, and a few tried to make everyone else look bad so they would look good. I was working long hours doing something I didn't care about and making very little money. There was constant tension. I had a few inconsistent friends and spent most of my time alone. I knew I was gay since I found a passage in an old dusty mid-twentieth century Encyclopedia Britannica that described "homosexual" in the sterile prose of the era. "Coming out" had been less of a personal journey for me than for others. It was nothing more than simply finding a gay club by accident one day and wandering in on Saturday nights. I never bothered to tell my family I was gay. They had not been part of my life for years and were not part of my support system since I graduated from high school. I didn't care what my family thought.

The one speaking engagement I agreed to after graduate school led to many more. Soon, I was traveling around talking about the new "gay disease" to anyone who would listen. Gay groups had an inherent interest and were easy to work with. A few social service organizations started to understand the potentially devastating nature of the developing epidemic. Medical groups occasionally took an interest. I developed some comfort with speaking as I worked with these supportive groups. I was also learning to relax, think, and most importantly, breathe—something I rarely felt that I could do as I grew up. Learning to breathe as I spoke made for more educationally valuable classes for the learners. These training sessions were also invaluable for me since working with hostile groups was soon to come.

Legionnaires' Disease had appeared a few years before, primarily in older men, after a conference in Philadelphia[1]. The public health response had been swift, and the cause, diagnosis, and treatment were quickly identified. It seemed that the same response would be forthcoming with this new and deadly disease. Instead, there was only silence.

---

1 The very early days of the AIDS epidemic are intimately tied to two significant events that happened in close proximity to the first recognition of a new disease. An obscure medical publication, *Morbidity and Mortality Weekly Report* (July 3, 1981), was the first recognition of an evolving new epidemic. Just five years before, in 1976, there was an alarming outbreak of a severe pneumonia in Philadelphia after a Legionnaire's Convention. A rapid and well-coordinated public health response quickly identified the cause, diagnostic criteria, and treatment. Within a year, Legionnaires Disease could be diagnosed and treated, and the public health system was credited with saving many lives. We were lulled into a false confidence that the same thing would happen with AIDS. As the months and years passed, it became clear that the public health system was fully capable of addressing an epidemiological emergency but not a social or cultural catastrophe. No effective nationwide response occurred, and what happened on a local level was often poorly coordinated and misdirected. While we reflected on the response to Legionnaires' Disease and waited for something to happen in response to AIDS, there were thousands of people becoming tragically and unnecessarily infected.

The other closely related event was the election of Ronald Reagan in 1980. His inauguration represented a profound cultural shift. Gay men had very little civil rights protection, and they certainly did not fit into the new conservative narrative. The public health community clearly understood what was occurring with the new epidemic, but the new federal government did not want to appear to have any association with sexual minorities. The response was silence. Street protests that started during this time used the tagline, "Silence=Death." This was both true and prophetic. The ensuing years of silence slowed an effective response but also allowed misinformation and false narratives to develop. Conspiracy theories abounded. Many people outside of the at-risk communities not only didn't understand what was happening but received inaccurate information that hardened into beliefs. Those beliefs became action and were fertile grounds for the counter protests targeting people with AIDS. The push for quarantining had its start in this toxic mixture of ignorance and fear of the unknown.

Months passed, and the silence continued as I started to get an uneasy feeling. Why was no one talking about it?

The state public health department asked me to talk at a community meeting, primarily advertised in the gay community. It was the first organized attempt to address what was mostly being whispered about. The meeting successfully brought everyone with a common interest together on stage, but the audience wanted no part of it. It was becoming very clear to me that the disease was sexually transmitted, which meant people needed to modify their sexual behavior. Some audience members saw it as an attempt to strangle the advances in a developing gay culture that had begun in the late 1970s. Halfway through the first presentation someone stood up and yelled obscenities while proclaiming that he was not going back in the closet. The audience was angry, we were unprepared for the response, and everything collapsed into a yelling match. I was always conflict-avoidant, and this was the worst possible situation. I fled the building and stood in the alleyway confused and afraid. My first attempt was disastrous, but it was a place to start. At least we gathered interested people together in the same room, and everyone could put names to faces.

The gay community on the East and West coasts were already experiencing what we were seeing. The federal government was ignoring the epidemic and refusing to fund research, education, and treatment. State and local public health groups were paying some attention, but the anxiety about being associated with gay people kept everyone at arm's length. The federal government coined the term "homosexual agenda" and fabricated a lengthy narrative around subversive activities within the gay community meant to spread the disease and use it as a tool to further special interests. AIDS was touted as a result of something gay men were doing (drugs) and ignored the clear epidemiological evidence to the contrary. A bizarre rumor that disco music was somehow involved circulated for a while. Many religious communities had already lined up to condemn the developing gay culture. They preached against the behavior of gay men, and AIDS was seen as a just outcome of the behaviors they preached against.

There were two successes that were finding some traction in the larger cities[2]. Local "AIDS projects" were tapping into the diversity of the gay community and partnering with any local organizations that had an interest in

2 I had the opportunity to travel to San Francisco to observe and understand their response to the developing epidemic. They benefited from several advantages prior to AIDS. Gay men had already achieved some notable advances in the late 1970s. Civil rights protection had been extended to sexual minorities, and city hall had seen the election of an openly gay supervisor (Harvey Milk) and a strong ally as mayor (George Moscone). The city had a robust health care delivery system with the world-renowned University of San Francisco Medical School, San Francisco General Hospital, and a progressive medical community. They were able to move quickly toward developing a compassionate and cost-effective system for managing patients. Outpatient clinics were established that consolidated care in one place and brought the best care to the patient. Hospitals established wards dedicated to the care of people with AIDS. Home care expanded, allowing more services at home. Activists pressured the political system to provide more funding and people to meet the increasing demand. The populace was comfortable with gay men, and the vicious backlash seen in other places never materialized in San Francisco. I learned the value of dedicated AIDS clinics and community-based AIDS projects and took those lessons back to Minnesota.

medical issues and were able to look past the stigma. We had some strong leaders in the gay community who were able to bring all of the interested parties together for meaningful problem-solving sessions. We were also lucky to live in a progressive community, and building bridges to established medical and political groups was met with some success. I was following the proceedings with interest and excitement until one day I got a call from our AIDS project organizing committee. They wanted me to be on the board of directors. I knew everything there was to know about the disease (which was still very little) and had developed some comfort with public speaking. I had no idea what a board of directors was, much less what I was expected to do. A trip to the business section of the library explained what a board did and the responsibilities of the directors. Yikes! I didn't feel I could do any of the things they discussed. The interim president of the board reassured me that he would help me hone my skills. I couldn't come up with a real or fictitious excuse not to join, so I agreed while still looking for every reason to back out. My default way out of frightening situations was to cut off my emotions. I hoped no one could see that I was a fraud. Confused and self-isolated, I kept moving tentatively forward. No one told me to stop.

We received reports about the successful opening of AIDS clinics in high incidence areas. In the early 1980s, health care in general was very fragmented. Patients were expected to travel around to access care and to advocate for their needs without the tools to stand up for themselves. AIDS clinics brought all of the health care deliverers together at one time, which facilitated better communication and put the patient at the center of the process. The AIDS clinics had supportive caregivers, which insulated patients from the increasingly hostile health care delivery system that was becoming hysterical about their personal risk of contracting AIDS from the patients. Patients were free to work on their own health, and caregivers could relax in a safe environment that didn't ostracize them. I felt a sense of belonging and freedom.

I became comfortable with the local Minnesota AIDS Project and found the other directors to be good mentors. I visited the AIDS clinic, which was providing good medical care but also showed me what it meant to genuinely care for patients. It was my first experience with empathy. At the end of the day, I would ask myself what I was doing, and again, I was certain that I would be found to be a fraud. What did I know about AIDS? I had only read the six articles from grad school and the handful that had been published since my original research. I continued to feel rudderless, overwhelmed, and often fearful. My direction was about to become clear.

Funding continued to be an issue. Federal funding for education was almost nonexistent, and any money that was available came with a rider explicitly forbidding use of the funds to "promote homosexuality." That included speaking about homosexual behavior, condoms, and less risky sex acts. A meeting was planned in Washington, DC, to address this and argue for funding for education. My nascent speaking skills were improving, and the board decided that

I should be the one to represent our region. All I remember was my panic and considerable gnashing of teeth. All of my familiar defense mechanisms rose to the surface. I could flee, feign illness, or miss my flight, but I kept myself moving forward. Walking into the meeting felt ominously similar to my grad school lecture hall and my first painful attempt at public speaking.

The meeting was facilitated by a well-dressed and attractive young man with a long title that assured us of his high status in the administration. He proceeded through the agenda with aplomb, handily listening to, and dismissing, the gathered experts. He also flirted with me—subtly during the meeting, more boldly during breaks, and explicitly in the restroom. I naively thought that our "connection" would bode well for a good outcome to the meeting. I excitedly watched his behavior as we returned for the remainder of the conference. At the end of the meeting, he snapped his valise closed and coldly explained to us that the administration could not be seen as supporting the "homosexual agenda." Funding would not be forthcoming, and he was sure that we understood why. He also whispered "faggot" in my ear and sneered as he sashayed out the door with his retinue in tow. I was bewildered and frightened. The enemy was clear, and it was us. This was to be the first of many painful examples of the power of internalized homophobia. We were beginning the war on AIDS. There would be an exhausting number of battlefronts.

As the door closed behind "Mr. Faggot," it became crystal clear to me what needed to be done. I had spent 20 years wandering aimlessly through my life. Learning about AIDS gave me direction. My compass was now laser-focused. The next 20 years, I would be totally engaged in fighting the good fight against AIDS and all of its corollaries. Beneath my evolving ironclad facade, I would still be the timid, insecure, and poorly socialized me. Eventually, that would come back to bite me, but that was still another 20 years away.

Our colleagues on the coasts were correct. A grassroots AIDS project and establishing AIDS clinics in every community were critical to our mission. We were blessed with strong leaders in the community who were gay or were our strong allies. They brought leadership to the table as we figured out what we were doing. An amazing person rose to the surface at the AIDS project, Eric, the first executive director. The project became the central clearinghouse for all things related to our cause. It was also where I would learn the ropes of leadership in a supportive environment with a dedicated team. I could relax and breathe. There was never any lack of people who wanted to help. We usually needed to triage what we did and hold some people back from being too enthusiastic. I sometimes felt a twinge of optimism. Later experience showed me that all organizations were not as functional as this one, which would temper my optimism. AIDS clinics were for the patients. They were protected from the hostility evolving about AIDS in society and health care in particular. Care was always excellent in the clinics, and the model was duplicated as a way to provide care in a cost-effective way in any clinical situation. Our initial optimism was soon to be dashed as clouds were gathering on the horizon.

Public fear drove the first wave of hostility towards us. It was clear to anyone in health care that AIDS was a sexually transmitted disease, probably a virus, but we didn't know for sure. The needed research was throttled by strict federal limitations on funding. People were genuinely afraid of contagion, but the link to sex and homosexuality made for a toxic mixture that we called the "afrAIDS." Education was my answer. I deduced that if people were informed, they would be less fearful. Knowledge may be power but the association with sex, particularly gay sex, took the conversation to an entirely different level. Along with an enthusiastic speakers bureau, we traveled the state talking to everyone who would listen.

The groups that we spoke to were small but generally curious at first. Medical groups, public health folks, and educators were courteously interested. My terror around speaking was waning, and I was more comfortable engaging with the audiences that we were attracting. The question-and-answer segments were lively, but I often felt a little distance between the speakers and the attendees. They assumed that the problem was in another place and would not affect their community. Questions were usually in the third person. There was an occasional hostile side comment. When I was discussing confidentiality, one physician muttered, "What about our rights?" An audience member noted that "they" were responsible for the consequences of "their" behavior. Someone else exclaimed, "Oh gawd," when I was explaining condom use. The comments were isolated at first, and I fell back on my old habits. I moved on without comment. I was comfortable denying the situation because then I wouldn't need to engage emotionally with the comments. I was also not addressing the real questions. Difficult situations made me tense, but I simply pushed on, which turned out to be a mistake.

Three emotionally charged situations arose in the same short period of time. First, the Catholic diocese wouldn't allow a funeral for one of their members who died of AIDS. Then nursing homes were uniting against admitting AIDS patients, and finally, a local physician started a campaign to defund the AIDS project, claiming that it was really a "cottage industry" promoting the homosexual agenda. Against this background, patients were showing up at our doorstep who were sick, isolated, and scared. Waves of opposition seemed to be sweeping over us from every direction. I was losing my confidence, and tentacles of anxiety were finding their way into my veneer of confidence. I dreamed one night that there was a knock at my back door. I looked out through the window to see a black shroud covering a human form. When the shroud was pulled back, there was a skull whose face was that of a friend who recently died. I recoiled and awoke in a cold sweat. I was feeling pressed by the need to push back against the social resistance but was clueless about how to proceed.

My first real test came with a community meeting in a small rural town. The initial inquiry was innocuous and appeared to come from the local health department. They were looking for speakers to address a community forum. There were a few representatives in the state legislature that were very vocal in their opposition to our work. Unknown to me, the most vociferous opponent represented the area where we were doing this presentation. He discovered our plans and wanted the presentation canceled. The organizers were prevented from getting flyers printed, and the venue owners were getting scared about hosting the forum on their property. The organizers wanted to proceed but warned us that this guy meant trouble. My co-presenters quickly backed out. I spent a day wavering between denial and sheer terror. The voices in my head said to run away, and every time I tried to talk to someone about it, I hyperventilated. The organizers called me the day before and told me that the venue owners were going to allow us in. They begged me to carry through with the presentation. I agreed.

The drive took a couple hours, and I could focus only on the road and my breathing. When I arrived it was dark and cold and the parking lot was empty. There were a few figures silhouetted at the lighted door as I approached. Two of the men had guns. I recognized the organizer of the event, and she nervously escorted me in. There were no more than 10 people in the room, and I could see the state representative sitting in the front row. He adjusted his seat closer to intimidate me and stayed there. The look on his face was pure hatred. I took a deep breath. With my heart in my throat, I recited my now familiar lecture while trying to be calm and intelligible. He was clearly expecting me to either leave, fail, or quit and was perplexed when I continued. There were no questions, and everyone filed out an hour later. The drive back felt like an eternity as I processed what happened. I had found the answer to the wave of hostility that was sweeping over us. We had to incrementally push back in whatever way we could. It was about this time that I read a quote from Maggie Kuhn. “Stand before the people you fear, and speak your mind even if your voice shakes.” My voice (and the rest of me) definitely shook, but it was time for me to push back. My friends and my community were dying, and I needed to do something about it. So I pushed back, and I shook a lot. I was an advocate for those who could not speak, albeit an improbable advocate.

The speakers bureau was to be our strongest tool. Fundamentally, the fear that people felt was rooted in ignorance, and knowledge could combat ignorance. I naively thought that we could make sweeping changes in attitude with large forums conducted in immense auditoriums. Now I knew I had been wrong. Minds were changed during the smallest of conversations between the fewest number of people. We had to be elated when someone invited us to talk to them. Nothing monumental changed after one interaction but the cumulative strength of a repeated, clear, consistent message slowly moved the needle toward justice. At this time, it was less than 15 years since the speech Martin Luther King Jr. gave at the National Cathedral when he reminded us that “the arc of the moral universe is long, but it bends toward justice.” Sometimes it felt like the arc didn’t bend for us. I found myself in classrooms, rural churches, fraternal organizations, senior centers, continuing education classes, morning glee club gatherings, and more. Sometimes I spoke to five people, and sometimes I spoke to 105, but the individual connections were what made the difference. The memory of the hate-filled state representative that nearly derailed me when I came to speak in his district became the driving force behind my work. I gave a speech to the legislature a few years later, and I saw him lurking around in the shadows with the same sneer on his face. He was defeated in a later election and died of AIDS several years later. He attributed his infection to a needle prick that he received at some indeterminate time in the past.

I had a complicated relationship with the medical community. There were some genuine and selfless people who gave their full support to caring for patients and supporting education. Some caregivers had a vested interest in the epidemic because of their sexual orientation, their connections in the community, or their deep feelings of empathy for affected family or friends. My heart was always warmed when I was in their presence. Goodness and light seemed to pour from them. Sadly, some caregivers were there for personal aggrandizement. They saw the chance for fame or fortune from researching the disease or giving eloquent speeches about what they knew. It was easy to see through their motives. Even so, I hoped their research would prove useful eventually. The majority of care providers were only interested when a question arose during their continuing education requirement but otherwise saw it as someone else's problem. At first these people would ship a newly-diagnosed patient to me immediately, which I took as an honor. I was proud to be of service. I realized, as time went on, that the referral was a way of disposing of an unwanted burden. They didn't respect me as much as they saw me as a dumping ground. I felt disrespected and excluded but took solace in the care providers who were doing good work. Some caregivers, and one physician in particular, used their position to spread misinformation. This physician, *Dr. Smith* for this writing, and his cronies tried to make it appear that the information we were providing was false or created to further our agenda. He and I had a few run-ins, but I mistakenly tried to ignore him. I was invited to a community forum, and he was to be a co-panelist. The audience was likely to be sympathetic to his message, and backing out was my first reaction. I was haunted by my insecurities. He would tout his credentials and mock my sexual orientation as the motive for my work. The day before the forum, I was wound into knots. There had been a spate of deaths the week before, and one of my closest colleagues, Julia, despaired that every day was like walking through her personal graveyard. She asserted that she would never quit this important work but felt so inadequate. All I needed to do was argue with a wimpy little doctor while she was suffering from the weight of caring for a clinic of desperate patients. I was clearly the inadequate one. The next morning, we went to the community forum together. The presence of Julia, this warm and smiling heterosexual woman, disarmed most of their arguments, and the audience fell in love with her. I could not be defiant in the face of a hostile community, but I could find a surrogate who could. We became a force to be reckoned with.

The faith community proved to be another vexation. Before coming out, I had never identified with any particular faith and had a "live and let live" attitude with people who did. After I started identifying as gay, my experiences with Christian denominations were secondhand but were not positive. What I read and heard was generally negative, but I was never confronted personally. A series of events pushed me to act. I was invited to speak to the congregation at a local church. I was met by the pastor at the front door. He unapologetically told me to leave. The members had heard that I was gay, and I was not welcome. I sheepishly retreated. Old feelings of shame bubbled up in me, but I buried them and moved on. It was easy to dismiss the situation as an aberration. I had met with homophobia before, but this was the most blatant. After all, the sign on the church had said that Jesus loved everyone.

Another interdenominational group convened a meeting to discuss a pastoral response to AIDS, and I was invited. The central organizers were from the Catholic diocese, and the conversation was upbeat and positive with a nun, Sister Ann, identifying herself as a point person for the discussion. In the course of the conversation, I mentioned my sexual orientation, and the room suddenly went cold. There were only blank stares coming my way. Discussing a health issue was tolerated but sex, and certainly homosexuality, was not acceptable. There were a few general comments about the need for pastoral services, and Sister Ann ended the meeting with a vague commitment to schedule again in the future. I attempted to make contact with the group again but was ignored. Shame and confusion overflowed, and I comforted myself by stuffing whatever feelings I felt. I became numb whenever the discussion of faith came up.

The AIDS patients needed something else. Many of them were close to their religious communities and wanted to continue those important relationships. This was particularly acute when planning end-of-life care. I tried asking and begging, but the major denominations would only be part of the AIDS care team on their terms. Their terms insisted that the patients denounce their sexuality. I did not understand Christianity, and I didn't speak their language. It was impossible to bring them into the fold.

A well-known leader in the gay community died of AIDS, and a celebration of life was planned at an event center[3]. To my horror, a local conservative congregation arrived with hateful signs denouncing the event. No one would cross the line of protestors. Public confrontations were definitely out of my comfort zone, and I retreated to my car. A friend heard about the ruckus and drove to the center. She

---

3 Coming from a culture that forced us to be invisible, there were few "gay" leaders. We were blessed with some natural leaders from the beginning of the epidemic. Many of these people had sharpened their skills while working on other progressive causes. Some were young people with innate people skills. There were the expected struggles as the younger ones learned what it meant to lead. It was the experienced leaders that made the difference. The 1960s and 1970s produced a crop of thoughtful and charismatic elders. They led the way as we made our way out of the darkness of social invisibility. We lost many of them to AIDS precisely when we needed them the most. Brian, the community activist I referred to in the story, was one of those experienced leaders that we lost. Losing gifted, long-term leaders took a toll on the community and forced new leaders to grow up fast.

knocked on the window of my car. She had a pile of sheets and wanted me to hold one up in front of the protestors[4]. If I did this, she hoped others would follow along. My voice was shaking again, and my heart was pounding. I started hyperventilating. The media had shown up. I would be on TV holding up a sheet while "God hates fags" was chanted in the background. Maybe I could wrap myself up in one of the sheets! No, that was not the idea. I needed to stand up in front of the world and be visible in a way that I had never imagined. I was shaking so hard that the sheet fluttered like it was in the wind. Immediately after I took my place several other people walked up next to me. In a few minutes the protestors were surrounded with sheets. We looked like angels. The paradox was unmistakable. I am no angel, but I got to be one for one day. The protestors shuffled off. We had won. Faith communities were still slow to join our movement, but there were signs of change. A regional meeting of Lutherans had a session on the AIDS response. The keynote speaker eloquently noted that Christians had made themselves irrelevant in the care of those in need, and that was not an acceptable position. Local churches started to welcome our patients and openly welcomed those from mainstream denominations, much to their chagrin.

The most painful battles to fight were within the gay community. In the early 1980s, gay men were just starting

4 Shielding mourners from the protestors with white sheets had been used before. It was both effective and symbolic. The practice was copied by others and was highly visible when parishioners from the Westboro Baptist Church tried to disrupt Matthew Shepard's funeral several years later.

to win some degree of recognition and were beginning to define a culture that was unique to them. Growing up in a fiercely heteronormative society came with an emotional price. The unrelenting message that we were wrong or somehow fundamentally flawed caused deep emotional damage. The term "internalized homophobia" was coined as a catch-all phrase that encompassed this damage. There were many complex facets to internalized homophobia, but the sexual behavior that so many men engaged in was part of what made AIDS risk so tricky to manage. Shame and guilt lead to anonymous sex. Years of repressed sexual needs led to multiple unsafe sexual encounters. There were many complicated intersecting psychological issues, but these were the basic problems I saw. That was the important factor in the spread of the disease. Alcohol and drug use further complicated the picture. Thousands of men were infected before we heard of AIDS, but even more were getting infected after we recognized the danger. If I said, "Don't have sex," a few people listened, but more often I was ignored or labeled as a messenger of the dominant society trying to foist moral beliefs on others. It was agonizing to see my own community killing themselves. Talking wasn't working. A dear friend got infected after an alcohol-fueled, impulsive, and stupid mistake. I had been unable to help him and convince him of the danger. Unfortunately, he felt that his freedom was more important than seeing himself as deserving of care.

We started taking the message (and the condoms) to where the risk was. Suddenly, our group of peer educators was in bars, bathhouses, restrooms, dark alleys, deserted basements, and more. I frequented a local park and strategically placed condoms where they might be needed. The police found out what we were doing and thought we should report what was going on and help them with arrests. Instead, we continued our work but were quieter about it. Bearing witness to the high-risk behavior that continued to occur was painful, and it was easy for me to despair. I remained defiant in the work, and we took the message wherever it was needed. Our presence became a local joke, but the rate of sexually-transmitted diseases went down. I believe that we saved many lives but still rue the many we were unable to reach. Later we extended the same logic to intravenous drug users by sponsoring needle exchange vans. We would appear with clean needles and share the same AIDS risk reduction procedures with another high-risk group.

Violence was a constant concern. People were frightened that they or their loved ones might somehow be at risk. Talking about homosexuality was threatening to people who felt that gay rights meant fewer rights for them or that they would be personally diminished in some other way. Discussing homosexuality created dissonance for many and triggered hostile responses. Others were scared that discussing sex would make people more sexually active. There were loud voices supporting the view that people with AIDS were getting what they deserved. The toxic mixture of misinformation, fear, and personal vulnerability caused anger that was not expressed in healthy ways. Caustic arguments erupted, sometimes at community meetings and sometimes in the media. For a guy like me who avoided discord, I did what I could to avoid those situations, but the situations usually came to me. I knew nothing about debate, but I learned. De-escalation worked, as did strength in numbers. Physical intimidation would generally abate if I backed off. Situations would rarely get beyond that, but guns were my biggest fear. Abortion providers had been shot and killed. Guns would appear at our meetings, or threats would appear in media postings. There were direct threats made against me and other activists. Traveling to remote parts of the state was important, and I never shied away from it, but I was always situationally aware. If there was a large group that seemed restive, I took an inventory of who could be my ally and where all of the exits were. I was never afraid to run away.

As a skinny, timid, and shy person, I expected to grow up to be an invisible adult. Looking at a picture of the "before 1980 Scott," you would see me as the perfect candidate for a back office desk job. Someone in college commented, "That is Scott. He is smart. Weird but smart." Shy and weird, yes, but nobody would have ever seen me as an advocate. The isolation of being gay in the 1970s sensitized me to the feelings of other marginalized people. I knew the sting of microaggression even before the word was coined. My childhood traumas caused a litany of unhealed emotional harm but also forced me to develop resistance in the face of adversity. I could at least deflect criticism and harmful emotions. I wasn't devastated by every real or perceived slight. Intelligence has its advantages. I knew my facts. I developed effective speaking and debating skills. Intellectualization was very familiar to me. I also knew when to be quiet. Eventually, I achieved some degree of success by simply showing up and defying adversity. A mentor once told me, "The winner is the one who shows up." I was the most improbable of advocates, but I showed up. I learned to breathe, kept pushing ahead, and found I could believe in myself.

Scott Strickland (he/him) was born in northwest Portland and lives there again 70 years later. He spent as much time as possible in eastern Oregon while growing up. Oregon was home for college and graduate school until a job in Minnesota took Scott on a 20-year ride in AIDS care and research. He was drawn back to the beauty of Oregon and a less stressful job in 1998. After a stint in prison, Scott has settled into a quiet, peaceful existence in the place he loves.

A Young Man's Song

By Eric Zimmerman

Prelude

I am 4 years old. Using all my strength, I climb up the door jamb in the hallway of our house, clamping the woodwork between my legs. It feels great to be up high. The sensation of warmth between my thighs feels good as well.

My mother shouts at me to get down, and I feel ashamed. I associate the shame with the warmth in that part of my body.

My babyhood attachment bonds with my parents have already been ruptured. My mother has untreated depression and has been partially bedridden. My father's emotions are shut down, and his ambitious work schedule keeps him away for long periods.

My heart has grown a self-protective callus, and I shy away from physical touch, the very thing I want most of all. I am ashamed to be me.

The Song

He has kind eyes and a sweet smile. His hair is light brown with a gentle curl, unlike my dark brown, straight locks. He's wearing tan slacks, and his thigh is almost touching mine as we sit side-by-side in the cramped airplane seats. I can feel his body heat. I need touch. I want it so much. We will sit here side by side for hours as we fly from Los Angeles to the East Coast, but then I may never see him again. We introduce ourselves. His name is Brad. I force myself to chat, and he answers easily, comfortable with our small talk. His smile reassures me.

It's now or never, Eric. Make a move! Single at age 24, I have never had a lover. I long to exchange caresses, kisses, and full-body embraces with another man. And, just maybe, to feel what it might be like to fall in love.

I put my hand on his thigh .... Yes! He rests his hand on mine. Success! And the warmth of his leg under my hand feels really good. Our conversation continues off and on through the long flight, along with our gentle touch.

It's October 1979. Brad and I, along with others on that plane, are traveling to Washington, DC, for the first national March[1] on Washington for Lesbian and Gay Rights[2]. My foray into political organizing began that summer with sidewalk leafleting on Santa Monica Boulevard in Hollywood. The idea of doing something that's never been done before excites me. To my delight, one of my leafleting buddies had been at the Stonewall freedom riots[3] 10 years previously.

As our plane nears the East Coast, Brad and I promise we will spend time together during our stay in Washington after my side trip to New York City.

A few days later, I board the train from New York to DC. The March organizers have arranged homestays for us. I want to spend the night with Brad, but I have no way to

---

1 The first National March on Washington for Lesbian and Gay Rights was a large political rally that took place in Washington, DC, on Sunday, October 14, 1979. It drew approximately 100,000 people to demand equal rights and urge the passage of civil rights legislation. On Monday, October 15, approximately 500 March participants went to the Capitol and met with 50 Senators and more than 150 Representatives.

2 In these notes, I use modern inclusive nomenclature, e.g., LGBTQ. In the earlier decades during which this story takes place, terminology (and attitudes!) were less inclusive. I have preserved this earlier language in my story for historical accuracy.

3 The Stonewall uprising was a series of spontaneous riots and demonstrations against a police raid in June of 1969 at the Stonewall Inn, a bar in New York City. Although this was not the first time that queer Americans had fought back against official persecution, this unrest sparked a new and bolder phase of the struggle for LGBTQ rights.

reach him. My overnight host is a slender, handsome, young man, very friendly. That evening he takes me into his bed as a matter of course, and we fall into a brief sexual embrace. (I have already experienced a handful of encounters like this, but they have meant little to me or my partners.) I don't feel safe enough with this man to fully relax and feel relief when the sex is done. I fall asleep missing Brad.

Then comes the evening before the march. I've located Brad amidst the hubbub of arriving marchers. What a relief! Now I have someone to share this novel experience with. I don't want to feel alone amidst the throng.

It's dusk. He and I stroll side by side onto the grass of the National Mall. The Washington Monument looms above us, beautifully spotlighted and encircled by American flags. The white marble of the Lincoln Memorial gleams in the distance. It's a mild, pleasant evening.

Looking around, I suddenly realize that the others I see walking nearby are also here for the march. *I am with my people.* I reach for Brad's hand. I have never done this before with another man. He grasps my hand and holds it with a warm, sure clasp. We walk hand in hand. It feels so different, yet so right. To my left at the edge of the lawn 100 men are raising their voices in strong and beautiful song. It's a gay chorus! My heart swells with joy.

That night: another pre-arranged homestay. I go to mine (a different host this time). Brad goes to his. I fall asleep feeling lonely and missing him.

The following morning is the day of the march. I ride the subway to the center of town and emerge into bright daylight and a festive crowd. Colorful banners and signs proclaim our pride and name the places from which we have come—from all corners of the nation. Announcements from megaphones pierce the noisy, dusty air. It's a happy confusion. Brad is nowhere to be seen, but that's OK for now. I feel exhilarated, excited. Then we're off! We stream through the streets. My stride is sure, strong, and powerful. Here is the White House. It looks just like it does in the news. We keep marching.

Now we arrive back on the mall to assemble as one big throng. The crowd swells, larger and larger. Many thousands of us are here, gathered on this sacred land at the heart of our democracy to demand full citizenship from the nation we love. Picnic blankets and food appear, but I'm too excited to sit down as the amplified voices of march leaders and other dignitaries roll over the crowd from a stage up front. Finally, my excitement wanes. I start to get cold and decide to leave.

That night: Brad's host has given the OK for me to join Brad in the guest bedroom. I can finally relax. We cuddle and talk softly. Our touch is slow and gentle, exploratory. This suits me well. His kisses are soft and sweet. Our sex is warm and leisurely. I am at home in his arms as we drift into sleep.

* * *

I'm back in Los Angeles. I see Brad regularly, enjoying his gentle company, getting more accustomed to what sex is like with him. One evening we even experiment, giggling, with an unfortunate cucumber ....

And I had discovered there were gay men's choruses! Seeing and hearing that chorus on the National Mall with Brad the evening before the march had made a deep impression. I learn that a chorus has recently started in L.A. It's called the Gay Men's Chorus of Los Angeles[4]. I track down the rehearsal time and location.

On a mild November evening, I drive from my apartment in West L.A. via busy Santa Monica Boulevard to Plummer Park in Hollywood. After parking and walking past the basketball courts, I enter the rehearsal hall. It's a large, rectangular recreation room, walls painted dull brown, with a raised, wooden platform on one side. Dingy ceiling tiles

---

4 The Gay Men's Chorus of Los Angeles (GMCLA) was founded on July 12, 1979, when 99 men showed up at the first rehearsal. Over the following decades, GMCLA has garnered international acclaim while remaining rooted in service to the Los Angeles community and beyond by promoting civil rights and acceptance through music. Critics have hailed the chorus's musical excellence on numerous occasions. GMCLA is the first gay men's chorus to perform for a sitting president, Bill Clinton, and has also performed for President Barack Obama. The 200-member chorus has toured nationally and internationally, has released 15 albums, and has commissioned numerous new compositions. GMCLA has also received accolades for its Alive Music Project, a music education outreach program serving middle and high school students, which uses song to create a powerful, anti-bullying message.

During the peak of the AIDS epidemic from 1982 to 1996, more than 150 chorus members died from the disease.

Current information about the chorus may be found at www.gmcla.org.

complete the ugly setting. But I don't care because here in front of me are over 100 gay men—mostly young (like me). Many are gorgeous (unlike me).

Wow! I feel scared, overwhelmed, and excited all at once. The hubbub of greetings and conversation is loud. Do these men all know each other? I don't know any of them. Anxious and impatient, I await the start of the rehearsal.

To my relief, the director, Harold Kjellberg, takes the stage. We stand in rows facing him. But before the vocal warmup[5] begins, Harold tells us, "Turn to your right and give a backrub to the man there." A long minute later he says, "Now turn the other way and do the same." I'm being touched by other men, and it feels so good. And I'm rubbing the shoulders and upper backs of two men I haven't even met yet. Heavenly! I've been touch-starved for so very long. "Now exchange a couple of hugs." Even better!

The warmup is hard for me. I'm not used to breathing deeply, and my stomach feels tight. It's hard to fill up my lungs all the way. It's been years since my brief introduction to choral singing in college. But I do my best, and sure enough, the exercises help me relax.

Music sheets are passed around, and we begin to sing. Gratefully, I recall that it was my mother who taught me how to read music notation as a kid. I think I can do this! My voice sounds pretty good to me, and the sound of all

---

5 The human voice does best when it is prepared for singing by means of a few minutes of breathing and vocal exercises beforehand.

these men singing together is grand. Strong at times, then faltering, we slip in and out of tune or tempo. Harold stops us, coaches and restarts us, and we sound better, little by little. It's hard work for me but fun as well. At times, I catch the emotion in the sound and the words, and my heart soars. Two hours fly by.

My drive home that evening is infused with hope. For a couple of hours, I'm freed from shame and anxiety, my near-constant companions.

Emotions from our first performance the following month: I'm nervous and excited beforehand. I feel pride and strength on stage. Then I'm giddy and celebratory afterward. My parents come to the performance and take me out to dinner afterwards. What a treat. Their support feels really good, and I recall with gratitude how they assured me of their continuing love when I came out as gay some years ago.

We resume rehearsals in preparation for the next concert. I'm in the bass section. I enjoy the way our tones mesh with the higher notes from the baritone and tenor singers. I like the sensation in my chest when I sing a low note. It feels good. And hearing our whole section hit the low notes—wow, that masculine sound feels powerful and sexy. I'm more comfortable with the rehearsal and performance process, and my voice feels stronger. I'm making some friends, but I'm still shy, hesitating to approach the men whom I find most attractive. I continue to like the backrubs and hugs.

It's 1980. Harold has retired, and Jerry Carlson is our new director. He challenges us to sing more skillfully and tackle harder music. We move to a nicer rehearsal hall.

A year passes. Brad and I have gone our separate ways. We part with no hard feelings. I remember his warmth and gentleness with gratitude.

So I am single again.

I gather my courage and walk into a bar in West L.A. This is only the second gay bar I've explored. It's a big place called Apache West. I stand awkwardly, nervous and afraid to look at anybody.

A man comes over and introduces himself. His name is Lavell. He is a solid fellow, a little older than me. He is self-assured, with skin like nightfall and short, black curly hair. His voice is gentle, but I sense strength in him. He wants my body, and I'm pleased and relieved to let him take charge. I give him my address, and he follows me home. We have sex that night, and several times thereafter. It's hot—intense in a way I haven't experienced before. The physical pleasure is astonishing. I've always seen myself as passive, accepting what is, rather than taking charge of my life and changing things for the better when they aren't going well. I'm ashamed of this and judge myself harshly for it. With Lavell, I'm starting to see that inside my passivity lies a paradoxical strength. When our bodies connect, I learn that I can let go *at will* with delicious consequences rather than adverse ones. The unmistakable evidence of his attraction for me makes the sex work—icing on the cake.

However, I'm not curious about him. I know very little about what he's up to when he's not with me. I'm 26 years old and don't care about that. I just want to touch and be touched ... any way I can.

A couple months later, it's time for a routine visit to the doctor. I sit on the examining table. Dr. Weisman[6] confirms all is well with my body. And then he shocks me by saying that it's best to not let a fellow put his cock up my butt because of a new disease going around.

Awww, I'm just learning to enjoy that with Lavell! I feel surprised and afraid. I also feel confused. A recently-published book entitled *The Joy of Gay Sex* includes my new favorite bedroom activity among its list of recommended sexual pleasures, mentioning no adverse consequences. Nor have any of my sex partners, though there haven't been many, darn it.

I leave the doctor's office and drive back to my lonely apartment feeling chastened. That night I write down Dr. Weisman's advice in my diary so I won't forget it.

I slow down the frequency of my dates with Lavell, then I stop seeing him. I miss the pleasure we enjoyed but

---

6 Thank you, Dr. Weisman. Yes, I remember your name after all these years. You may have saved my life. Joel D. Weisman, a gay man, was one of the first medical professionals to identify the pattern of illnesses that was ultimately diagnosed as AIDS during his work as a general practitioner in Los Angeles. He later became an advocate for the development of treatments and prevention of the disease, including establishing the AIDS Project Los Angeles (APLA) in 1983 and developing Southern California's first AIDS unit at Sherman Oaks Hospital.

As of 2025, HIV/AIDS has caused more than 42 million deaths worldwide.

feel relieved that I'm no longer putting myself at risk. I also feel resentful. I've only had a taste of this new kind of touch before it was snatched away.

* * *

It's a chorus rehearsal evening in 1982. I realize I'm fed up. It's because of the casual misogyny bantered between rehearsal announcements and during conversation when we're not rehearsing. It also pops up in skits and impromptu talent shows at our rehearsal retreats. I am disgusted by this denigration of women's bodies, their mannerisms, even their *smell.* I think of admirable women like my sisters, my mother, my stepmother, and I wince. This contempt is wrong and needs to stop. I've learned that gay male culture is full of this ugliness. It's not unique to the chorus.

I go home and bang out a rant on my typewriter, calling out this prejudice and challenging chorus members to stop engaging in it. I walk to the print shop at the end of the street, and they print me a stack of copies. I bring them to the next rehearsal, showing up early. When nobody is watching, I put them on the table near the door where we all pick up new music and announcements as we enter the rehearsal hall. Each man takes a copy as he comes in. Even though my editorial is unsigned, hence anonymous, I feel anxious. They're all going to read it. What if they hate it, demand to know who wrote it, and expel me? My conscience will force me to tell them I wrote it. Maybe I'd have to leave the chorus forever.

Nobody says a word.

Later: My missive worked. My words are taken to heart. Expressions of misogyny have nearly vanished. It feels good to discover that my words have power.

It's 1985. By now, we've toured the nation, performing in San Francisco, Portland, Seattle, New York, and Washington, DC. Even better, we've traveled to smaller cities, such as Fresno in the Central Valley of California. This agricultural area is far removed from our usual big-city environment. Our visits and performances spark interest and gratitude from folks in these rural areas. It touches our hearts. We're helping gay and lesbian residents there find each other and planting seeds of community outside the big cities.

At rehearsal one night, our director, Jerry Carlson, tells us he's been infected with the newly identified virus, HIV. My heart sinks. He looks healthy, though. He'll be OK, right?

* * *

Jerry takes a leave of absence. A series of interim directors take charge. They're competent, but it's not the same as before. That electric energy and joy I used to feel are gone. And we get a nasty surprise: one of our performances right here in Hollywood is picketed. During the quieter moments of our concert, we can hear the demonstrators' angry shouts from outside. I never learn who they are, but I can guess why they came. The new disease rouses the fearful and the hateful against our kind.

I show up at rehearsal one evening, and the men already there are standing in little clumps, murmuring to each other. My stomach sinks. I feel afraid, wanting to know what's happening. At the same time, I don't want to know. Someone tells me that Jerry has died. AIDS. I feel hollow, empty. This can't be true ... can it? What now? Will the chorus survive?

* * *

The chorus hires a new director, Jon Bailey. He's a tall, slender, energetic man in his fifties with close-cut thinning hair. His enthusiasm is reassuring, inspiring. Maybe we're going to be OK after all.

* * *

It's been a couple of years, and I have come to really appreciate how deft Jon's leadership is. When choosing our music, he creates an emotional journey for our audiences. It invites the listeners to experience sadness (so much death is happening around us these days), remembrance, humor, and even joy. The chorus is playing a shamanic role in the community, helping us all through a tough time while still insisting on celebrating the beauty of our "tribe." Jon told us that his first choice in college was divinity school and that only later on did he decide to focus on music. There is a quality in him that I can only describe as spiritual. It shows up in the manner in which he leads us in rehearsal, the way he relates to the audience in performances, and even the quality of the sound he summons from us singers.

AIDS is everywhere. I see it in the ashy skin and gaunt appearance of some of my fellow singers. I now know what Kaposi's Sarcoma lesions look like because I see them in person. One night a singer comes to rehearsal towing a flimsy metal structure behind him. Nobody wants to embarrass him by making a fuss. I'm bewildered. I'm guessing these pieces of metal have to do with his illness, but I don't deduce their purpose at first. Then I realize ... it's an IV stand.

Small groups of us singers go to hospitals and stand at the bedside of one desperately ill man after another, singing gently, lovingly. It's a sweet, tender experience for me, and it breaks my heart.

We are invited to sing at fundraising events to fight AIDS. The government has dropped the ball on combating this plague, so private individuals and non-profits are struggling to pick up the slack. Many such efforts are fueled by luminaries from the television and movie industry right here in Hollywood. Most are women. We share a stage with Elizabeth Taylor. A regal presence, she speaks with passion to the audience. Backstage at another fundraiser, I catch a glimpse of Madonna leaving the stage. I'm surprised at her small stature.

As we work with these individuals, and others, I see that they are gracious, *very* hard-working, and respectful of us and the community we represent.

We sing in churches that want to be more welcoming of LGBT[7] people. I feel this is a great way to fulfill the chorus's mission. When we sing in a hall of worship, I can feel the trepidation of the congregation melting away in response to the inviting sounds we work so hard to make. I'm learning that it's better to persuade via the heart than the mind—a potent yet gentle process.

It's 1990. I'm seized by inspiration: I will bring the Heart Circle process to the chorus. I was introduced to it by my father and also found it in the Radical Faeries[8] this past year. It is an opportunity to share from our hearts and encourage the shy individuals among us to speak up. We will sit in a circle and pass around a talisman, the bell that Jon rings to signal the start of rehearsal. The person holding the talisman has the opportunity to speak. Everyone else listens, with no crosstalk. We'll pass the bell from one man to the next until it has traveled around the circle. It's a simple process, but it has profound results. Deliberately setting aside the usual back-and-forth of regular conversation empowers the speaker with quiet courage. He often will surprise himself with intimate and heartfelt sharing, encouraged by the kind, loving eyes of the others. What's said in the circle remains confidential.

---

7 Yes, our language is becoming more inclusive as the years go by, so I reflect this here.

8 The Radical Faeries are a loosely-affiliated worldwide network and countercultural movement blending queer consciousness and secular spirituality since the 1970s. Sharing various aspects with neopaganism, the movement also adopts elements from anarchism and environmentalism.

The chorus leadership is receptive to my proposal. During our next retreat, 90 men choose to participate. I feel anxious. Can I do this? What if it goes out of control and does emotional harm? Maybe I shouldn't have offered to do it. But I forge ahead, introducing and describing the process once we've settled down in our folding chairs, forming a big circle.

As our talisman makes its way from person to person, my anxiety subsides. It's working! My ground rules are being honored. We are in need of this. We've lost so many members to AIDS. We shed tears together in the emotional safety I've helped create. I feel awe and gratitude that I've been able to give this gift to the chorus in our time of need.

Heart Circle becomes a part of future chorus retreats.

Now it's 1991. California governor Pete Wilson, a Republican, has reneged on his promise to sign the LGBT civil rights bill that was just approved by the state legislature and sent his way. I've heard that his administration is considering rounding up infected gay and bisexual men into internment camps. I'm frightened, but mostly I'm angry. It's too much—the dying, the hatred that keeps coming at us.

I join with tens of thousands of others as we take to the streets, blocking traffic in leaderless, illegal demonstrations, night after night. A new direct-action political group called Queer Nation has inspired these demonstrations[9]. We

9 The Queer Nation meeting format was similar to that of a Heart Circle. Decisions were made mostly by consensus rather than via a more traditional hierarchical process.

shout, yell, and bang drums and other noisemakers. I don't care that I'm breaking the law. This is the apocalypse. We carve a jagged path through our familiar city streets, changing direction as we please. This baffles the police who are forced to follow rather than stop us.

On one such evening, as we gather at Ventura and Laurel Canyon Boulevards, I realize that familiar territory lies to my west. I grew up in that part of town. I walk over to that side of the crowd, hollering and waving my hands, urging us to move in that direction. Others feel the same way, so we collectively decide to do so. As we stride westward on Ventura Boulevard, our mood turns celebratory. The police are helpless to stop us. By owning the pavement of the busiest arterial in this part of the city, we are saying, "Enough is enough." We will not tolerate any more broken promises by craven politicians.

We reach Van Nuys Boulevard, another busy street. A few moments later I hear people in the crowd saying, "Shush. We're coming to the hospital." And so we are: here is Sherman Oaks Hospital, a bland, red brick building to our left. I've driven by it countless times over the years. Many men with AIDS are here. We must not disturb them.

We fall silent as we approach the hospital. Then all at once, as if we have received a telepathic command, we stop motionless in our tracks. *We are utterly still.* Complete silence envelops the scene as we wordlessly honor the men fighting for their lives inside the hospital. I look at the drivers whose vehicles we have temporarily surrounded. They sit motionless in their cars, silent as well. For a long, breathless moment all is quiet. And then, as one, we resume our march up the boulevard.

Another night, another demonstration: we are gathered on a scrap of lawn outside the Century Plaza Hotel, one of a cluster of high-rises in the western part of the city. Governor Wilson is inside hosting a political fundraiser. A couple of chorus members are here, and Misha, a singer in the bass section, has suggested that we wear our chorus tuxedos "to mess with people's minds." I had done so. But now I don't see any sign of Misha or the others, and my formal attire stands out like a sore thumb among the other casually-dressed demonstrators. I start to feel uneasy. I see a *lot* of police stationed nearby, well over 100. They're dressed in black, leather uniforms and wear heavy, black helmets. Some are on horseback.

We mill around on the lawn, shouting. Then some demonstrators run over to the hotel entranceway and attempt to shatter the heavy glass doors with wooden clubs to force their way inside. Now I feel frightened. I don't belong here. This isn't right. In front of me, several demonstrators pull out an American flag and try to set it on fire. The big snout of a TV news camera swivels around to hone in on the scene. I feel ashamed of what they're doing to the flag. I try to block the camera's view of it with my body, saying, "*Please* don't do this." But they persist, and the flag begins to burn. Other demonstrators shout, "Sit down, sit down," in an attempt to calm the situation. I think this is a good idea, so I sit on the damp grass.

The police now have us completely surrounded. Suddenly, they charge directly at us, horsemen in front. The horses loom above me. Their bodies are *big.* I scramble to my feet and back away as the mounted police wade into the crowd. They're swinging their batons one-handed, landing heavy blows onto the heads, shoulders, and arms of the demonstrators in front of me. Other police press forward on foot and begin shoving us backwards with their batons. Shouts and screams erupt from the crowd. It's bedlam. I continue to back away. Then something inside me compels me to pause so that a policeman nearby will approach me. He does, and I look directly at him. I see confusion in his face, and he stops his advance. He's noticing my tuxedo, and I surmise he's wondering whether I am a latecomer to the governor's fundraiser who is caught up in the chaos by mistake. Maybe he's thinking he'd better not strike me with his baton. His hesitation gives me the moment I need to step back into the now-retreating crowd.

The police continue their advance, shoving us through shrubbery, across curbs, retaining walls, and other uneven surfaces. They chase us into an adjoining open-air shopping mall, *through the entire mall,* and out its other side onto a side street.

And then they are gone. The crowd also melts away into the night. I stand still in the now-deserted street trying to collect my thoughts. I decide to get the heck out of there as well. I'm trembling with fear and anger as I walk to my car and drive home.

Several days later, I see a flyer showing where the next Queer Nation meeting will take place. It's at Plummer Park in the same room where the chorus used to rehearse. What a deja vu moment. I'm seated in a large circle along with the other attendees as the meeting begins. We are debriefing the events at the hotel. One by one, each of us has an opportunity to speak. When it's my turn, I say, "I don't think it was right to engage in violence." I'm referring to the attempted hotel break-in.

A man to my left interrupts me, his voice tight with anger. "That was *property damage,* not violence." To my shock and dismay, I see a large bandage on his head. He's one of the people who was beaten by the police. Pointing to his wound he says, "*This* is violence!" Consumed with shame, I want to crawl under my chair. He's right. I slink out of the meeting as soon as it ends, speaking to nobody.

I force myself to go to the following week's Queer Nation meeting and apologize to the group for confusing property damage with violence against persons. I receive perfunctory nods of acknowledgment for my belated political awakening. Still feeling ashamed, I depart promptly and never go back.

I join a class action civil lawsuit brought by the American Civil Liberties Union (ACLU)[10] against the City of Los Angeles and Police Chief Daryl Gates for brutality and reckless endangerment. As I say to my friends who weren't

---

10 The ACLU has been a legal champion for civil rights for everyone in America for over 100 years.

there, we demonstrators were the targets of a police riot that night. The police lost control of themselves, acted in anger, and violated their professional rules of engagement with the public.

During the legal process I'm deposed for two hours by hostile city attorneys, an unpleasant experience. But I have no regrets. My deposition is recorded and transcribed word-for-word by the court reporter, generating a thick paper file, which I receive in the mail afterwards. And in that transcript I see I have succeeded in finding the words to describe how it felt to be physically endangered by representatives of the state who swore an oath to protect me. I feel betrayed by the country I love. Why else would I go to all this trouble to help make America a more just and equitable nation if I don't feel a primal identification with it in the first place[11]?

In 1992, Governor Wilson reverses course and signs the anti-discrimination legislation.

* * *

We depart on a performance tour to Europe. It's grand! We are welcomed wherever we go. We sing in the capital cities of Hungary, Czechoslovakia[12], Denmark, Austria ... and Germany.

11 The lawsuit was eventually settled out of court. Each plaintiff received a settlement check.

12 In 1991, this nation had not yet separated into the Czech Republic and Slovakia.

We perform a concert with the Berlin gay men's chorus. They're a small group and welcome us warmly. They invite us to visit Sachsenhausen with them the day after the concert. Sachsenhausen was a concentration camp near Berlin where many gays and other minorities were taken from the city and murdered by the Nazis during the Third Reich.

After roaming Berlin all night in a fruitless quest to get laid, I show up at the bus with my emotional defenses down from lack of sleep. It's an oppressively hot July day. The bus takes us through lush, green countryside. The trip doesn't take long. We arrive at a large, unmarked dirt parking area and exit the bus. There is no signage. The site is deserted. The air is still. It is very quiet.

We walk under the iron archway of the camp entrance upon which is inscribed, "Work shall set you free." What grim irony. There was no freedom here. Inmates were worked to death or just murdered on the spot. The ground inside the camp is hard-packed dirt. There is no vegetation at all. We stop at the kitchen, now just a rectangular hole in the ground. Germans and Americans, we stand side by side and sing our grief, raising our voices in honor of the men murdered here because they were gay. We are told that *nobody has done this before,* even after all these years. A film crew is with us. They are making a film about the chorus and its tour of Europe. I feel deep pain, but I also feel strangely blessed. History is being made here, and I am a part of it.

After we sing, there is time for personal reflections. I surprise myself by speaking a few simple words. I feel something within me forming the words, and I just let them flow. The film crew continues to record the scene. I weep and wish I had brought more tissue to blow my nose.

As we walk silently back toward the parking area, we pass the ruins of inmate barracks to our right. I glance at a window in one of the barrack walls that's still standing. *I see a man's face in the window.* This is impossible. My skin crawls and the hair rises on the back of my neck. Has my lack of sleep and the emotional intensity I've experienced triggered a hallucination?

We walk back under the iron fretwork to the still-deserted parking lot, get on the bus, and return to Berlin.

It's a winter evening back in Los Angeles. With my brothers in song, I'm rehearsing a new piece commissioned by the chorus to commemorate this time of death and resilience. Entitled *Hidden Legacies*, it's composed by Roger Bourland with lyrics by John Hall. It directly addresses the AIDS epidemic. The second movement is a ferocious denunciation of the institutionalized prejudice that is exacerbating its terrible toll. Among the many artistic attempts to grapple with this historic, still unfolding event, we are the first, *anywhere*, to capture in choral music the raw anger and grief that so many feel. We stumble and weep through the jagged harmonies and swirling storm of words. It is the hardest music we have ever attempted, but we are up to the challenge. We bring *Hidden Legacies* to audiences in Los Angeles, Dallas, and Denver, in performances that are etched in my heart. Other choruses across the nation pick up the baton.

We perform Leonard Bernstein's *Chichester Psalms.* Some of us bass singers are invited to try out for the falsetto part in the final movement. I've been curious about falsetto ever since I learned that bass singers can be taught to use this technique to sing very high notes. It has something to do with how the vocal cords can be manipulated, and bass singers are more likely than baritones or tenors to be able to do it ... and I can! With the others selected for the falsetto part, I experience the exquisite pleasure of singing Bernstein's high, clear notes, soaring above the other four voice parts in the finale of the work. Wow.

It's 1994. The chorus travels to New York City. One of my three hotel roommates is Bill, a tenor in the chorus. He's from Portland, Oregon, and has come to Southern California for work. I haven't really gotten to know him yet. He's an openly gay pastor in the United Church of Christ, a small Protestant denomination. I admire his courage.

The chorus performs at Carnegie Hall. I'm in awe that I'm here, on stage in the most famous performance hall in America.

We continue the tour to Washington, DC, for another performance. It's good to see the city again. Fond memories of the 1979 march, and of Brad, come surging back. The day following our performance is set aside for rest and sightseeing. A group of chorus members is going to the Holocaust Memorial Museum, and I decide to accompany them. As we begin the museum tour, each of us is given a slip of paper bearing the name of an individual caught up in the Holocaust. At the end of the tour, we will find out whether that person escaped or was murdered by the Nazis.

We descend a ramp into a large, dimly-lit room and walk between two piles of shoes. There are thousands upon thousands of them. They are piled into heaps higher than my head. I see that some of the shoes are much smaller than my own.

We walk through one hall after another. Here is a cabinet displaying small pieces of faded cloth. Among other shapes and colors, I see a pink triangle. Gays were forced to wear this in public as a badge of shame. I look at the small, pink cloth for a long time before moving on[13]. Next is a black-and-white video taken by Allied forces when they reached the death camps and liberated the inmates.

The images depict the aftermath of unimaginable depravity.

We walk onward, hall after hall, exhibit after exhibit. Finally, to my relief, the exit doors appear in the distance. I cannot bear to insert my slip of paper into the museum's print reader to learn the fate of the person whose name it bears. I put the paper in my pocket instead.

---

13 Similar to how Jews were forced to wear a yellow Star of David by the Nazis, gays were forced to wear a pink triangle. In the modern era, this symbol has been reclaimed and now signifies LGBTQ pride.

We exit the museum and emerge into the bright afternoon sunshine. My mind and my heart feel broken. I return to our hotel and lie down on the bed to catch my breath. Bill is there. My emotions overwhelm me, and I burst into tears. Bill holds me and gently strokes my back, my neck, my hair. I'm grateful for his presence, his reassuring touch.

* * *

That day in Washington deepens my budding friendship with Bill. After a few months, we become lovers. Getting to know a man *before* having sex with him is a new concept for me! Bill is tall and stocky, with sandy-blond hair and a generous smile. He is 18 years my senior. During the friendship phase of our relationship, I learn that he has a generous heart as well. His life journey has been marked by bravery, tragedy, and a consistent effort to live out his deep Christian faith. He has been a pioneer in his denomination, helping to open it up to LGBT people and to all people who have been excluded for one reason or another.

In the 1960s, during the early days of Bill's career as a (closeted) minister, he was outed, then fired by his church near Portland, Oregon. He therefore lost his livelihood as well as the relationships he had built with his parishioners. But his inner drive to be of service was too strong for him to give in to despair. He found work as an administrator for a senior housing non-profit while continuing to advocate in his denomination for inclusion of all people. He and other religious pioneers eventually succeeded. The congregation near Los Angeles that invited him to come and be their pastor in 1991 knew right from the start that he was an openly gay man.

Like me, Bill had a difficult childhood, and we bond more deeply because of this.

We move in together. Now, in November 1995, we are partnered in a commitment ceremony under a flower-bedecked arbor in the backyard of his church. Bill and I are wearing our chorus tuxedos, of course. In front of family and friends, we read our vows to each other, exchange rings, and kiss. It's a beautiful ceremony followed by a catered meal and lots of good cheer.

It's 1997, and the new HIV medicines are here. The dying has slowed to a trickle. The chorus continues to sing a wide range of repertoire, but our performances always include music that invites our listeners to feel the grief, the loss, that we still carry.

Now it's 1999. We're performing in a large hotel ballroom in Beverly Hills. The acoustics are terrible, but this matters not at all because we are singing for none other than the President of the United States. Bill Clinton is a gracious host, complimenting us after we finish singing and cracking a joke about our music's clever lyrics. He also tells the audience that the chorus is about to depart on a tour of Europe and Russia.

After his speech, Chorus members are invited to line up to greet and shake hands with the President one by one. However, the semen stain on Monica Lewinski's blue dress is still fresh in my memory[14], and in a surge of judgmental pique, I decline the invitation. I wonder if I will regret this later on. (News flash from the future: I will!)

Now we are on stage in Tchaikovsky Hall in the center of Moscow singing our hearts out. We have partnered with Alla Pugachova, a well-known Russian singer who is also famous for her outspoken civil rights advocacy.

And look! There are television cameras stationed in the aisles, filming our performance in this famous hall. We are told that our presence and our mission have captured the interest of the nation. Although small numbers of brave Russian LGBT activists have preceded us, our concert is the *first widely-noticed gathering of gay-identified people in the thousand-year history of that nation.* I'm trembling with awe and excitement as our performance concludes. I hope we have planted seeds that will sprout as Russia's young democracy matures.

After the performance, we board the overnight train to St. Petersburg. It's a stuffy ride in the overheated carriages, with friendly cockroaches to keep us company as we doze in our bunks.

---

14 The Clinton-Lewinsky scandal was a sex scandal involving Bill Clinton, then president of the United States, and Monica Lewinsky, a White House intern. Their sexual relationship began in 1995 and lasted 18 months. Clinton ended televised remarks on January 26, 1998, with the infamous statement, "I did not have sexual relations with that woman." Further investigation led to charges of perjury and to Clinton's impeachment in 1998 by the U.S. House of Representatives. He was subsequently acquitted on charges of perjury and obstruction of justice in a U.S. Senate trial.

In St. Petersburg, our performance takes place in a 100-year-old hall at a music conservatory, a space whose acoustics were specifically designed for choral singing. As in Moscow, we intersperse our music with conversation between Jon and the audience via the professional interpreter we've hired for our tour. The language on the marquee outside the hall translates as "Men's Chorus from Los Angeles." Apparently, there aren't any non-pejorative words for LGBT people in the Russian language. When Jon does his deft Q&A from the stage and the audience suddenly realizes who we are, a few people stand up and walk out of the hall. But the vast majority remain settled in their seats. They are music aficionados in a city steeped in culture, here to enjoy excellent music in a lovely hall. So that is what we now proceed to create.

Jon lifts his baton, and we are underway. We pay keen attention to his musical direction, his tempo, his gestures and phrasing, and we do our best to follow his lead, as always. The acoustics are glorious! I can hear my fellow singers with crystal clarity. The hall's marbled walls and high, wood-beamed ceiling are working their sonic magic as promised.

Midway through the concert, it happens: we are suddenly one indivisible musical entity. We singers are bending and stretching our phrasing, shaping our tempo and volume in new and wonderful ways. And Jon is following *our* lead. Or is it that *Jon* is catching fire with surpassing skill and *we* are following *him*? No—somehow, impossibly—we are co-creating the music together. It's akin to what a jazz band does when they're in their groove. But how is that possible here? We're singing classical music whose notes, tempo, and phrasing are specified in advance. It can't be done, *but we're doing it.*

Even before this performance concludes, I'm certain that these moments of musical transcendence will be etched in my memory forever.

* * *

Now it's 2002. Bill and I have been together for seven years. We live in the church parsonage with our cats, Delilah and Miss Sarah. Our county newspaper recently published a front-page Sunday article featuring Bill, his ministry, and our partnership. We agree they did a good job. I visit my state representative, a Republican. We have a nice chat, during which I show her snapshots from the commitment ceremony between Bill and me. She is a gracious host, but I don't know if my visit will affect her political viewpoint.

We continue to sing in the chorus, which is still going strong.

Bill has been pondering retirement lately. He misses Portland. We've discussed moving there together and have made several exploratory visits. I am charmed by the city, its political scene, and the beautiful Oregon landscape.

We decide to take the plunge. Bill bids farewell to his congregation. (His denomination will locate several available pastors to present to the congregation for their review and selection.) I resign from my computer tech job and will find new work in Portland.

At the first rehearsal of the chorus's new season, I step forward to say farewell. I've made beautiful music and shared tears, love, laughter, and unforgettable memories with these brave men for more than 20 years. It is a bittersweet moment.

In addition to bidding adieu to Los Angeles, I realize I am also saying goodbye to my young manhood.

And on July 2, 2002, Bill and I arrive in Portland. It's a gorgeous Oregon summer day. Our hearts are buoyant with hopes for this new chapter in our lives. Among many possibilities, one activity already stands out as a certainty.

Portland has its own gay men's chorus, and we are proud to stand with them and raise our strong, beautiful, defiant voices to the heavens.

Coda: 2025

That lifelong callus around my heart has softened over the years. No longer young, I've realized that living a heart-centered life is why I was put on this earth. Sexual touch is good, but it's not my ultimate destination.

Perhaps there is a cloud of invisible witnesses hovering above us, the ghostly presence of the hundreds of thousands of friends and lovers from those earlier decades who were cut down in their prime by prejudice-fueled disease and death. If so, may they fuel our determination to speak truth to power, now and always.

The wheels of American history have turned once again. Cruel, gleeful, powermongers in Washington, DC, and elsewhere are on the attack. To them I say: you cannot imagine the empowered defiance now springing up and coming your way. You have no idea. You live and thrive on lies. We speak our truth, fueled by love, which will win out in the end.

Eric Zimmerman (he/him) was born and raised in Southern California, where he participated in the flowering of LGBTQ culture in the latter part of the 20th century, including singing for over twenty years with the Gay Men's Chorus of Los Angeles. Now retired, he has lived in Portland since 2002.

A Young Man's Song

Acknowledgments

I am extremely proud of this unique collection of stories. Authors gave of themselves deeply and cheered each other on while we virtually workshopped our stories.

I am grateful to our observant beta readers, Sittrea Friberg and Rebecca Blair. They offered kind words that encouraged our writers to think bigger and explore deeper ideas in their stories. Their support played a key role in helping us grow as writers and create better stories for our readers.

Our returning copy editor team provided a deep, final review. My husband, Arnel Mandilag, and long-time friend, Laurie Olson, made a powerful duo. They were keen readers with an appreciation for a good story. They polished each story, while celebrating the unique voice of each writer.

Arnel also contributed his technological and design talents to this important project. He did all the formatting and typesetting and designed our cover.

My friend John Marenzana was an encouraging force that kept me inspired. I credit him for coming up with our book's tagline when I was stumped.

I also want to acknowledge one of our writers and one of my best friends, Jim Sutherland. Jim provided story coaching to writers with our first book, and was a contributing writer with our last book, Defining Moments. Sadly, Jim passed away last October. I dedicate this book to Jim Sutherland. I value our 30+ years of friendship and shared stories.

It's not possible to thank all the people who supported our book tour. Libraries, community centers, faith communities, local businesses and PFLAG chapters eagerly and bravely stepped up to support our message and create community dialogues. Just know we feel your love and support.

I deeply appreciate and respect our authors for their willingness to share their stories of defiance and trusting in our process. We must amplify our voices and support each other, now and in the future.

And lastly, I thank you for choosing our book. It means a lot to us that you decided to read our stories. Each story was carefully crafted to bring you authenticity, courage, or a sense of wonder. We hope that as you turn each page, you feel the love and effort behind every word. Our goal is to share these stories as a special gift, and we truly hope you enjoy them as much as we enjoyed writing them.

—Paul Iarrobino

Our Bold Voices

We encourage you to stay connected by visiting us at www.ourboldvoices.com to follow our current projects.

www.ingramcontent.com/pod-product-compliance
Lightning Source LLC
Chambersburg PA
CBHW060449030426
42337CB00015B/1527
9798990194038